THIEF OF HEARTS

www.meningitisUK.org

M & J photography

Find out more at www.mjphotography.co.uk

Joseph JP Lawlor

authorHOUSE®

AuthorHouse™ UK Ltd.
500 Avebury Boulevard
Central Milton Keynes, MK9 2BE
www.authorhouse.co.uk
Phone: 08001974150

First published by AuthorHouse 3/30/2011

ISBN: 978-1-4490-6788-5 (sc)

For Jordan, Keira, Jenna.

To Jessie

with love

From Joe x

ABOUT THE AUTHOR

The cards were never stacked in his favour. But nobody ever told him that. Born in 1963 in Birmingham, England to a very young, and frightened Irish Catholic girl, he was soon taken back to the land of his mother's birth and raised there by his Grandmother. He was educated in Churchfield National School in Cork City, where he loved to write  short stories on any subject that was given to him as an assignment. On leaving school at the age of fifteen having gained his national leaving certificate he immigrated to England; working at first, then later became the proprietor of several successful businesses. In 2001 he went back to school and studied arts, and humanities then law... In the late nineties a scandal broke surrounding the NHS in which it was discovered that thousands of young children's organs were being harvested illegally for study.

The author's daughter Kaine had died in 1989 from a meningitis related problem; he subsequently became aware that his little girl's organs had been taken without his knowledge. This is her story. The opening lines take you on a journey that only the author is qualified to take you on. Both riveting and compelling this is a deeply moving account of a father's love for his child and ultimate triumph over adversity. Written with a delicate balance that take you from tears to smiles, he proves that this is a story that had to be told, and also shows that no matter how much time had passed he never could forget.

ACKNOWLEDGEMENTS:-

Special thanks to. Ken Jones, for his invaluable help in the final production of this book. Nigel Lowe, who proved when the chips were down that he was no fair-weather friend. Thanks mate.

A TRUE STORY BY KAINE LAWLOR'S FATHER.

CONTENTS

INTRODUCTION

The decision to write this book was not an easy one to make. As an ordinary person, I have, with thousands of others, been caught up in a situation that has caused so much pain, bewilderment, and frustration; infant and child organ retention; all done in the name of scientific research; allegedly.

I am the father of a child who underwent such a fate and, as such, I felt that no-one was listening to me. Unless the person I was talking to had had a similar experience, I always got the impression that the information I was relaying was such an assault on the senses that my words went completely over their heads. Well, words have more meaning in the written form, hence the saying 'the pen is mightier than the sword' or in this case, the scalpel. And so I have made a decision to attempt to write about a subject that has been reported many times in the past, mostly by the media. Now I feel it is time to convey my thoughts and feelings on the matter. In doing so I hope to be fair where fairness lies, and to condemn only where the need arises. No doubt many people more-qualified than myself, both in healthcare and in law, will see me as a layman unqualified and ill-educated by their standards. Unless they though, as the saying goes, 'have walked a mile in my shoes', then on the primary matter of losing a child and the desecration of that child's body, I beg that they will seek to be as fair with me as I shall endeavour to be towards them. The effect this subject has had on me as a person and on my family is hard to put into words, but throughout the pages of this book, the full realisation of parental bereavement will become apparent. This book is being written not only for myself but also for the other families whose lives have been torn apart by the death of a beloved child. Add to that the further revelations of a massive cover up perpetrated by an institution in which ordinary people including myself put their entire trust, only to find that trust betrayed.

For those who have heard the stories of child organ retention and paid no heed; if they are listening now, the truth may be sometimes quite shocking. But now I am going to tell the story of my daughter. Her name was Kaine Helena Patricia Lawlor, she was a real person, not a statistic on a page, a report in a newspaper, a television news programme or radio broadcast. She mattered to us and this book is dedicated to her memory. May she, and all the other children who mattered equally and who also shared in her fate, rest in peace.

CHAPTER 1
Midnight the darkest hour.

Twenty-one years have now passed since that night in the Children's Hospital ward room in Birmingham; but for me, it might just as well have been yesterday. We were told that we had to wait in there for the final tests to be run on our daughter's condition. It was very late and I had Kaine in my arms as I dozed fitfully in and out of a tormented sleep. It was as if I was enveloped in a nightmare that wouldn't release me from its terrible grasp. The realms of semi-consciousness were cruelly interwoven with what I wished for and what was about to take place. Karen, my wife, was in a similar condition to myself; we had been awake for more than twenty-four hours, the strain was enormous. She sat in a chair a few feet from where I was sitting; she was asleep, then not asleep; that's the way it went, all night long. I remember looking at my daughter's beautiful face now spoiled by the ever-present oxygen tube which was the only indication that she was seriously ill. Had that not been there she would have looked as though she was in a peaceful sleep. It was of course a graphic reminder as to the awful reality of our surroundings. The constant beeping of the heart monitor and other instruments fulfilled the same function.

I opened my eyes and tried to focus my vision on the clock on the wall. Ten fifty-five pm, and I remember whispering to her, "not long now, sweetheart." We were waiting for the specialist to arrive at the hospital for the tests to be conducted on Kaine. I knew in my heart what the results would be and that is why I whispered to Kaine "not long now." Strange really how you feel at times like that; I didn't want to lose her but I knew I had to. It was inevitable. I resigned myself to my pain and grief and held her that little bit more closely to me for the next hour, for we had been told that the afore-mentioned doctor's arrival was to be around midnight. Not long now......

The time came for the tests to begin, and, as expected, the doctor and staff arrived around midnight. I can still clearly remember the doctor's face although I can't remember anyone else's from that night. I think this may have been because I was hoping that this man could perform some kind of miracle. He had a distinct look about him; Middle Eastern maybe; I was not quite sure. He had a round face with dark skin and curly dark hair greying at the temples; forty-ish I would have guessed. He wore round glasses and a bow-tie that set him apart from everyone else present. He quickly went to work asking for reports and readouts from the monitors in situ. I could feel my heart sinking; the time we most dreaded had finally arrived. I sat there, holding Kaine; I felt so helpless. The room was now brighter, due to all the lights having been switched back on; stark reality stealing the surreal twilight of the previous few hours we had had. The good doctor's team quietly went about their tasks; they were getting ready to take Kaine from me to do those tests, those awful tests! Why couldn't we have been left alone just the three of us….. I heard a voice addressing me; it was the doctor. His tone was gentle as he spoke and I got the impression that this was a scene he had witnessed many times and that the impact of the situation upon myself and Karen was not lost upon him.

"I'm afraid you will have to lay her on the bed for me now." His voice was kind and he had one hand on my shoulder as he motioned with the other towards Kaine's hospital cot.

"We're ready." Those words cut me like a knife. Slowly I rose from the chair, Karen with me, I carried her to the little bed, and, as gently as possible, laid her on the mattress. We moved away from the bedside and I found myself standing at the top of the bed observing everything that now had to take place. The doctor was talking to me again, explaining the exact procedures taking place and what exactly they were trying to achieve. I can still vividly remember the syringe they were now using, inserting it into my poor baby's ears and injecting ice-cold water from it to see if some response was forthcoming, and, of course checking the brain scan monitor to chart any brain activity. "How long before we know anything?" I heard myself ask. "We have to make sure we have completed the tests thoroughly", was the doctor's reply. And so we stood there; all adults, surrounding a small bed with a small child lying on it who no-one could now help.

My prayers to God, it seemed, had been in vain; there was no miracle response to the freezing cold water; the brain monitor readout remained unchanged. I prayed that she would open her beautiful sapphire blue eyes and be ok.

"I'm so sorry," the Doctor said as I slumped into a chair and held my head in my hands. I could hear Karen's sobs turn to a howl of anguish; she was now being comforted by some of the hospital staff who were present.

"The tests are now complete, and unfortunately we must conclude that there is no brain stem activity."

I had expected the worst, but the force of the spoken reality hit me like a ton of bricks. Kaine was dead; albeit still breathing with the aid of the life support machine. Karen and I clung to each other, overwhelmed with grief.

After some time the doctor's team slowly started to pack away their equipment. I was aware of activity going on around me, but it seemed to be in slow motion. People were speaking to me and it was as if they were all far away. I gradually became aware of the Doctor talking directly to me; he had sat me down on a chair and was now sitting in front of me, and his expression was pained. The intensity of our loss had affected him and others also present; tears were streaming down the faces of the nurses. I felt so small and helpless, as I had so many times those last few days. Fear had overtaken my body; I felt cold and weak I had never experienced anything like it before and I never want to again.

Karen by now had also joined me; we sat there holding hands. The doctor spoke to us; his tone was gentle, soothing. He began.

"All the tests are now complete; and sadly it would appear that your daughter has not responded to any of them. With no sign of any brain activity we must sadly conclude brain stem death has occurred. This unfortunately means that your daughter's bodily functions are not controlled by her; breathing is controlled entirely by the life-support machine, and, without that, I'm afraid it would be highly unlikely she would be able to sustain her own survival. Please understand the decision you must come to is entirely for yourselves to make; you will be under no pressure whatsoever from the hospital, you can take as much time as you feel necessary to decide; again I am so sorry for you both."

The implication was clear; we had to decide when to give our permission for the life-support machine to be switched off; the worst decision a parent could ever have to make. I asked if we could have a little time with our baby alone. The answer was, of course, in the affirmative, and with that they all left the room, leaving us alone with Kaine. We both stood by the bedside; we held her hand and wiped her brow, kissed her gently and through our tears we reaffirmed the love we had had for her from the moment she came into the world. And now it was time to say good-bye. How could this be? You're not supposed to see your child die! This couldn't be happening; but it was. Life's greatest gift was about to be taken from us. We spoke to her and told her how much we loved her; surely she could still hear her mom and dad. We told her how much we would miss her beautiful little face in our lives; and, most of all, that we would never, ever, forget her. We gathered her soft toys together and placed them in her arms so she would still have them with her. Kaine was only eighteen months old; this wasn't fair, and it wasn't fair her life was over. Both Karen and I would have gladly given our lives so that she could live. If only she could live. It was hopeless to think that this could be anything now but wishful thinking. Darkness descended on us; we had to accept the inevitable.

I spoke to Karen and told her I was going outside to speak to our families who were gathered in the waiting room. I would tell them that there was no hope and that we had no choice but to let the life-support machine be switched off within the next hour or two. As I walked down the corridor and rounded the bend, I was planning what to say and trying to keep myself as composed as I possibly could. Then I saw them all standing there with my mother at the forefront of the group, a look of expectancy on her face; half fear half hope etched on all of their faces. What was I going to say? My emotions got the better of me as I gave way to the awful strain I felt myself under over the recent days. My mom instinctively hugged me as the rest of the family gathered around. I told them the news everyone was dreading to hear. I explained about the tests and the results; then I told them we were preparing to say 'good-bye' to Kaine and that they should do the same. With that, I left them to make their own arrangements and made my way back to the little room where Karen and Kaine were.

When I arrived back at the room, Karen was sitting in an armchair holding Kaine in her arms, talking softly to her as if she were asleep. As I walked in, Karen looked at me and gave me a little smile. I smiled back at her and pulled up another chair beside her and we both sat there in silence. After a while the first of the members of the families came in. They came in twos; they held her hand, touched her face, and cried. 'Good-byes' were said and even though she couldn't hear them, pledges of love and remembrance hung in the air like suspended dreams.

After everyone had left we were once again left alone with our baby; and as before, we sat in silence. Prayer was of little use to us now as a means to save our child. The only thing we could ask of God would be to remember Kaine until we might be able to hold her once again. It is hard to describe how I felt at that moment of time; I remember being calm and collected, the sheer panic of the previous hours had now left me. I felt wide awake and alert even though it was early in the morning of the sixth of November. A few short hours earlier we had listened to fireworks exploding all over Birmingham, everyone it seemed had been celebrating Guy Fawkes Night; how could they have known that a young child had lost its fight for life and that Karen and I had lost everything? We hadn't a lot anyway, an old second-hand yellow Volkswagen Polo and a small house near Wolverhampton. We had struggled to buy it and interest rates at the time were crippling; but it was our home and we had looked forward to raising our child there. Now all our dreams for the future had gone.

After some time had passed, (I can't recall how long,) Karen and I looked at each other and we both knew it was time. Tears once again welled in our eyes and I got up from where I was sitting to summon the medical staff into the room. The doctor came to us and comforted us both as best he could. We then had to make the hardest decision of our lives; we could have sat there in that room for days, months or even years. The only thing that was keeping our daughter alive was a machine; unthinking uncaring, devoid of all emotion; with a flick of a switch it would stop. The doctor asked us if we were ready to go through with it. I looked at Karen and just nodded; barely audibly I said, "yes." His team solemnly went about their work.

Slowly and meticulously they separated Kaine from the life-support unit. From where I was standing I couldn't see everything, but then, just like a curtain opening they parted. I could then see Kaine laying there; the light above her shining down on her pale skin. Quietly, everyone left the room. Once again we were alone with our child. We both knew that she could not sustain her own breathing and that we would only have a few moments of precious time left until she passed away from our lives forever. We picked her up and gently laid her on the changing table close by; all we could do now was look after her in these last moments. We changed her nappy; although it wasn't soiled, it was important that she had a clean, fresh one on. This task we did together as we had done many times since she was born, except that this time there was no struggle to keep those flailing limbs under control. She lay there quietly. The room was quiet and we were both calm. Although I don't know why, it was then that I laid my head on her chest and listened to her heart beating. Karen did the same and together we heard the final beats of her heart that had been formed through the miracle of love between two people. Slowly the little beats diminished until finally they were no more. We both then gently kissed her and it was over....

Kaine had put up a brave fight through the many times that she was ill and had had to undergo many operations to replace the shunt that was fitted months earlier. Now the struggle was finally at an end. For this at least, we were grateful, for no longer would she feel any pain or be sick anymore. Strange really how you can comfort yourself with these thoughts, but when you add it all up it was a pretty poor bargain. I could hear it all in my head,

"at least she's not suffering,"

"it's for the best,"

"it's God's will."

But I didn't want her to suffer. Surely the best would be for her to be with us, and a loving God would certainly advocate life, not death. What would be the point of giving someone a treasure beyond compare and then snatching it away forever? It could not be so; and yet, here I was, with my wife, holding the now lifeless body of our little girl.

We could only do our best for her now; so we dressed her in a clean romper suit and placed her in the Moses basket provided by the hospital. There was a gentle knock on the door. "Come in," I said and the door opened. It was the nurses who had looked after Kaine throughout the time she was in intensive care; the pain they felt for us was evident in their faces.

"We've come to see if you're both all right?" How could we both be all right I thought; but I suppose that's all one can really say in such circumstances. They must have encountered this tragic scene many times before. It would be hard to imagine that anyone could get used to it, and as I have said, their faces really said it all, for no more dedication could have been shown by anyone to their little charges, I'm sure. It was all over now and a certain peace seemed to descend upon Karen and I. The nurses sat with us and held us both; we talked for awhile about Kaine, how lucky we were to have her and about the funny little things she did while her personality was emerging. She was a good baby and in spite of her illness she wasn't any trouble; she looked like her mother, she had beautiful blue eyes and blonde hair; she had a cheeky smile that lit up those gorgeous eyes. It was so hard to believe that we would never see that smile again. All our comments were reciprocated by the nurses along with caring smiles and nods of understanding; they were probably parents themselves, maybe thinking how blessed they were not to be in our position. I thanked them all in turn for the care and dedication they had displayed through all the days and nights we had spent at the hospital.

One person who was not there was one of the junior doctors whose unpleasant task it had been to inform us of Kaine's deteriorating condition. In the end, when all hope was gone, he had asked for a brief meeting between us; and in one of the small offices on the ward earlier in the evening, the first mention of our daughter's organs had become an issue. With an expression of intensity and anxiety he had sat down.

"I have to ask you both a very difficult question but I hope you both understand the reasons for me asking you this." I had guessed what was coming. As for Karen though, she hadn't seemed to grasp the enormity of what I had feared was coming next. The man had stiffened himself in his chair as if preparing to embark upon a difficult task, and had needed to brace himself for the job.

"I hope you understand that this would be a vital treatment for other sick children should you agree to my request….. would you be prepared to allow your daughter's organs to be used in transplant to other patients?" The words, although expected, had struck me like the repeated blows of a hammer. From Karen's expression it would appear she had felt the same. For although I knew my little girl's life was at an end; the fact had somehow been reinforced by the question of removing her organs. I must confess in the darker moments of the preceding hours I had given the matter some thought, and had tried to prepare myself as to the answer I would give when I had realised that there was no hope left for us.

"I think we need a little time to discuss this." I said.

"Of course," he had answered. "Believe me there is no pressure on from us to weight your decision. As this is a highly personal matter for you both to decide, I will understand entirely, whatever decision you come to." Kind words. Had I known the horror of what was to come, I would have made my wishes very clear there and then.

"When you have discussed the matter between yourselves just let one of the nurses know that you wish to speak with me." I had spoken with this young doctor on a number of occasions before; always, it had seemed his sad duty to inform us both of Kaine's deteriorating condition by degrees. By now, strangely enough, I was starting to feel sorry for him; it couldn't have been easy telling the parents of a little girl it was unlikely that their baby would ever recover to be a normal happy and playful child again. This, though, it seemed, would be the last bearing of bad news he would have to lay before us. Only two choices lay before Karen and me; Yes or No.

The decision was not mine alone to make. I knew what I wanted to do but Kaine was Karen's daughter also, and, as her mother, whatever she decided, would be my decision also.

"Joe I can't!" She seemed to guess what was on my mind, and as we sat there in anguish once again, I thought of all the times Kaine had been unwell and said to myself "enough is enough". Kaine had had enough intrusive surgery in her short life and now was the time for her to be at peace.

"It's okay; I'll go and tell them what we've decided to do." This I reassuringly told Karen as I got up to tell the Staff Nurse that I needed to speak with the Doctor.

"Have you come to a decision Joe?" He asked.

"Yes we have," I answered. Even though I was only a young man at the time I was not ignorant of the fact that organs were highly sought after by the NHS hoping to save another person's life, and this weighed heavily upon me as I gave my response. I felt almost embarrassed; as if my answer being in the negative was to extinguish the hopes of some other poor parents elsewhere hoping against hope that a heart, a liver, a kidney, or something would become available perhaps, to save their child.

Now here I was to prolong their agony by not having the courage to let them take my daughter's organs from her. Over the years that have passed I have often wished that I had said 'yes' to the question so that at least we could have some comfort from the knowledge that we had spared some other parent from the stomach churning, ice- cold grief that we were then going through. Also, in a way, I thought that Kaine would somehow live on; in that some child, somewhere, would have the gift of life from our daughter's passing. But on that night it was not to be; we had made our decision.

"I'm afraid the answer has to be no; we feel that she has suffered enough and to put her through any more is too much. All we want for her now is peace."

"I do understand, and as I said earlier the decision was an entirely personal one for you to make." I felt almost relieved at his reply, for by this time my emotions had taken such a battering; I felt so small and utterly helpless that my opinions and decisions counted for very little. Now it was done, I went back to Karen and told her that Kaine would be left alone.....

By now Kaine was dressed in a clean nappy and romper suit and all her soft toys were with her in the Moses basket. Her mum, as ever, had lovingly wrapped her in a blanket. She looked as though she was asleep. It then struck me how big she had grown; she was no longer a baby but a toddler. Maybe it was because I knew now that our time had ended that my mind was taking in every last detail about her, for I knew in a very short time we were to be parted, perhaps forever, as far as I knew. While I had been engaged in conversation earlier with the Doctor, one of the nursing staff had arranged with Karen to take Kaine to the chapel of rest within the hospital, and now it was time for Kaine to leave her room and make this short journey. The nurse had arrived with small trolley. This was of a different type to the ones I had seen being used in the hospital previously, and this was one that was reserved for a different purpose. It was stainless steel all over and a white cloth cover was draped over the completely flat surface. The absence of any guard rails on the sides emphasised to me that this device was used for transporting children who could no longer pose a risk of falling from it. One of the nurses put her arm around Karen as another gently lifted Kaine in her basket onto the trolley and slowly and solemnly we made our way toward the chapel.

When we arrived there our respective families were already present. The atmosphere was, as you'd expect; very heavy and subdued. After some time in the chapel, where again many supplications were made to God on behalf of our daughter, though now, instead of the miracle we had all prayed for and did not receive, we prayed instead for the life that we had lost to the ether, I can well remember feeling very confused.

Being a Catholic at the time, I was prepared to put up with the 'mystery' of God and why very bad things happen that bring so much misery to the Earth. We were told it was 'God's will' but wasn't it 'God's will' for people to have children? Then why take them away? Surely this would be the cruellest of deeds to perpetrate. My child would not grow up to know the blissful joy of innocent childhood or to witness her first snowfall or to look up at the sky in wide-eyed wonder. We would not see her bloom into adolescence and then into womanhood. She would now know nothing of falling in love, or music, or any of the simple pleasures every living person takes for granted. And yet I was being urged to give thanks for the eighteen months of her young life. Too much of that young life had known pain, but she had also known happiness. And now no more, for she was gone from us.

She lay in her Moses basket in front of the altar in the chapel. A statue of Jesus on the Cross was high above her on the wall. It seemed to me though that the unseeing eyes of stone could not discern or comprehend the injustice I felt in my heart, and that the unhearing stone ears of a statue could not hear the quiet sobs of grief coming from our families rising up to the heavens. Was this our sacrifice at the altar of God? I was being urged to give thanks and to be grateful; but for what? Many years later I would come to know the truth but at that time I felt total numbness, shock and anger as the enormity of the tragedy that had now befallen us slowly dawned on me.

My thoughts were now for Karen; how would she feel when she now saw other young mothers in the street with their children happily going about their business? Her sense of loss would surely be compounded at the sight of a mother leaning over a pram to ensure her child was warm enough on a cold day. These thoughts were now going through my head and although my own heart was breaking, I felt that I now had to try and be strong for her.

It was now around three-thirty a.m. of the morning of the sixth of November nineteen eighty-nine, a date seared into my memory. There was nothing more to do and everything that could be said had been said. I had been awake for some thirty-six hours or so, apart from dozing fitfully in the chair when I was holding Kaine earlier. I was now asked by the hospital staff for permission to remove Kaine's body to the mortuary. We kissed her as though we were kissing her goodnight, and although she still looked as if she were asleep, her skin now felt quite cool and the colour had gone from her face.

We stood for a little while now taking in every last detail of her as it was probably going to be some time before we would see her again. Everyone was now leaving quietly and respectfully until only Karen and I were once again alone together in the chapel, with Kaine. We then took a lock of her hair to remember her by and placed this in a small plastic tube for safe-keeping. Shortly afterwards they came to remove her......

CHAPTER 2.

But for Kaine, there was no new day.

Provision had been made for us to stay at the hospital throughout the duration of Kaine's illness, and we found ourselves making our way back to our room. One of the ward sisters came to us, and with a pained expression on her face offered us some strong sleeping tablets, saying that we might need them. We gratefully accepted and when in our room we duly took them, for in spite of the amount of time I'd been awake, I doubted either of us would have been able to sleep naturally.

Neither Karen nor I spoke; we simply got into bed and waited for sleep to overtake us. When it finally came it was a blessed relief from reality. If I had never woke again it would not have mattered to me at that time. At least I would have been with Kaine again.

Morning came, as it always does, and I awoke to a different world, at least for Karen and I; the pale November sunlight was streaking through the cracks in the blinds against the window. The events of the previous hours once again crept into my consciousness. I became aware of Karen lying next to me. I could sense that she was awake but we didn't say a word to each other. We just lay there for a time; we were not two whole people anymore for every parent's worst fear had torn through us. There was just the two of us again.

Somewhere within the hospital Kaine lay as well but for her there was to be no new day.

I had to get up and go to the bathroom, and while I was in there my emotions overtook me, and with the door locked, I sank onto the bathroom floor and allowed the pain I was feeling come to the fore, and there I wept uncontrollably for some time.

Karen later told me that she had heard me and had wanted to come to me but had decided to let me be; it was probably for the best because nothing could have been said to comfort me at that moment. Sometime later, when we had got dressed and had tried to pull ourselves together as best we could, we went onto the ward to find out exactly what was to happen over the next few days. Upon our arrival the doctor who had spoken to me earlier about donating Kaine's organs was waiting to speak to us. We duly met with him and he began to inform us about the procedures that must now take place.

"There will have to be a post-mortem to try and establish the exact cause of your daughter's death," he said. At this point I was unsure of everything I was now being told, as we had brought Kaine to the hospital only a few days before for what we had thought was just another routine operation to replace the failed shunt.

"Don't you know?" I asked.

"Well, we can't say for certain; this is why a post mortem is required so that we can give you a more accurate account of what happened to Kaine."

"When is this to take place then?"

"It will have to take place quite soon, perhaps within the next couple of days." The thought of this was really too much for us to bear and I asked if we could be excused in order to gather our thoughts.

I had to get out of there, and so I said to Karen that there was little point in being there now and that we would be better off going back to her mom's house. Karen agreed. The oppressive atmosphere at the hospital was becoming claustrophobic, so we went back to our room to gather our things together and make our way from that place.

As we walked out of the building and into the bright cold November day, it struck me how everybody was going about their daily business as usual. Didn't they know of the catastrophe that had befallen us? Of course they couldn't know. For as night follows day and back again, the world just keeps on turning with supreme indifference, along with its occupants. We walked through the car park to where our little yellow Volkswagen was, and as I opened the doors for us to get in, the empty child safety seat in the back of the car served as a reminder of whom we were leaving behind. Kaine had sat in that seat many times, gazing out of the window as the world of the time flew by.

As we drove out of the car park, I turned to Karen and told her that I didn't want to face anyone yet; and so we decided to drive around for a while instead of heading straight back to her mother's house in Walsall.

It was around lunchtime as the meandering route I had taken from the children's hospital took us into the West Midlands town of West Bromwich; a place both myself and Karen had frequented in more care-free days. It

occurred to me that neither of us had eaten properly for a few days now, and although food was the last thing I wanted, I suggested we stop off for something to eat. We went to a pub called 'The Railway' in the High Street and as Karen found a table, I went to get us a drink while we decided what we were going to eat.

We ordered the food and it was duly brought to the table; two simple meals of fish and chips with salad as I recall. Now West Bromwich wasn't known at the time for its culinary delights; however, the meals looked and smelled nice, and the change of atmosphere from the hospital earlier was indeed a welcome relief. While we were eating, it was then that a most extraordinary experience occurred. Karen stopped eating and was clearly becoming distressed. Just before I noticed Karen's sudden change in demeanour, I had myself been having a strange sensation around me. The only way to describe this is as an odour; one I immediately recognised as being associated with Kaine. During the last few days at the hospital while Kaine remained in a coma; she could not ingest food physically and was fed by intravenous means only. As I had held her closely to me in the last few hours of her life, I had noticed that her breath had begun to smell slightly. I later found out that this was caused by the lack of food going into the stomach over a period of time, which causes this distinctive odour to occur. As I have said, I became aware of this sensation around me but thinking that this was my imagination playing tricks on me, I didn't say anything to Karen sitting opposite. It was then that I noticed Karen had begun to cry and I immediately left my part of the table in order to go to comfort my wife. As I sat into her immediate presence, the odour was all around Karen also: but more powerful and more distinctive. This was the reason for Karen's starting to cry; she too had recognised the odour and had linked this to Kaine. The significance of this to us was that our daughter was still with us. At that time it gave us a small crumb of comfort to believe that Kaine was with us and would not leave us, and we certainly would not leave her.

We arrived at my mother-in-law's house later that day and we were very reluctant to speak to anyone about our experience that lunch-time. We had decided to keep this to ourselves as we felt that people would not, or could not understand; in truth it was hard to explain what had occurred in any reasonable way. We didn't want anyone thinking that we had become unstable or anything, and at any rate, we felt it was an entirely private matter for us to decide how we felt about it, and this we did.

It is worth saying that this is a factual account of my daughter's story, and after long and thoughtful consideration, I felt that to omit this episode would be unjustifiable. The same experience happened on a number of occasions over the following weeks, but it differed in that it had happened to us both while we were apart, but the experience happened to Karen much more frequently and usually at times when she was in great distress. This would often serve to comfort her greatly for according to our beliefs at the time we thought that Kaine was still with us as a Spirit. These events culminated one day when Karen was alone in our house. While she was sitting on our bed she became upset, as the grieving process was taking its toll. The experience previously described happened again. The odour was very distinctive, and somehow much stronger this time. Realising she could no longer look out for her physical well-being Karen and I had talked about her spiritual well-being in light of these appearances. It was with this in mind that Karen began to talk to Kaine and tearfully explained that she must go to God: who would care for her and love her as much as we did and that she would never leave our thoughts and hearts. After a while the presence eventually faded away and neither of us has experienced it since.

Over the next few days we decided that we couldn't face going back to our house. We stayed at Karen's mom's bungalow that she shared with Karen's stepfather Roy (my employer at the time) and Karen's younger brother Lee. Arrangements had to be made about the funeral, and so a few days later I made an appointment to see an undertaker in All Saints Way in West Bromwich. We also had to decide on the final resting site; and as Karen came from an area of the West Midlands called Stone Cross and I came from Hampstead, Great Barr; central to these two areas was a church called All Saints; or, as everybody locally knew it, 'the old church' since as I believe, it was built some hundreds of years previously. I was then a Catholic and Karen was Church of England so the choice was not one of religious conviction. The church itself stands adjacent to the traffic lights at the junction leading into West Bromwich from the Newton Road and from Stone Cross. I'd always liked the area as it is situated at a high point overlooking part of Sandwell Valley and the surrounding fields; and as anyone who lives in the industrial areas of the West Midlands will tell you, green fields are a refreshing sight. This also formed part of our decision for Kaine's, and ultimately our own, resting place.

A few days later, after a number of phone calls, we found ourselves in front of a very nice lady whose name was Francesca. She had short dark hair, a posh accent, and a very nice disposition; probably a little to sunny in her outlook for my mood that day but, however, that was the woman's personality and so we proceeded with our meeting. Francesca explained that it would be her role to conduct the funeral service and to that end we spent some time talking about our lives so far with Kaine, the circumstances surrounding her illness, and ultimately her death. Francesca was a kind woman, obviously very touched by these events; we made a further appointment for her to meet us at Karen's mother Pat's house a few days later. She explained that she would have to sort the paperwork and so on in order to make sure that everything would proceed as planned. We said our good-byes and left for a further appointment I had made with the director of Gibbs funeral home, a mile or so away from 'the old church' also situated along All Saints Way. And so we found ourselves for the second time that day sitting in an office quite unfamiliar to us in our every day dealings in our lives up until that point. The conversation with the funeral director seemed strangely practical. I'd never in my worst nightmares dreamed that I would be arranging my daughter's funeral; it's safe to say that is a task you expect your children to do on your behalf. And yet here we were. And no matter how painful, certain practicalities had to be addressed, and so the choice of coffin was discussed.

He informed us that this would have to be specially made as he remarked

"children don't die so much these days." I was not sure how I felt about that comment although I wish to stress that it was in no way said in a disrespectful way; it was more of a professional observation on the man's part. I think his words just reinforced in me how unlucky we were that our daughter was in that sad minority of children who did. The other issues addressed were; where Kaine was, and what jewellery, if any, was on our child. On the night she passed away I was wearing a gold crucifix on a gold chain around my neck; it seemed appropriate to put this on her. Karen removed her wedding ring and placed it on the chain as well and so she had two items personal to us both to be with her always. These items the undertaker carefully noted, and he informed us that he would ensure everything was still in place at the time of collection of her remains. This struck me as quite strange at the time as I could never imagine anyone stealing anything from a deceased child. However, I was young and relatively naïve and the world and its ways were still to make serious impact on me. Years later, we were to find out that we were indeed robbed; but not of anything as trivial as material silver or gold but of something far more precious; of which neither Karen nor myself nor the unsuspecting undertakers would ever have thought of checking....

A couple of days later Francesca was at Karen's mother's house. I remember the day well. It was a beautiful bright sunny day for November; the bungalow was warm and one could be forgiven for thinking it was the height of summer, were it not for the bare appearance of the leafless trees outside the living-room window. The evening before,

Karen and I had spoken about the church service. As we were both in our early twenties at the time, the thought of just old fashioned hymns being sung didn't appeal to us; and so we went through a list of songs that we liked and decided on a couple that we thought were appropriate for the service. The songs we decided upon were 'Girl I'm gonna miss you' by Milli Vanilli, and 'Don't want to lose you now' by Gloria Estefan; these two songs, we felt, suited how we felt perfectly. During our meeting with Francesca we requested that these songs be played; the former on entrance to the church, and the latter as we exited. After playing the afore-mentioned songs for Francesca the conversation was then centred on the service itself, which prayers were to be said; in which order, and, traditionally, a few hymns were to be included. There was also to be a memorial service on the following Sunday at Evensong where Kaine's name was to be read out along with the names of other parishioners of that church who had passed away. Francesca was a kind woman, as I have said, and tried to offer some words of comfort and encouragement to get us to carry on attending church; as I had in my youth been a regular church-goer where I lived in Cork City in Ireland. This attendance, though, I must say, was the result of being brought up in sixties/seventies Irish society and after reaching my teen years the parish priest, Father Murphy-O'Conner had seen less and less of young Mr. Lawlor.

I nevertheless appreciated the sentiment, and as I was really looking for an answer to all this, I said that I, along with Karen, would give due consideration to the encouragement being offered. And so with the arrangements made, Francesca took her leave and drove away in her brown Fiat Panda.

As we cleared away the cups and plates from the tea and biscuit offering, my mind turned to another matter. We knew that Kaine's post-mortem was very soon to take place; and to ease Karen's apprehension, I telephoned the Children's Hospital a little later that morning and was put through to the appropriate department. A male voice was on the other end of the line and in answer to my questions I was assured by the man that Kaine's post-mortem would be carried out with the same care and respect as would be afforded to a living person being operated upon. I thanked him for his kind words for this also eased my mind. I then told Karen what I'd learned and she also seemed a little relieved at this. The only clue I had that the information I had been given by the person on the other end of the phone was a lie came a few days later when we went to the hospital to see Kaine's remains for the last time before the funeral took place.

We went to the part of the hospital where the mortuary was situated and we were politely asked to wait by a sympathetic looking nurse while she made sure everything was ready for our visit. As the minutes ticked by I could feel myself starting to become apprehensive. A little while later she reappeared and asked if we would like to follow her. We walked down some corridors and then we were ushered into a small waiting room.

"Before you go in," she began, "I would like to say that you might want to prepare yourselves. Kaine has undergone the post-mortem and has been in the mortuary now for a few days. Her physical appearance may not be the same as you last saw; so if you want to take a minute or so before you go in…..?"

Karen and I both looked at each other. I indicated that we were ready to enter. And so, with that, the nurse opened the door for us and just myself and Karen entered. The door was quietly shut behind us. The room was small with what appeared to be a window with heavy-looking short curtains which were drawn. A small bed was the focal point of the room, upon which our little girl was laid. Two chairs were placed at the side of the bed, and there was a little side table with a Bible placed on top. The significance of the size of the bed didn't hit me until some time later when it was with dismay that I realised that only children would ever lie there. The concept of a child-sized bed in a mortuary viewing room was another sad fact of life I had now been taught.

Our attention was immediately on Kaine, and we were both indeed shocked by her appearance. When we last saw her she, as I have said, looked merely to be asleep, as if the slightest noise might awaken her from slumber. In my mind's eye this was still how I imagined her to be before we entered the room. How wrong I was......(I have agonised as to whether to describe what we both saw and have decided not to include this detail in the narrative of this book.) Suffice to say she did not look the same...... [The description is in the handwritten draughts of this book and will remain there until any need for it to be seen, legal or otherwise, is shown to me as the author of this document.]

.....Kaine's little soft toys were carefully placed on the bed with her, and my gold crucifix, with Karen's wedding ring on the chain, was around her neck. The other significant difference to when we last saw her was how she was now dressed. Instead of the romper suit we had dressed her in on the ward, she now had on what appeared to be a cotton night dress which was sleeveless to the shoulders. The gold of the ring and the crucifix was condensating and this, oddly enough, sparked the curious, or not so curious, reaction of us both to how she was now dressed; for she was cold; and even in death, a parent would look out for the well-being of their child. It seemed that even though we knew she could no longer feel anything, the natural instinct for us, as parents, was to want to protect her from this. But we couldn't.....

Although I can describe what I saw, what I felt is an entirely different matter. We sat there both of us crying and holding her now cold hands. I wanted Kaine to know that we didn't want to leave her there and that we wanted so desperately to take her home with us. But mere words were now rendered impotent as the intensity of her death and appearance now engulfed us. We left the hospital in a terrible state. I, for my part, never wanted to go back there again! And I never did go back to that place, although years later I would have to go to the new children's hospital renamed The Diana, Princess of Wales Children's Hospital, located in the city centre following the closure and refurbishment of the old building into modern apartments just off the 'Five Ways' traffic island on Broad Street. But I will come to that later on in this book.

As we drove back down the motorway I said to Karen that I didn't want to see Kaine again as I had honestly thought that she would have looked no different from the night that she had died. Now the shock of seeing her like that had really upset me. Karen felt exactly the same and had had similar thoughts prior to our visit to the hospital.

We had already decided with the undertaker on the arrangements for Kaine's funeral, and what route it was to take to the church, and subsequently Kaine's final resting place. This involved the funeral procession starting out from our house in Willenhall so obviously Kaine would have to be brought home for one last time. We both felt that we wanted to preserve the memory of her sweet little face as we remembered her, and so decided that the coffin lid would be closed. This we reasoned would be best for our friends and relatives who would also be attending.......

CHAPTER 3.
Mother Nature's rage.

A few days later the day of the funeral was upon us. It dawned cold and grey; the previous bright and sunny days had vanished. And so the darkest day of our lives was to have an appropriate backdrop of bleak November mist. We had breakfast of a sort as my appetite was not good, got ourselves ready, and; as we were still staying at Karen's mom's house, decided at what time to start out to make the fairly short journey to our house. This I was not looking forward to as I had not been back since Kaine's death. Karen's mother Pat had been there; to pick up clothing for us, and to prepare everything for the reception after the funeral, as we would be having a number of people back for the customary drink and something to eat.

As I walked in through the open front door, the feeling came over me that the home we had had was now just a house again.... The atmosphere was tense; no-one really spoke more than they had to. It wasn't long before the flowers and wreaths started to arrive one by one, and, as seems to be the tradition, were laid on the front lawn. We had ordered a white teddy bear made of white carnations and a bed of pink carnations spelling out Kaine's name. As all the flowers were arriving, I remember standing there in my suit, just staring at them, feeling very numb. Flowers were coming from everywhere; friends, neighbours and relatives had all contributed.

Finally the moment I had been dreading arrived. Karen's mom had been looking out of the living room window she turned to me and quietly said,

"Joe, they're here."

I could feel my stomach turning over. The funeral cortege had come into view at the top of the street and was slowly making its way down. We watched as the leading car, almost silently, glided along and came to a halt directly outside our house. The cars for family and close friends were directly behind, followed by a seemingly endless convoy of cars belonging to more friends and relatives. Through the glass panels of the lead hearse a small white coffin was in full view. The numbness I had felt earlier was still present within me as I watched. It seemed as if a film was unfolding some grim tale as the undertakers slowly opened the hearse door and gently removed the coffin from inside. While all this was taking place, a small stainless-steel trestle was being set up in one corner of the living room by another one of the undertakers, and as they brought her in and gently laid her on it my thoughts were, that at last, my little girl was finally home. Everybody stood there in silence, each with their own thoughts. As requested by Karen and I the coffin lid wasn't removed. I, along with Karen, found myself by Kaine's side, and once more tears came. I rested my hand on top of the coffin, and touched the little silver plate that had been attached to it. It simply read,

KAINE HELENA PATRICIA LAWLOR who fell asleep on November 6th 1989…. If only she were just sleeping.

The time came for us to leave, and for Kaine her final earthly journey was to begin. The closest family members were all in the funeral cars and friends and relatives took their places in the sad convoy behind. I sat next to Karen looking out of the car window as we wound our way through the streets on our way to the church. People going about their business on that bleak November day hardly gave a second glance at the cortege, apart from an old- timer who stood and removed his cap, as was the tradition of a more courteous era that had long since faded into obscurity. I saw two young mothers, who happened to notice the colour of Kaine's coffin as we passed mouth the words "that's a baby." The shock on their faces bore testimony as to the rarity of infant mortality.

We were approaching our destination and as we neared the church gates by the main road, I could see a large group of people gathered there. All were people we knew, and more relatives as well. I was shocked to see how much the death of our daughter had affected so many people, and I could feel a lump in my throat as emotions once again rose within me. As we stepped from the car I was conscious that all eyes were upon us. I could almost read people's thoughts, and I have to admit it was very uncomfortable to be in such a position; to be the focus of so much attention under such circumstances. Kaine was once again taken from the back of the hearse, and a small fold-away trolley was deployed as a means to take her from there into the church. I can remember people starting to cry as the little white coffin came into their view for the first time. Slowly, we made our way into the church behind Kaine, and as we entered, the song we had chosen for her on entry was playing. The air was emotionally charged as everybody took their seats and Kaine was placed at the foot of the altar with Karen and I a few feet away at the head of the congregation. The church by now was full.

I looked up, and saw Francesca for the first time in her official robes. After a few moments had passed to allow everyone to settle, she began to speak. What she said mattered little to me, for words were of no use. All I knew was that inside the little white wooden box that was now the focus of everyone's attention, lay the body of my daughter, who was our world for an all-too-short eighteen months; just six seasons. Words counted for very little......

The service inside the church drew to an end and now it was time to take Kaine to her final resting place. As we filed from the pews, Gloria Estefan's "I don't want to lose you now" played, and this song, I felt, said it all. I had wanted to carry my daughter to her rest but I was afraid that my emotional state would not allow me to complete the task; and so we walked behind, Karen and I, hands entwined in our mutual grief, followed by the others as the trolley used to take Kaine into the church was employed to take her the short distance to the cemetery.

When we arrived at the graveside, Francesca took up her position and everyone gathered around in a semi-circle to bid our daughter farewell. The weather by now had deteriorated. The wind had increased and violently tugged at Francesca's robes and vestments; it roared through the leafless trees making a shrill whipping sound. It was as if Mother Nature herself was enraged at the sight of a child's coffin waiting to be lowered into the earth. Francesca had to raise her voice against the wind.

"Go forth now Kaine Lawlor on your journey unto God, may he rest you in peace until the day of the resurrection through the Lord Jesus Christ. We commit this day the body of our young sister to the ground to await your calling. May she be granted peace at last. Amen."

As these words were spoken, the undertakers lowered Kaine from our sight forever….

We solemnly made our way back to the car park, a few minutes walk from where the funeral had taken place. I was not aware of anyone else around me at the time save my wife Karen, whose hand was in mine again as we climbed into the waiting funeral car. It would be some minutes before we could be on our way as the amount of people coming back to our house would take time to get into their cars. Some were unsure of the way and so we waited for them. Karen sat beside me and we didn't, couldn't say anything to each other. Once again I found myself staring through the car window. The raindrops that began to form and run down the glass matched the tears that ran from my eyes for the child I had left behind. I can't really say how or what I was feeling at the time. Emotionally I think I was drained of all feelings, and in my mind I felt myself returning to one of the happiest days I could think of….

CHAPTER 4.

Nothing now could stop her.

Just twenty-seven months earlier, I had arrived home from work tired and ready to flop into the chair in my living room. My job at that time was as a butcher in Birmingham's Indoor Market underneath the old Bull-ring Centre. The hours were long, seven until six and nearly an hour to get home by bus if the traffic was bad. But I was happy to work there, I loved my job and the atmosphere of the market was great. My work colleagues were a good bunch and although the days were long, they were filled with laughter for most of the time. My boss Alan Doherty and his brother Paul were top rate guys; really I couldn't have wished for better employers. Karen and I had only been married for a few months and we were living in a spacious council flat on Yew Tree estate in Walsall. It wasn't the best of neighbourhoods but then again it wasn't the worst either. For myself and Karen, in our newly-wed state and now having our own place; we were blissfully happy there. We had decorated and furnished the flat to our own tastes, and I can remember just having bought a brand new Hinari remote control television. It was only a sixteen-inch screen but it was mine, I was immensely proud of it, and envisioned myself falling asleep late at night in front of the TV with my slippers on my feet. We hadn't really got a lot but in later years I would come to realise we had had everything.

I'd just sat down and was reaching for the remote control when Karen said,

"Before you turn that on, I've something to tell you."

"How much have you spent now?" I asked jokingly, thinking she'd been out shopping and spotted a bargain.

"No you idiot, it's got nothing to do with shopping, but maybe a trip to Mother Care wouldn't be out of the question," was her reply. I stared blankly at her as Karen's sense of humour could be on the cryptic side and I wondered if she was having me on over something.

"I'm pregnant," she said, slightly annoyed that I hadn't gotten the Mother Care reference.

It was indeed earth shattering news to a twenty-three year old who was just getting used to being married to be told he was going to be a father as well. We hadn't really planned this or really talked about starting a family. I think we both assumed we would leave it up to nature and cope with things as they happened; and now it had happened. The news took a minute to sink in, and like most men when news like that is thrust upon them, I felt obliged to turn into a gibbering idiot.

"How, how did that happen?" was my response.

"Well if you don't know by now, then I aint gonna tell ya!" Karen laughed at my idiotic question.

"No,…. I meant, I don't know what to say."

"Well, don't say anything then and come and give me a hand with the tea!" I got up in a daze and proceeded to do just that, slowly coming to terms with the idea that instead of just the two of us, there would now be three.

"Congratulations dad!" she said to me, smiling. It was then that the reality hit me. I was going to be a dad! What a wonderful Feeling! Up to that point I had only given the thought of fatherhood scant consideration, in the past and now it was real.

"Well? Are you happy?"

"Of course I am, just give me a little time to get used to the idea."

Karen went on to tell me that she had been suspicious for a couple of weeks as she had been late, but had decided not to say anything to me until she was sure. She said that she had been to the clinic for a pregnancy test and that 'nothing now could stop her', to quote a line from a squeeze song. And so that night, after we had eaten our evening meal, we sat down to discuss an entirely different future to the one we had planned for ourselves before we had our happy news. We made plans to turn the spare bedroom into a nursery and when we went to bed later that evening, I slept the sound sleep of a happy man.

In the morning my usual alarm call went off at five o' clock. I rose and followed my usual routine of having a wash and shave. As I put my shirt and tie on, my thoughts turned to work and the lads. I thought to myself "I'll tell them all my good news when I get in." and so off I set with a bit more spring in my step than usual on that early morning walk to the bus stop. I arrived at work at about ten-to-seven; normally I was the first one in closely followed by Nobby and Ian. Alan and Paul would always arrive in at seven on the dot. We also had two young youth training scheme lads, Mark and Rodney. Rodney wasn't his real name (this escapes me now probably due to the lack of any real use,) so I hope the lad forgives me for this; but due to his resemblance to Del boy's brother from the television show 'Only Fools and Horses', the moniker was applied and stuck. No amount of protestation would then cause its removal. In fact, the opposite effect would be the result, and the name would be used even more vigorously than before. We went about our normal morning routine, (one that you would expect to see in any busy city-centre butchers shop,) getting trays of meat from the chillers, and chopping and cutting fresh meat and joints for our window displays. I loved the routine as the whole place had a busy urgency to it as we raced every morning to get the cabinets filled up and the whole pitch ready for when the Market Hall doors opened at nine o' clock. As was the case every morning, conversations would start amongst ourselves, ranging from the previous evenings television viewing to news items of particular interest to our market-hall butcher's philosophy. It was my job to prepare the second counter, Alan's was the first. Since I'd started working there, the counter that was my responsibility had seen a steady increase in trade, and I was pleased that my efforts to build this trade hadn't gone unnoticed by Alan. My weekly wage packet reflected his appreciation and a monthly bonus paid without fail ensured that our little band of brothers was indeed a happy one. This morning was no different to any other and the good natured banter began, with Nobby and Ian extracting the urine from each other as per usual. As Ian, shall we say had a slippery relationship with the truth, his nightly exploits were always met with derision by Nobby who found the endless supply of material very useful in the extreme as a way of steering the conversation, with the skill of a hunter towards a trap he would always spring in order to catch Ian out. This morning however after twenty minutes or so had passed and the laughter was getting louder, I thought I'd tell the boys my bit of news.

"Hold up lads, got summat to tell you."

"Oh! sounds a bit ominous Joe. An announcement this early in the morning's got to be important. Are you finally admitting you're gay?" said Alan. This was followed by howls of laughter from the lads.

"Nah, not yet Al', I'm waiting for you to come out the wardrobe first!" was my answer as it was my experience to fire back with a joke for joke in a shop full of comedians.

"No, seriously though, I got in last night and Karen told me she was pregnant."

"Who's the father?" asked Nobby, to more howls of laughter.

"Ha! Ha! very funny. No seriously though, lads, I'm gonna be a dad, and as I'm gonna have an extra mouth to feed Al', it looks as though I'm goin' to have to ask for a rise." Alan didn't see the funny side of this, but the rest of the crew found it hilarious. And so the morning went; congratulations were offered all round and the topics of conversation veered, as always, between the sublime and the downright ridiculous.

Anne and Carol were our two female counter hands who also worked with us in the shop. They didn't usually start until nine o' clock and so when they arrived, I told them of Karen's pregnancy and, as you would expect, a woman's reaction to this news was completely different from that of the good natured leg-pulling of earlier on.

"Great news Joe," said Carol, who worked with me on my counter. She was a lovely woman, with dark hair and a great sense of humour. Anne who worked with Alan and also a lovely woman was equally as pleased for us both.

The Market Hall opened and the steady stream of customers filed past. We were used to selling a lot of our produce by outcry and it was part of my job to attract and sell to our customers. Over the months I'd been working there I'd been doing just that, and, as I said earlier I had increased the trade on my counter significantly. A lot of my customers were of Afro-Caribbean descent and as Birmingham is a multicultural society, the mix of Irish, Jamaican, Chinese, Italians all made for a colourful and varied flow of people. Being of Irish blood myself, I found I had a talent for engaging in a fairly decent repartee with the various types of people I found in front of me on a daily basis. It is said that butchers, for some reason, have a reputation of being jolly and cobblers for being miserable; I was more than happy to be lumped in with the former. As a result, a lot of my regular customers became very friendly and they were aware of me being recently married. Some of the older dears took a keen interest in both myself and Karen, and of course I was only to happy to tell them of my good news. The reactions were of wide smiles and congratulations, and a few wagging fingers laughingly telling me that I was a naughty boy! Over the ensuing weeks and months these very same people would take a great interest in Karen's pregnancy, and, for my part, I was only too pleased to tell them of the growing bump that was our unborn child.

At home one evening, we were discussing the subject of babies' names. Karen had taken out a book from the library on this subject. We were pretty convinced that we were expecting a boy. So we looked down through the lists of names, going backwards, and forwards, disagreeing with each other over a few. I liked the boy's name Kane. [Karen liked the name also] and as we were convinced it was a boy in Karen's womb this was the one we settled on. It was only after some weeks into the pregnancy that Karen and I went to the hospital for an ultra-sound scan and were asked if we would like to know the sex of our baby. This was still relatively new technology at the time, and so we said 'yes'. It was then we were told that we were, in fact, expecting a girl and not a boy after all. We were also told that the baby was growing and developing normally and so we were happy and pleased that this was the case. The only disappointment I can remember feeling was that we would have to change the choice of name. I had my heart set on Kane and so I suggested to Karen that we keep the name and just alter the spelling, Karen agreed and that is how our daughter was given her name as we simply changed the spelling to Kaine. This sounded like a Gaelic name to me and so I was pleased at that. I was more pleased though that she was developing normally and healthily.

The weeks went by and the bump was getting bigger and Karen was blooming in her pregnancy. My daily routine of going to work at the market continued without break. The second bedroom of our flat was nearing completion now as a nursery; we had purchased and assembled a lovely white cot complete with mobile. Everything was in readiness. Karen used to work at Coral the Bookmakers in Wednesbury a small town a few miles from where we lived. It was only a part-time position and the money wasn't great but it certainly helped, and through our combined wages we found that we managed quite adequately. It was now nearing the time for Karen to leave work and concentrate on what was coming next. That would be as a full-time mom, our excitement was growing.

As I mentioned before, my regular customers at the market hall took a keen interest in our expected arrival; this resulted in my coming home on various evenings with baby clothes bought for us by kindly folks. We were beginning to amass a fair collection. Every thing was going so well for us at that time. The shop was busy, my side of the pitch was increasing steadily and my relationships with my workmates and customers alike were going from strength to strength. I was an expectant father and I couldn't have been happier.

I remember one night at home when we were in the nursery and it was two weeks from Karen's due date which had been predicted to be sometime in late April of 1988. We had emerged from the winter of that year and into the spring and as the weather warmed and new life once more sprang forth from the earth and leaves were beginning to bud in the trees, my attention was focusing on the new life created by us and starting to run out of room in her mummy's tummy.

"It must be getting a bit cramped in there by now don't you think?" I said smiling as I gently patted the bump.

"She had better get her skates on then and hurry up and come out." Replied Karen, and we both laughed.

I was looking at the collection of baby clothes bought for us in anticipation of their wearer. My finger ran around the neckline of one particular little set and as it did so I pondered on the next two weeks of waiting. And by the time the third week had passed I reasoned that my as yet unseen child would soon be occupying this garment. This was a little reality check for me, for in a few weeks or so the real work would begin and I would be responsible for another human being. Yes, it was getting close.

And so the day dawned of the 26th of April 1988. As always I got up and went about my routine of sticking some bread in the electric toaster whilst I got ready to go to work. As it was early Karen slept on undisturbed as I was went about my usual preparations. I went into the bedroom and kissed her good-bye as I always did and set off for work. The dawn was breaking and light was beginning to grow in the morning sky. I loved being up early in the mornings, I always have done, its 4.30 am as I write this so things haven't changed in that respect for me. I walked to the bus stop and as you might expect there were very few people about at that hour. This suited me, the morning larks were my only company as I walked the ten minute or so journey to catch my bus. I liked the forty minutes of solitude in the mornings as I sat upstairs, usually at the back, and I would sit there with my hands in my pockets if I hadn't got a book to read, listening to the engine as it revved and subsided again as the driver went about his work. I would get off at my stop and it was another ten minute walk to the underground car park of the Market Hall. As I walked down the ramp, the distinctive smell of the place was so familiar to me. I would make my way to the goods lift situated deep in the bowels of the car park and ride up to the first floor. I would hear tuneful whistling coming from within the market hall area made by some of the other early-morning risers as they went about their routine. This I found to be peculiar phenomenon, as most people who get up early, usually against their will, can barely grunt a 'good morning' at such a time. And yet different tunes, whistled by different lips, gradually filled the air as people arrived to start their day.

To-day was no different. I arrived at work at my usual time and began to put on my white coat and striped apron, the traditional butcher's garb. Nobby my good mate, arrived at his usual time just a few minutes after me as his bus ran just behind mine. Always a laugh, you could depend on him to lift your spirits in the blink of an eye if you were feeling down. His love life was as complicated as a Swiss watch and normally would be the first topic of conversation brought up. Everyone else started arriving and the usual 'good mornings' were proffered and reciprocated. We were a good-humoured bunch and I can't honestly remember a single incident of anyone arriving to work in a bad mood. Looking back nostalgically, the atmosphere created in that shop contributed to some of the happiest times and funniest moments in my life to date.

The well oiled routine of the shop cranked itself up, and soon each man was busily going about the various tasks to be performed, the urgency of completion once again taking precedence as the opening time of the hall drew near. This it did and again our wares were ready and waiting for the good hard-working people of Birmingham and the Black Country. I took up my station and as always went about my morning with my customers needs being attended to as a matter of priority. It was my goal that each and every customer of mine felt special in the attention that their custom required, and at times both counters would be three deep with people making our task easier as regards to shifting our produce. And so we all prospered.

The morning advanced at its usual hectic pace. The previous day Karen had told me that she was going to Sandwell Hospital for a routine check up. As I would be at work, she had said that she was going there with her mom. She was on her due date and so I was told to expect a phone call at any time. Our shop phone situated at the rear of the pitch was behind a partition where all our personal belongings were kept, and as you would expect from a busy little place like that, the phone rang fairly frequently. In my heightened state of expectancy, this didn't do my heart much good, as that morning, more than any other, I had my ear tuned for the 'ring ring' of the expected call that would send me on my way to fatherhood.

It was around twelve thirty or so when a call came through and one of the girls answered. The resulting comment of 'Joe, it's for you' sent my pulse racing. I picked up the receiver.

"Joe, I think you'd better leave work and get yourself up here." It was my mother-in-law Pat. "Karen's waters have gone and she's gone into labour."

"I'm on my way," I said, and quickly put the phone down while at the same time undoing my apron strings and taking off my white coat.

"Right, I gotta go," I said as I urgently put on my jacket and made my way to leave the shop.

"Good luck Joe!" called Alan as I made my headlong dash through the busy market.

"I'll ring you later!" I shouted back as I disappeared into the throngs of people and headed for the Market

Hall exits. I emerged into the bright April day, made my way down to the bus stops and got on a bus for West Bromwich where Sandwell Hospital is situated ironically along All Saints Way, cursing the driver for being slow and why were so many people getting on and off the damned bus? Didn't they know I was in a hurry to greet my new baby! The minutes seemed like hours and I didn't want to miss my girl's entrance into the world. I needn't have worried; I got to the hospital and met Pat who took me up to the room where Karen was lying on a bed.

"How are you feeling?" I asked as I sat down next to her.

"A bit uncomfortable but ok," was her response. It was going to be awhile yet before baby Lawlor was ready to make an appearance. We had had an overnight bag for Karen packed and ready at the flat but Karen had neglected to take it with her that morning and so I needed to get back to pick it up. Karen and her mom had gone to the hospital in our car a Vauxhall Cavalier; this was now parked on the car park. So I took the keys and along with Pat, I drove back to the flat to pick it up.

When we got to the flat Karen's mom sat in the living room whilst I quickly got changed out of my work clothes and grabbed the bag. I came back into the living room and told Pat that I was ready.

"Your lives are going to change forever after today Joe," she said, smiling at me in expectancy of Kaine's arrival. She had no idea how sadly prophetic those words would prove to be.

We drove back to the hospital and went straight into Karen. By now she was a bit further along and was beginning to feel the birth pangs now causing her to grimace as they took hold. We spent the next few hours awaiting the final stages of the pregnancy, and as nature dictates our child would come only when she was ready to do so. This time came about eight o' clock in the evening of the 26th. Her delivery was normal apart from a cut that was inflicted on the top of her head by one of the young midwives who did this in order to deliver Kaine. The sight of this was a bit too much for me and I'll confess to feeling a little woozy and had to open a window to get some air. When I had recovered I went over to Karen who was now holding Kaine in her arms. She was still attached to her umbilical cord and apart from the slight wound on the top of her head she seemed fine. Her mom had a look of pleased satisfaction and relief about her. I looked at my daughter and said, "So you're the one who's been causing all this fuss then." I was a happy man. She was here and she was fine, or so we thought. Karen was, as expected, a very tired woman by this time and so the midwives were arranging to get them both onto a ward for the night. When this was done I accompanied my wife and new-born child to the ward and saw them both to bed. I then had to return home so I kissed Karen and my new daughter goodnight and said that I'd see them both in the morning. Karen's step-dad Roy had been up to the hospital earlier in the evening and drove Pat home. I got back to the flat and watched a bit of telly for an hour or so before the events of the day began to take their toll. I went to bed and slept soundly.

The next morning I woke early as usual, one of my first tasks was to phone my place of work and tell them of our good news. I'd phoned my mom and the rest of my family from the hospital the night before and needless to say everyone was delighted that mother and child were doing well. My morning that day consisted of me getting myself ready to go to the hospital, having first phoned ahead to find out what sort of night Karen and Kaine had. I was told that everything was fine and that Karen was nursing Kaine as she had been up with her during the night. I arrived on the ward later in the morning to find Karen looking relaxed and pleased after her first night as a mother had passed successfully. I looked at Kaine now sleeping peacefully in her baby tank at the end of Karen's hospital bed.

"How was she last night?" I asked quietly in order not to wake her up.

"Fine, she's a greedy little thing though," Karen answered. I then enquired as to when we could take her home and Karen said that it would be a day or so before she would be allowed home with our little charge. I couldn't wait to take her home and show her all the preparations we had been making in expectancy of her arrival. And so it was that two days later I was at the hospital to take my wife and daughter home. Friends and family had all been up to see Kaine, and I was expecting more to arrive at our flat in the coming days so I thought we'd better stock up with tea coffee and biscuits.

It was indeed prudent to do so as the never-ending stream of relatives and close friends descended upon us over the next few days and 'cooed' and 'ahhed' at the sight of our baby. It was my job to keep the tea and biscuits flowing. This I did uncomplainingly and waited for the evenings to arrive when we could be alone with Kaine....

CHAPTER 5.
The first signs.

Those first few days and evenings were so very special. We cared for her like she was the only thing in the world that mattered, and of course she was. The midwives called on a daily basis also during this time to check on both Karen and Kaine. As I was there for the immediate days after Kaine's birth, I was witness to whichever midwife was on duty at the time showing Karen the skills of nappy changing and how much sudocrem to apply etc. and also explaining to us the importance of keeping baby's bottom clean and fresh in order to avoid painful nappy rash. Everything seemed fine, Kaine was feeding well and we were adjusting to our new roles as proud parents. The weather at the time of year was good and I remember that weekend we decided to take our daughter out into the May sunshine. It was a beautiful Sunday morning when we went out for our walk. Looking at Kaine in her pram on that lovely day we saw no indication of the illness that was soon to take a terrible grip of our child. The days progressed and everything seemed normal.

That was until one night when Karen was changing Kaine's nappy. She was lying on her changing mat when suddenly Kaine stretched out her arms and legs and seemed to strain her little body; the other physical thing we saw was that whilst this was happening, her colour went a deep red, from her face to the rest of her body. We thought she was straining to release a bowel movement, this did not happen, and although I think natural instinct told us this was not quite right, as this was over within a few seconds we reassured ourselves that it was simply that Kaine had strained to release the afore-mentioned bowel movement. In hindsight, I though, in all honesty was worried that all was not well. Even so we managed to put it out of our minds......Until it happened again.

I went back to work. In the following days, the midwives were calling on a fairly regular basis on Karen and Kaine. My days were as before; my customers asking about mom and baby and of course plenty of cards and more baby clothes. These I took home every night to our flat.

When I arrived home one particular night, I was met by Karen with a worried look on her face, I immediately enquired as to the cause of her concern and she told me that what we had witnessed with Kaine a couple of nights before had occurred again. Except that this time it was for a longer period. Karen's mom Pat was with her the second time. I asked if she had phoned the hospital and she had.

"What did they say?" I was now as concerned as Karen.

"They just said it was probably wind," Karen answered; her voice was a bit shaky.

"That isn't wind, I'm gonna ring 'em now," I said. I got on the phone and rang Sandwell Hospital and asked to be put through to the midwives department. The person on the other end of the line didn't seem to share our worries regarding our daughter. She asked if there was anything untoward with Kaine as we were speaking. I answered that she looked okay at that moment but that I was concerned as what had happened as it didn't seem right. She repeated the other midwives telephonic diagnosis of saying it was wind, adding "kids do all sorts of funny things with wind." She said that someone would call and take a look. I put the phone down and went over to Karen who was cradling Kaine in her arms while sitting on the settee. I looked at her and she looked fine nestling in her mom's arms with a contented look on her face.

"How has she been feeding?" I asked.

"She's been feeding ok; apart from that happening, everything's been fine."

I reasoned with myself that she must be feeling okay if she was feeding well as common sense would otherwise dictate that her appetite would be off if she didn't feel right. In the event, a midwife turned up at the flat about an hour after the phone call I made to the hospital. Karen explained to her what had happened earlier with Kaine. The midwife asked for her to be placed on the ready changing mat and to take her baby suit and nappy off in order for her to give her an examination. She then checked her over, took her temperature and examined her joints, hands and feet. She asked about Kaine's bowel movements and how she had been in general. Karen explained that as far as she could tell, as a new mother, that everything was as it should be apart from the straining, which we thought as yet was still unexplained. The midwife concluded that all was well, but as for the reason for us calling her out, she was silent on that one. After she had left the flat, we still had an instinctive, uneasy feeling about this episode.

We decided that we hadn't really got a satisfactory answer that night, and so in the morning Karen went to visit our GP. He examined Kaine and said that she seemed fine. The straining was beginning to become more frequent and we subsequently found out that these 'straining bouts' were, in fact, fits which Kaine was suffering from as the illness was tightening its grip. The weekend had arrived and it was on the Sunday that we found that the fits were getting more frequent and intensifying. Karen had learned quite accidentally, that if she blew gently on Kaine's face this would result in calming the effect of the fit. However at the time we had no idea at all what was happening to our daughter. We were getting more and more frustrated with the midwives who were calling at the flat; we were explaining what was happening to Kaine, but as these attacks were completely random, it would or could be any time when she took a fit. Other than that she looked completely normal. One of the more experienced midwives who called a few times could sense the growing anxiety we both displayed and sensed that all was not right with Kaine. She put a call in herself expressing a concern that Kaine should be looked at again by our doctor. He arrived at our door; we showed him through to the living room. He examined Kaine by checking her heart and looking over her little body.

He finally clapped his hands close by Kaine, I'm guessing to gauge for an unusual reaction. I can't be specific as I am not medically qualified. His conclusion? He pronounced Kaine fine. I asked "what about the straining?" and his reaction was one of puzzlement, again no answer to this! As I write I can feel my anger burning in me. If this collection of incompetents had, at some point even, took the precautionary measure of sending Kaine for elementary tests it may not have been my task now to write this story. As young parents we were dealing with mature medical people who were telling us that our baby was fine. Two doctors' examinations and numerous midwife visits had all concluded that we were imagining things! Who was to be proven right?

It was unfortunate that we were.....

The weekend merged into the new week, and we were increasingly worried that things weren't right. The week wore on. This was the second week of Kaine's life. The fits grew more and more regular and now yet another midwife came to our flat and examined Kaine. I had had enough, as my wife had, of being told that nothing was wrong. After looking over our baby, the midwife got up to leave, and it was at this point that I snapped. I said to her, "you are not leaving this flat until you SEE what's been happening to our little girl!"

She looked shocked that I had lost my cool. As if on cue, Kaine then took a fit right in front of this woman. Almost immediately she reached for our phone and dialled the hospital for an ambulance. This was the first time anyone else, apart from Karen's mom, had seen this. I didn't know whether to be relieved or not; relieved that something would now be done and fearful as to what was so wrong with Kaine that prompted the ambulance to be called immediately.

The midwife wouldn't or couldn't give us any details. The ambulance arrived and we found ourselves heading for Sandwell Hospital once again. Only this time anxiety had replaced the happy feelings of our expectancy of two weeks previously. We arrived at the hospital and were shown onto a ward accompanied by the midwife who was explaining to one of the medical staff what she had seen at our flat. The machinery of the NHS now took over and Kaine was taken from us and a series of tests began in order to determine the cause of the fits that we had witnessed many times and seen more recently by the midwife. The look of concern on her face will stay with me forever more. We were for the first time since Kaine's birth, both of us, without her. We anxiously waited for news of our daughter's condition, and, as ever, we were in the dark about progress, without even anyone to ask., with hindsight, I've often felt that the lack of communication between the hospital staff and us as parents was deliberate policy, stemming from the old saying of 'knowledge is power'. I would have thought that if they were ever in the same position they might have realised how desperate one could be for even the smallest piece of news.

After a considerable period of time which we had spent pacing the waiting room, a doctor approached us and began to explain the procedures and tests they had been going through with Kaine. He explained that they had performed a lumbar puncture to draw fluid from her spinal column for testing; these tests would now take time to complete in the laboratory. And so again we waited and waited.

It was around three o' clock in the morning or so when the news reached us of Kaine's diagnosis. The previous few hours my mind were occupied by the thought of the lumbar puncture, it had sounded so painful for a little tot to endure. Of course I'd never even heard of the procedure before that night, now the term is burned into my mind.

The same man came to give us the bad news. I think by this time now we were prepared for the worst as we were both very tense at this point.

"We have run all the tests we needed to in order to make a diagnosis and then treatment procedure," he began. I was hanging on his every word, as was Karen. The latter part of the man's sentence was the most prominent in my mind though. Treatment, this was hope to us.

"Your child is suffering from a viral infection; the area of infection is in the fluid in the spinal column. This also affects the brain, hence the lumbar puncture. I'm afraid your daughter has contracted meningitis." Meningitis! I'd heard of the disease and from the look on the doctor's face I knew it was serious, but as for what it did I had no idea at all. Karen spoke first,

"Is she going to die?" she asked with tears welling in her eyes.

"You mentioned treatment," I said, latching onto the words of his previous sentence.

"We hope we have caught it in time to prevent death, but I'm afraid we cannot tell as yet if the disease will, or has, caused any damage within your daughter's brain or body. The treatment we have Kaine on at the moment is anti-viral antibiotics administered to her intravenously. It will be some time before we can say for certain when we will see an improvement in her condition."

"Can we see her?" we asked anxiously.

"Yes of course, I will arrange for you both to go to the ward." And with that he left us alone in that room. We couldn't have known then that the course of our lives had been irrevocably altered. And from that point onwards nothing would be the same as it was before.

Our state of mind was one of complete turmoil, we had no idea what to expect. Was our child of two weeks going to be alive by the time the sun rose? Or were the doctor's words to prove that they had caught the disease in time? But then the worry of Kaine being damaged mentally or physically or both was the new spectre that had invaded our consciousness.

These were questions only the following hours and days would answer. At least we knew what was happening, and as of yet, the anger I was to feel towards those who had ignored our pleas when we knew in our hearts that Kaine was unwell, had not risen to the fore. I was now, as was Karen, more preoccupied by the treatment that our daughter was receiving. We were taken to the ward where Kaine was being treated, she was lying in a hospital cot and she appeared to be asleep; the intravenous drip with its life-giving fluid was attached to her. There was no sign of the midwife who had accompanied us to the hospital earlier. It was late and I reasoned that she must have long since gone home. To this day my feelings for her on that evening are mixed. She had, in fact, been responsible for Kaine being taken to the hospital and so may even have saved her life. However if she had left as she was about to do prior to my insistence that she stayed, she may well have joined the others whom I condemn as irresponsible in the treatment of our child.

Is it merely a speculation on my part which I should lay to rest? Maybe so, but I can't help feeling that if our pleas to the professionals had not gone unheeded, then the outcome of our lives may have been quite different and that is all I am going to say.

We were informed by one of the nurses that a bed could be provided for Karen to stay with Kaine. This obviously Karen wanted to do; as for myself, however, no such provision could be made at that time. So we decided that Karen should stay whilst I made my way home to pack a bag for Karen's needs. I left the hospital ward and made my way down to the foyer where the payphones were situated and rang for a taxi. This arrived within ten minutes and I found myself heading home, minus wife and child. Maybe the taxi driver picked up on my mood or maybe he wasn't the chatty type anyway, but little was said between us apart from destination on my part and the resulting fare by him.

I entered my flat. All the lights were still on as we had left in a hurry. The quietness of the place gave me a further uneasy feeling as I recall. I switched the lights off and headed for my bed; although my mind was preparing itself for the trials that we had still to go through, I guessed sleep, if it came at all, would be of little benefit to me. This proved to be the case, and when I got up the first thing to enter my mind was Kaine's condition. I immediately telephoned the hospital and was put through to the ward Karen and Kaine were on. I was talking to Karen and enquired as to how Kaine was and how she looked.

"She seems to be sleeping well, she's not had any more fits but as yet I'm waiting to speak to one of the doctors," she said.

"Ok, I'm gonna pack your bag and make my way up in the car, do you want me to get you anything to eat?"

"Erm, yes, bring something with you from the shop." I then put the phone down and went about packing a small suitcase with underwear and toiletries for Karen's use and some clothing for her and Kaine. As I was doing this, the thought that a very sick child was a very heavy yoke to wear entered my mind. It seemed only a short time earlier that the biggest problem I would have would be a large gas bill or something as equally trivial. I didn't feel my twenty-odd years that morning, more like one hundred and twenty.

I completed the job of getting the suitcase ready, I then got myself washed and dressed. I left the flat, car keys and case in hand and got into my car to drive the twenty minute or so journey to the hospital; a place I would find myself getting familiar with over the following few weeks.

I arrived on the ward after first stopping off to get Karen a sandwich,

some sweets and a drink from a local paper shop. I immediately enquired how Kaine now was and Karen told me that the doctor had been round to check on her progress. Although it was early in her treatment it seemed that Kaine was responding to the antibiotics; we weren't going to lose her, thank God. However whilst we were obviously pleased that her condition was stabilised, we were still looking at the prospect of a disabled child, as I mentioned earlier meningitis was virtually unknown to both myself and Karen. I had heard of it but as this was my first encounter with the disease, it was obviously something about which I needed to know more. We asked to speak with a doctor who could explain exactly what the disease was and it's ramifications. This meeting was arranged a few hours later and we went to a small side office where a doctor was waiting for us. We sat down and he began to explain to us what exactly meningitis was, how there were different strains of the bug and described its destructive presence in the body. I listened in horror as he explained that meningitis caused blindness, amputations, deafness, brain damage, and in some cases, death. We were out of the woods it seemed as to the latter; it was to be a little time before we were to find out how this horrendous thing was to affect Kaine. Reassuringly he told us that in cases of meningitis, it was fairly common for a full recovery to happen. This olive branch we readily grasped at. And we prayed that this would be the same for our daughter.

There was little we could do at the hospital except to be there and monitor Kaine's progress and hope and pray that the doctor's last words to us would prove to be true in our case.

I remember sitting in the hospital room provided for us with a separate bed for Karen's use. The weather outside was beautiful, bright sunshine was filling the day; this was to me in stark contrast to the darkening clouds that had now filled the previously unblemished horizon of our future. I had to go home for a few things and while I was there I rang Alan, my boss, and gave him the news of Kaine's illness. I had, whilst at work, told him of the unusual behaviour Kaine had been displaying and, of course, the man was concerned for me, as were the rest of the staff. However, I didn't tell my customers of this as I am a private person, and I was still, at the time, hoping that all this would turn out to be nothing at all.

"Joe, if you know any prayers say 'em," was his response to the news of Kaine's illness.

"Obviously I won't be in tomorrow Al' and if you want to tell the rest of the gang for me I'll be grateful," I said.

"Okay, Joe, you just get that little girl of yours sorted out." This I assured him was my intention and that I would keep him informed of any and all progress. This glorious Sunday ended with my going back to the hospital where I spent the evening with Karen carefully watching as Kaine was making slow progress fighting the disease that would eventually and cruelly claim her....

CHAPTER 6.

"Your lives are never going to be the same."

As Monday morning dawned, I awoke alone in our flat. My normal routine would have been to rise early and get ready to go to work. However it was to-day that my routine would be broken, and the first signs of my mother-in-law's prophetic words that our lives were to change forever were beginning to show. I got myself ready to go to the hospital. All the time my mind was focused on Kaine. I could take a little comfort from the fact she was now in a stable condition, but my mind couldn't tear itself away from the terrible possibility of brain damage, and so the worry went on.

I arrived at the hospital around half past nine, I went straight to our room and enquired after Kaine. The news was that she was still holding her own against the disease and so I felt slightly better. Karen looked tired and I told her that if she wanted me to stay at the hospital for a while or overnight to give her a break, that would be okay. But she was a dedicated mother who loved her child and so she wouldn't be without Kaine for a minute. I understood how she felt and our next course of action was to find out if any damage had been created by the meningitis bug. To this end we needed to speak with one of the paediatricians at the hospital. Kaine was now being closely monitored by the nursing staff. As she was barely two weeks old, it was not really possible to determine if she had been affected mentally by the bug; this would only be seen as she grew and developed.

There were some very positive signs which we felt were very significant. Her eyesight remained unaffected, as were her reactions to stimuli. Her hearing also remained unchanged. And so all these positives we used as little bricks to build our house of hope that she may have been lucky enough to have emerged unscathed from this potential killer-bug. An appointment was made for us within the hospital to see the paediatrician; it was to be around two o'clock that afternoon. I was eager to speak with this person to put my mind to rest even more. So far the signs remained good. Kaine's limbs, hearing, sight etc were unaffected and we thanked God that her life was no longer in immediate danger. The last hurdle of possible brain damage though, seemed to be the biggest to get over. There were some ways that could determine the general condition of her health at that age, but as for the higher functions of the brain such as developing speech, numeracy, cognition and general normal development all this was yet in the future and so this was of major concern to us.

Our appointment time came and once again we found ourselves in what was now becoming an all too familiar place, the doctor's office. We had approached the doctor's door at precisely two o' clock, I had politely knocked and the female voice from within had bid us 'enter' and so we found ourselves in front of a woman who was to take a great deal of interest in our little girl. She was smallish in her late thirties I'm guessing, with short dark hair. Her manner was very pleasant and refreshing, not at all stuffy; I immediately liked her as she had the ability to put one at ease in a tense situation, and I think this could be classed as one of those situations. she introduced herself as Doctor Andrea Mayne, Consultant Paediatrician at Sandwell District General Hospital. It was her role to oversee Kaine's treatment and recovery. She had in front of her all of Kaine's notes to-date and other papers to which she referred as we spoke; she informed us that the type of meningitis Kaine had contracted was a type categorized as meningitis group B STREP, and that this type was not the type to cause loss of limbs or skin. This was an obvious huge relief to us both but the other problems mentioned such as blindness, deafness and her development as a normal healthy child had still to be addressed. As I mentioned earlier, the signs were that her sight and hearing were unaffected, so I was feeling more buoyant that we would indeed be fortunate and that Kaine would make a full recovery and remain unscathed.

"We're very concerned about possible brain damage doctor." I said.

"The initial prognosis is that Kaine has not suffered any brain damage that we can tell. As paediatricians, we deal with children of this age all the time and it would seem that, so far, although very early in her treatment, we are very hopeful that Kaine will not be affected by any damage; but as I have said, her long-term development will highlight any abnormalities." We were hopeful but not completely reassured by her comments. It would seem that we would have to wait and see.

After our meeting we went back down to the ward to take up our places by Kaine's bedside. Karen's mom and step-dad came up later that day, and obviously were very concerned as to how she was. At least we could give them some good news that she was holding her own, that the fits had stopped and that she was being kept sedated for a few days in order for her treatment to work to the full. Her feeding was being done by tube and as Karen had intended to nurse Kaine herself, the result was that nature's body clock was now dictating the time her feeds should take place. And so Karen had to express this surplus milk that Kaine would have consumed. At night I was heading home to our empty flat, and the late evenings were taken up by my taking and making phone calls to concerned friends and family.

The days following that, Kaine was allowed to wake up and start feeding normally again; and it was obviously a source of great joy to us both when she opened her eyes and her mom offered her up to the breast and she hungrily took to it. We reasoned that if she knew where to get her food then there couldn't be much wrong with her brain. The hospital had to do more lumbar puncture procedures to monitor how the anti-viral antibiotics were doing; each time they did this Kaine was again sedated. We viewed this as a necessary evil she had to go through to make her well again. The results of these tests were good; Kaine was winning her battle with the disease and we hoped that we would be able to take our little girl home with us again very soon. In the event, it was to be a further two weeks before she was finally discharged from the hospital. Doctor Mayne had visited Kaine many times during this period to check on her progress and had become quite friendly with Karen and myself.

As Kaine was making progress, I decided to go back to work as she was improving daily, and I still needed to earn a living to keep us. Alan, my boss, had not deducted any money from my wages in my absence and I thought it was only fair not to have too much time off as the bulk of the crisis now seemed to have passed. After work I would make my way to the hospital to attend to Karen's needs and also to see how our little treasure was doing. And she was doing fine. My customers at the shop had obviously missed my presence and had been kept informed as to the progress Kaine was making; and so on my return to work the true nature of ordinary people was laid bare in the form of dozens of get-well cards and teddy bears and soft toys of all descriptions which had been passed over the counter on a daily basis from the time they had first learned of Kaine's illness. I was truly touched that so many people cared, and soon we were running out of room in Kaine's nursery back at the flat with all of these offerings now piling up.

I was now able of course to keep my customers informed myself of how she was doing. The day was drawing near for Kaine to leave the hospital and I was looking forward, as was Karen, to resuming our lives the way they were before our daughter was taken ill.

The longed for day finally arrived, and so I took the day off work in order to bring our little girl home again. The worries of the previous two weeks were fading in to the back of my mind and both myself and Karen were optimistic that Kaine would make a full recovery; this was what we hoped for. I awoke that morning with a different outlook, for I was now thinking that we would be able to resume the life we planned for ourselves; that of course being the raising of our child worry free. I got into my car and drove to the hospital. This had become an all too familiar place over these last two weeks, I would be glad to see the end of it as would Karen. At least, for myself, I had had the opportunity to get a break by going back to work and of course returning to the flat every night. Karen, by contrast, had more or less been at the hospital full time, the only break that she had taken had been to come back to the flat to pick up some clothing and toiletries, this of course bore testimony to her dedication to her baby.

It would be good to be home with all three of us again; our flat had become a lonely place in the evenings on my return from the hospital. And so I arrived at the ward to find Karen all ready to go, we were bidden farewell by the hospital staff and Doctor Mayne had made a special visit to Karen to wish us well.

Of course that would not be the end of the hospital visits as appointments had to be made at the out-patients department to monitor Kaine's progress. But that morning we were free; it was a lovely day in May and we were just glad to be getting out of there. We placed Kaine in her pushchair and made the short journey down into the car park. Karen sat in the back cradling our baby as I put the pushchair in the boot. I really couldn't wait to start the engine and soon we were driving home, the three of us together once again.

We arrived home and I remember thinking she was safe and sound with us I didn't want anything to hurt her again. We settled in and all was left to do was watch her grow; the last two weeks would soon fade into the back of my mind and we thanked God that our daughter had survived this episode in her thus far short life.

The first indications that that all was not as it should be occurred just a few days later. Kaine had started to go off her feeds and become quite miserable and when not like this she was very drowsy; so without taking any chances calling the midwives out, we went straight to the hospital where Kaine was now admitted immediately due to the recent meningitis bout. Our fears came flooding back and once again as we found ourselves in very familiar yet relatively-speaking unwelcome surroundings. The reason I say this, is because in spite of the care she received there, we really didn't want to find ourselves at the hospital again, and especially so soon after leaving.

Kaine's condition remained the same and we feared a return of the bug that had come close to taking her from us. She was examined by one of the paediatricians on the children's ward. He ruled out a return of the meningitis bug and maintained that what was wrong with Kaine, was as a result of her recent illness. He, however, didn't want to speculate as to what the cause might be until a more detailed examination could be made. The most obvious pointers on the exterior though; were that when he measured the circumference of Kaine' head, it was found to have increased much more rapidly than it should have done for her age. And her fontanel, (in layman's terms the soft spot in her head) was quite tense. Kaine was sent for an ultra-sound scan the results of which were not made known to us until the following day.

After a sleepless night at the ward for Karen, and for myself back at the flat, morning came and after I'd arrived early, we impatiently waited for the results concerning our daughter's condition to be made known to us. Kaine was still drowsy and non-responsive and this state was a source of great concern to us. A meeting was scheduled with Doctor Mayne, and so we found ourselves before this lady once again; our growing confidence of the previous days broken and battered by this unwelcome turn of events. Doctor Mayne explained to us the results of the ultra-sound scan. She went on to say that Kaine's head circumference was now the key to what was wrong with her. Apparently her head had been growing normally, over the last ten days however a marked increase had been noted and this, coupled with the tense fontanel, prompted the initial diagnosis of hydrocephalus. In lay-man's terms again, this is more commonly known as 'water on the brain'. The ultra-sound scan had also revealed that due to the meningitis bug, the ventricles within her brain had become blocked up.

I will attempt to describe this condition as it was relayed to me in the hope that readers without medical training might understand the cause and effect on Kaine's well-being.

In the centre of the brain is a chamber which contains the fluid that travels up and down the spinal column and in and out of the chamber itself. There are two small tubes which allow this fluid to pass to and fro from the chamber; the meningitis bug was in this fluid and thus degraded or blocked these tubes. This spinal fluid was prevented from travelling its course and so a build up of fluid within the brain had occurred. This condition is known as hydrocephalus. The result of all this was the drowsiness described in Kaine earlier, and the obvious miserableness that she felt with being unwell, and, as would be expected the lack of feeding as well.

This news was, as you might imagine, very upsetting to us both and as we sat there she went on to explain what exactly could be done to relieve Kaine's suffering. An operation would be required but this was not to be carried out at Sandwell Hospital but at Birmingham Children's Hospital. This was a significant development for us at this time; our lives had now taken another sharp turn and I personally felt that it was no longer us in charge. Fate itself was now controlling the events in which we were to find ourselves becoming deeper and ever-deeper embroiled.

CHAPTER 7.

"Manna from heaven."

We left the meeting having thanked Doctor Mayne for explaining in detail what had to be done to make Kaine well again and indeed the reason for her being unwell; for as I said earlier information to those starved of this can, in some cases, be like manna from heaven. In our case though we had mixed feelings about this turn of events, I was very uneasy about the operation involving the most delicate and intricate of organs in the human body. I could have felt easier, I think, about anything else. Broken bones heal as they do, and skin repairs itself in its usual fashion; but as for neurosurgery, this was a fearful event for me to contemplate for my little girl. I kept my thoughts to myself as I didn't want to alert Karen to my fears.

An ambulance had been arranged to take us to the Children's Hospital in Birmingham, and so on our return to the ward we found Kaine being prepared by the nurses for her journey there. As Karen gathered her own and Kaine's things together, I arranged to follow the ambulance in our car, as the route to the hospital was unknown to me that time; and why should it have been? For neither I nor Karen had any reason to ever go there prior to the birth of our baby. It was, though, to become a well-travelled path which we would take many times more than we would have wanted to, I'm sorry to say.

And so a short while later, I made my way to the car park to get my car and rendezvous with the ambulance at the exit of the hospital. Karen stayed with Kaine in the back of the vehicle. It set off with me following behind, we made our way up All Saints' Way and down the dual carriageway to join the M5 motorway. As we entered the slipway and then onto the carriageway, the ambulance increased its speed and I struggled to keep up with it, eventually arriving at Birmingham Children's Hospital. The ambulance, of course, went straight to the emergency entrance whereas myself, in a private vehicle, had to find the public car park. I eventually did so and then had the problem of finding out exactly where they had taken Kaine in that large ominous-looking building that was so strange to me. I parked the car and made my way toward the public entrance having had to ask for directions on the way from some other people who had reason to be at the hospital. When I eventually found my way and walked up to Reception, some twenty minutes or so had elapsed and I was a little hot and bothered by having to rush. I spoke to a nurse on Reception and explained to her that my daughter had been transferred by ambulance from Sandwell children's ward, was somewhere within the building and that I needed to find both her and her mother. After some internal phoning around, the nurse eventually traced them to a ward and gave me the directions I needed. I expressed my gratitude, and set off in the direction of her pointing finger towards the elevators situated at the end of a long corridor.

I eventually made my way up to the ward and having first stopped off at the nurse's station to ascertain that I was in the right place, eventually found Karen and Kaine a little further along. When I got there I was slightly breathless and more than a little agitated as I think the stress of heading into Birmingham, trying to keep up with a speeding ambulance through the notoriously busy 'Spaghetti Junction' and then trying to find my wife and sick child in that huge edifice was starting to get to me.

Karen was taking to a tall, balding, dark-haired man whom I learned was Mr. Hockley, the Consultant Neurosurgeon at the hospital. Kaine was lying in her hospital bed and was obviously the intent of his focus. Karen looked at me on my arrival and seemed at ease compared to when I left her at Sandwell.

"Ah, you must be dad," he said in a surprisingly light hearted-tone.

"Yes I am," I answered. I was a little tense as I have said, but the man had an air of supreme confidence about him that seemed to ease this feeling in me. He reached out his hand to grasp mine and introduced himself.

"I'm Anthony Hockley, I'm the Consultant Neurosurgeon for the hospital. Your daughter has actually been placed in Mr. Hamilton's care, who is my partner here. Unfortunately he is on leave at this moment in time so your daughter will temporarily be in my care until he returns." He must have picked up on the way I was feeling because he added reassuringly that everything would be fine and that we were not to worry; this would be an entirely routine operation.

I must have exhaled noticeably at this because he patted me good-naturedly on the shoulder and smiled as a kindly father would with his inexperienced young son. He turned his attention to Kaine once again who was very pale and non- responsive. Her fontanel was bulging noticeably and he delicately touched it with his fore-finger.

"This is the immediate problem we will have to sort out. We are going to have to take her away for a little while and as soon as we are done, she will be brought back feeling a lot better, I can assure you both." At this I could have kissed him as I'm sure Karen could have done also. He left us and on his instructions, a very short while after that, the nurses came to prepare Kaine for whatever procedure Mr. Hockley was to perform. The porter came with the wheeled stretcher and they removed Kaine from us and took her away. All we could do for now was wait. It wasn't too long before we had our daughter back with us, and to my surprise, she was looking so much better compared to what we had observed in the previous hours gone by. The first and foremost difference was that the bulging of her fontanel had gone down noticeably to what would be classed as normal, and as the decrease in pressure inside Kaine's head was taking effect, her colour had returned and her eyes were now open and she seemed more responsive to what was going on around her. This, as you can imagine, was to our great relief. The only noticeable result of the procedure performed on her was a small red dot in the centre of her fontanel just above her forehead. Common sense told me that this was but a temporary solution to the problem though, as obviously the main reason for Kaine's condition were the blocked ventricles, as explained to us by Doctor Mayne at Sandwell. I was to be proven right in my assumption, and as the nurse was settling Kaine into her hospital cot, Mr. Hockley came into the room

to explain what he had done, and what must be done, to relieve the build-up of fluid in Kaine's head on a more permanent basis.

He went on to explain to myself and Karen that all he had done for now was to simply insert a hypodermic needle into the fluid chamber and draw off the fluid that was in excess and causing the pressure inside the cranium. This resulted in an immediate improvement in Kaine's condition and as the man had said that when she was returned to us she would be feeling a lot better, this indeed proved to be the case.

"So what happens next then?" I asked him.

"Well we will have to operate fairly soon as the fluid-build up will return as the natural drainage within the brain isn't working, so an artificial means to do the job will have to be employed."

He went on to explain that in years gone by, before a treatment for hydrocephalus was developed that children with this condition were unlikely to live for very long. For as the build-up of fluid caused the cranium to expand more and more, the weight of the enlarged head became too heavy for the neck muscles. This resulted in their not being able to support the head and, as a result, they became more or less entirely wheelchair bound, or carriage bound for the duration of life. The pressure on the brain would increase and this would eventually result in death. This was not what we wanted to hear, but he was talking in the past tense, and so we were understandably keen to hear what could be done to prevent this happening to

Kaine. Mr. Hockley explained that an operation would have to take place to fit a ventricular-peritoneal shunt; this was to be the artificial means by which the fluid would then be drained away,

Essentially a shunt is a small white rubber type object. It is tubular in shape and has a series of drainage holes at the upper end. Also it has two small little buttons which can be manipulated manually in an emergency. Tubes are attached to the shunt, one for draining fluid from the chamber within the brain and the other to get rid of this fluid. I believe in Kaine's case, this was drained into her abdomen. Essentially a shunt is a valve that works on pressure, when the fluid builds up the valve opens and drains it away. Mr. Hockley having explained to us as much as he could he then excused himself as he had other duties to attend. Before he left however, he said that the date and time for the operation would be handled fairly shortly by the administrative department of the ward on his instructions, and that we would be kept fully informed as to this.

All this was extremely worrying to us as we had hoped for the best on Kaine's release from Sandwell Hospital and now we were faced with a potentially life-threatening condition and a brain operation on a very small child. We comforted ourselves however in the knowledge that Kaine was in good hands here at the Children's Hospital, and that was the only thing that we could really cling to in order to keep our spirits afloat at that time. In the next few hours Kaine started to behave normally and began taking her feeds hungrily again and so this was a good sign for us to see. That evening, as I was now growing more accustomed to, made my way back home alone and settled in for the night fully aware that the next day I would again be back at the hospital. Worry was now my constant companion; it was an unfamiliar acquaintance up until this time and one I would have rather done without.

The usual phone calls were made to keep everybody informed and after that I went to my bed feeling more exhausted that night than if I had done a full week's work without a break. The next day I rose early got ready and made my way into Birmingham. The hospital as I have said was situated close to the city centre, and so in my mind, in order to relieve the tension of being constantly on the ward, I thought that at some point during the day if circumstances would allow me, I would make my way down to the Bull-ring Centre to the Market Hall to see my employer Alan and the lads. If the truth be told, I longed for the time when our trivial chit-chat was all that occupied my mind and those care-free days seemed so far away now I wondered if the sun would ever rise again without this constant worry weighing heavily on me. When I arrived at the hospital and went onto the ward, Karen was feeding Kaine and she looked relaxed; so this in turn relaxed me as well.

"How is she?" were my first words.

"She's okay, she's been feeding properly and seems content," answered Karen.

"That's good, any news on the operation yet?"

"No, not yet, but it's early and we're expecting the doctors to do their rounds at ten o' clock, so they might tell us then."

"Well, it looks like we'll just have to wait and see then eh?" I said. "Later on to-day I was thinking of going into the market to see Alan and the boys and let them all know first hand what was happening. It's only down the road a bit and I shouldn't be too long. Alan will want to know how soon I will back at work so I'll be able to give him some idea as soon as we know what's happening here."

"Yes, do that, and say 'hello' to Anne and Carol for me when you get there." Karen had got to know my work colleagues from the many times she had come to the market on a Saturday evening to drive me home from work.

"Yeah, I will do. But I ain't going nowhere until I know what's going to happen here though." Ten o' clock came and a short while later the doctor in charge of the ward came to check on Kaine. He looked at the nightly record and checked her over physically as well.

"Well everything seems fine so far, I'm still waiting to hear from Mr. Hockley's office as to when Kaine's operation is to be scheduled, but as you can see, we are monitoring your daughter very closely and any change in her condition will be dealt with immediately."

These were comforting words, and I began to relax a little more as my previous thoughts that Kaine was in good hands were being more and more reinforced by the care and professionalism I could see before me. A few hours later the same doctor came back and informed us that the operation on Kaine was to be the next day on morning theatre. My apprehension began to rise within me again at this news, but at least now we knew exactly where we stood and could plan accordingly. Karen suggested that this would be the best time to go into work and let Alan know what was happening and this I readily accepted as I never really did like hospitals and still don't to this day. I kissed Kaine gently on her forehead, as I was holding her at the time and gently passed her back into the care of her mom.

"Right then," I said as I pulled on my jacket.

"I'll see you in a while and I'll say 'hello' to the gang for you as well." Karen smiled and said "'bye' as I headed for the door. I made my way down through the ward, passing the rows of beds containing other poorly kids of various ages, I couldn't concern myself too much with other people's plights as my own was upper in, and foremost on my mind. I went into the lift which took me down to the foyer and out onto the street, I made my way through the city centre down the familiar streets and found myself by the Bull-ring centre. I entered the Market Hall at the Saint Martin's Church entrance our pitch was only a hundred yards or maybe a bit less from the doors. The noises and smells of the market hit me as I entered and I found Alan in his usual position with a tray of steaks in hand turning on the charm for a prospective punter.

"Hello Al'," I said as I walked onto the pitch. "All right lads?" I enquired of the others at more or less the same time.

"Bloody 'ell Joe, what you doin' 'ere?" Alan said, surprised at my sudden appearance.

"Just came to let you know what's going on," I replied. By now the lads had gathered round, as pleased to see me as I was them.

"I'll stick the kettle on," said Nobby, who was eager for a break.

"Good idea Nobby, you can do that while you're sortin' out that fore-quarter on the block!" said Alan sarcastically.

"Ok mate," was Nobby's reply, and as myself and the rest of the staff and more especially Nobby knew, Alan's pet hate was being called 'mate', it was a sting-in-the tail reply to which he knew he could do nothing about as everybody sniggered, including me. It was a welcome relief to the strain I'd been under to see that at least some of my world remained intact and as sardonic as ever. To make matters worse the prospective punter that Alan had entrapped with his formidable sales pitch, had taken full advantage of this brief intermission to decide that the five or six quid Alan wanted for the steak might be better off spent in the pub, and so had quietly slipped away.

"Now look what you've made me do!" shouted Alan, clearly annoyed that a customer had escaped.

"What 'ave I made you do Al'?" asked Nobby feigning concern in his trademark high-pitched voice.

"That punters sloped off cos you distracted me!" shouted Alan again whilst banging the unsold tray of steaks down on the counter.

"Oh, sorry mate," answered Nobby with a hint of a smile on his face that told he was as far from being sorry as he was from becoming the next Pope, and even more pleased that he'd got a second 'mate' in on the word duel.

"Prat," was all Alan could mutter to himself, knowing he'd been soundly beaten and no doubt wishing he'd just let Nobby put the kettle on when he'd first mentioned it.

Anne was the first to speak concerning Kaine. "How's the baby Joe?" she enquired. The mood changed to a more serious tone as I went on to explain that Kaine would be having an operation the next morning.

"What's that entail then Joe?" enquired Alan. I went on to explain that it was to be a neurosurgical operation to fit the shunt and that according to the doctors at the hospital it was a routine operation and that everything should be fine. Obviously any operation concerning the brain has a degree of seriousness and this fact was not lost on all concerned. I could detect an undercurrent of fear for myself and Karen in our conversation regarding this. I wanted to change the subject and for a little while forget that I was now a father with a sick child and wanted to be just one of the lads cracking jokes with my mates as we had done before all this happened; and so I spent the next forty minutes or so chin-wagging with the lads about their scrapes and encounters that I'd been missing while I was at the hospital.

When the time came for me to return to the ward, I told Alan that as soon as I got any news to tell them I would ring and let them know exactly what was happening, Alan, although sympathetic to my problems, was keen to have me back at work, as all the hard graft of building a decent trade on the other counter was starting to slide somewhat in my absence. I assured him that at the earliest opportunity I would be back in the saddle, so to speak, but for the moment I could concentrate on little else than what was going on with Kaine at the Children's Hospital. This he accepted of course and I understood perfectly that the man had a business to run and that it all was very much akin to a well oiled-engine and that if a part was missing it didn't run quite so efficiently and this as I mentioned previously was what we all strove to do.

I left the market a little saddened at having just a brief taste of my old care-free life and now the worry of this operation once again returned. My thoughts turned to my wife, and I thought to myself that it had been a little bit selfish of me to have taken a break from it all when she was constantly at the hospital without let up. Of course Kaine's physical needs regarding her feeds played a primary part in Karen's attentiveness but even so I know for an absolute fact that even if Kaine had been bottle fed and that a nurse could have taken over for awhile that Karen would not have left Kaine's side for a minute so strong was this bond of love between her and her daughter.

On my return to the ward I found Karen sitting in the armchair reading a magazine, looking relaxed and fairly happy in spite of the operation to take place on the morrow. Kaine was sleeping peacefully in her cot a few feet away, having not long been fed by mom.

"Everything okay?" I asked already knowing the answer from Karen's demeanour.

"Yes, everything's fine. The doctor wants to see you though regarding the operation tomorrow."

"What about it?" I asked, a bit surprised that he wanted to see me.

"He said something about signing the consent form in order to carry it out. I told him that you'd gone out for a while to see your boss and that you'd be back later but I didn't know when. How's everybody at Alan's anyway?"

"Still the same, you know what Nobby and Ian are like for winding Alan up, I said 'hello' to Anne and the gang for you. Carol had gone home as she only works part-time. Anne sends her love though."

"That's nice of her; you'd better go and find the doctor to get that form signed then eh? We don't want any hiccups."

"Yeah, too right, I'll go and find out where he is and get it sorted out." I left the room again and heading for the nurse's station I told the sister that I needed to see the ward doctor to sign the consent form for the next day. She rang his office and found him there and informed him of my presence back on the ward to which he asked if I could go and see him straight away. I then went to the office and found the good doctor sitting at his desk.

"Ah, Joe there you are, I've been looking for you."

"Yes, I know. Karen told me as soon as I got back, and I came straight here."

"Well it's nothing to worry about; however it is important that we have all the paper work sorted out before Kaine's operation tomorrow."

"Yes, Karen mentioned something about a consent form that you need me to sign."

"Indeed, I have it here. Assuming you have no objections to the operation being carried out by the hospital, it's just a legal requirement that we have to go through in case anything goes wrong."

"Anything goes wrong?" I asked, suddenly concerned at this negative connotation.

"Believe me Joe this is an entirely routine operation, fairly simple by neurosurgical standards and Kaine is in the hands of the best, I can assure you of that."

Knowing that Mr. Hockley himself was carrying out the operation I knew that this was the case, and so I felt slightly easier, although I still wished he hadn't mentioned the possibility of anything going wrong. I was tense enough with my own fears and these I felt didn't need adding to.

"Yes, of course, I have no objections whatsoever, it's just that I'm a little well, you know jumpy."

"Of course I can understand how you feel Joe; this can't be easy for both you and Karen."

"Okay, I guess we'd better get this form signed then." He placed the form in front of me and passed me his pen. This was the first time in the history of my life when the responsibility of another human being was in my total care, and I felt it. If it were just me having to go under the knife I may have felt slight apprehension but in this case I was granting consent for my little daughter to be operated on, and so the apprehension I felt was compounded. However I knew that this was all for her good in spite of the natural worry that gnawed at my insides. I took the form in my hand and briefly read it; it wasn't in any way complex with legal jargon. It was just a simple consent form. I signed it and passed it back to the doctor who dated and signed it as well making the consent legally binding.

"Good, now that's all sorted we can go ahead and get on with the real work of getting Kaine well for you to take her home," said the doctor, smiling at me.

"Thanks doc', that means a lot to me." I shook his hand and went back onto the ward to where Karen and Kaine were.

"How did you get on?" asked Karen upon my return.

"Fine, it was just as you said; he wanted me to sign the consent form for the operation."

"Did he say anything about tomorrow?"

"Only that she would be in the hands of the best and that it was fairly routine and we weren't to worry unduly." I told Karen reassuringly. At this Karen smiled and looked a little bit more relaxed. I suggested that she take a little break now that I was back and Kaine was asleep, by popping out and having a look around the shops on Broad Street. She looked a little pale from the lack of fresh air and I thought it would do her good as well to experience a little normality in life even if it was just for an hour or so.

Reluctantly she agreed, yet I had to keep telling her that Kaine would be fine and that she was to go and do what she was good at.

"What's that then?" she asked me, slightly puzzled.

"Looking in shop windows of course!" I laughed.

"Cheeky git, it's a good job we ain't got much money or else you wouldn't be laughing when I came back!"

"I know, that's why I said it. Now go on get lost!" I wanted to relieve the tension as much as I could and Karen felt the same,

she gently bent down, kissed Kaine and smiling at me, she left the room for a brief respite.

About an hour later Karen returned. By this time, Kaine had woken up and was quite happy to be in my arms as I sat in one of the armchairs provided by the hospital. She was looking up at me and I was talking to her in that baby talk we seem to think they can understand but, of course, made no sense to either of us. Her eyes followed my finger as I moved it across her vision, once more satisfying myself that her eyesight remained unaffected by the meningitis. As I passed her back to Karen her arms flailed slightly and she took a little sharp intake of breath upon happy recognition of her mother. This we both laughed at as we were becoming more convinced that, although she hadn't come through the meningitis entirely unscathed as we'd hoped, it seemed her development as a normal baby remained unimpaired.

"How did you get on having a look around the shops?" I asked Karen.

"Would 'ave been better if I'd got money to spend," she replied, laughing.

"I know, Broad Street isn't exactly the bargain basement when it comes to prices is it?"

"You can say that again!" She replied, once more laughing, but I could tell that she was only too glad to be back with her daughter once again.

The afternoon wore on into the evening. The only noticeable change we could detect so far was that Kaine, although still remaining lucid and responsive, was now showing signs that the pressure in her fontanel was building as it differed from when the excess fluid had been drawn off earlier. It was starting to bulge slightly again, reminding us both of the urgent need for this operation. If unchecked, the pressure would build once more to a level that would induce the tell-tale signs of drowsiness and refusal of feeding. It eventually became time for me to leave and yet again make my way home to the flat. The morning would bring a new day and I was hoping for an end to our troubles. With this thought in mind I said a little prayer that this might be so.

I arrived back at the hospital early next morning; sleep had largely evaded me as it had Karen, as she told me on my arrival. The nurses were busy preparing everything for Kaine to be taken into theatre and Karen had been told not to feed her for some hours before as this would satisfy the nil-by-mouth requirement where all operations requiring anaesthetic are concerned. Kaine's fontanel was even more prominent than the day before and she was 'cranky', this, I reasoned, could be a combination of not feeling well again and being denied her feeds. The nurse in charge filled out the little name tag that was to go on Kaine's wrist; double checking her full name and date of birth and adding to this the name of the operation, this being abbreviated to v. p. shunt. At last she was ready to go to theatre, I looked at her, she was so little and delicate amongst the group of people now milling around in a sense of controlled urgency. I wished to God she didn't have to go through this but it had to be done, and soon she was taken away from us again.

"Try not to worry," said one of the nurses to Karen as Kaine was being wheeled away. Easier said than done, I thought to myself at that point, I grasped Karen's hand gave her a little reassuring smile.

The following couple of hours or so seemed the longest of my life as we waited for Kaine to return from the operating theatre, and when finally she did, we were greeted with the pitiable sight of Kaine being brought in on the gurney and being lifted gently from there onto the hospital cot. A brown iodine stain ran from her neck up behind her left ear where a gauze dressing covered several recent stitches which had been inserted into a small incision. Underneath the skin, I could make out a little bulge where the shunt had been fitted. Obviously Kaine was not fully conscious as yet due to the anaesthetic. My eyes immediately fell on her fontanel, and I could see straight away that the recent bulging that we had seen had gone; so the shunt valve appeared to be working properly. Karen had looked for this too, and silently I thanked God that she was okay. Our relief was palpable as the nurses now took care of Kaine's post operative welfare. They moved her onto her side and brought a small bowl of water along with what looked like small sponges attached to plastic stems. One of the nurses dipped the sponge into the water and put it to her dry lips. I was amazed to see an immediate response from her as she licked thirstily at the liquid. She must be parched, I thought to myself but I was glad it was all over and I was hoping that this would be the end of it for us.

Our immediate instinct was to want to pick her up, but we knew, of course, that she had to stay where she was and be closely monitored by the nursing staff until the full effects of the anaesthetic had worn off.

"The best thing for her right now is to sleep," one of the attendant nurses told Karen. "It will be a while yet before she feels like she can wake up properly." Karen nodded in agreement.

"You can give her water as we're doing now, she'll be conscious enough to know how much she wants, and when she's had enough she'll stop taking it from you; but it's important to keep her hydrated, so keep offering it to her until she wakes up properly and starts to want to take a feed." She looked so small and helpless but for now the worst was over.

Over the next few hours Karen did exactly as the nurse had outlined and gradually Kaine started to come round more and more. The nursing staff were in attendance every thirty minutes or so to keep a close eye on Kaine as she came back to full consciousness. All I could really do was to be there with Karen. I did however go and make the necessary phone calls to our families to keep them up to date on events and obviously put their minds to rest. I also put a call into work to let them know, as promised, how things had gone with the operation, and I told my boss that, all being well, I would be in work the next day. I was relatively close to the Children's Hospital and figured that if Karen needed me, I could be there in fifteen or twenty minutes from the city centre.

"That's good news Joe," was Alan's response to both the successful outcome of Kaine's operation and my imminent return to work.

All I wanted now was for Kaine to make a full recovery and for Karen and I to take her home, so that we could resume our normal lives once again and watch her grow. In the hours that followed Kaine was a little 'cranky' once more but this was to be expected as the operation's effects were probably still with her; but on the whole, she appeared to be recovering quite well and was feeding normally too. I told Karen that I was planning on going into work the next day and that if she needed me to just phone straight away. Karen was fine with this as her mother would be coming over the next day as well to keep her company for a few hours, and obviously, as soon as I had finished work, I would come straight there also. That evening as I made my way home, there was a sense of relief that Kaine had come through the operation, was recovering under the professional care of the staff at the hospital and that Karen was there to keep a watchful eye on our daughter. So, exhausted, I went to bed early, hoping that the interruption to our normal routine was at an end or very nearly, and slept soundly until the alarm went off at five am. I awoke and as I went about getting ready for work, my thoughts returned to my young daughter. I wondered how she had gone through the night and if everything was well. I had the telephone number for the Nurse's Office on the ward but I thought it a little early to ring. I also figured that everything must be okay as I would have heard from them had it not been so. The best thing to do, I reasoned, would be to go to work and ring from there a little later.

As I left our flat that morning it was already light, the beautiful blue canopy of the early morning sky stretched out above me, and the rising sun in the east was of deep orange red, its early rays painting the few clouds on the horizon a beautiful reddish golden colour. I must have witnessed the early dawn many times in the past, but this morning, of all mornings, the new day seemed more beautiful than ever before. No doubt the contentment I felt at Kaine having come through the trial she had done enhanced my mood. I made my bus on time and took my usual seat upstairs and settled in for the journey in to work. Still I felt this nagging in the back of my mind that I wouldn't be happy until I assured myself that all was well at the hospital.

When we had completed the preparations for the shop, with about fifteen minutes or so to spare before the Market Hall opened to the public, I grasped the opportunity to ring the ward to ease my mind. I was put straight through to the nurses' station and spoke with the ward sister regarding Kaine's post operative-night. She immediately put my troubled mind at ease by telling me that according to the night staff's report, she had had a comfortable night and so had Karen. Apart from waking up for feeds everything had been fine. I asked to speak to

Karen but was told that she was asleep and so I just said to tell her that I'd called and that as soon as she woke and was convenient she could give me a ring at work. And so with my mind easier now I went about my work picking up from where I left off, dealing with the customers old and new.

At the end of that first day I felt like a broken record player, after the umpteenth time responding to my regular customers' enquiries as to how Kaine was and explaining the type of operation she had just had. Of course this was to be expected, I was somewhat touched as to the good nature of people in general; their enquiries were a reflection of the concern they felt towards my wife and our daughter. Karen had called earlier in the day as requested and I had been able to pass on the good news that everything was indeed fine and Kaine was doing okay for now. That day's end couldn't come quick enough and as soon as I was free of work I hopped on a bus to take me to the hospital to see first hand how Kaine was.

I arrived on the ward about half-past six that evening and went straight to our room where I found Karen, with Kaine lying in her cot awake and content. The tenseness that had been evident in Karen's face over the past days had gone and she looked more relaxed and at ease.

"How is she?" were my first words on seeing her.

"She's fine, been good as gold all day, haven't you sweetheart?" answered Karen as she reached over and gently caressed Kaine's tummy.

"That's good." I joined her by the side of the cot looking at Kaine who in turn was looking back at us. Reflecting back now I wonder to what degree children of that age can recognise the people who are most important to them at that very early stage in their lives. One thing I know to be certain though is this; from the moment a child enters the world the instinct we feel as parents to protect and care for our children, in most cases, never fails.

"What's the doc' said then?" I asked.

"Mr. Hockley has been to see her today and he's really pleased with how she's doing. He said in a couple of days, if everything continues as it is, we can go home, can't we mate?" said Karen happily, as she again looked at Kaine.

"That's great; I didn't expect to hear that news so early on. I can't wait to get us out of here, I think we've had enough of hospitals to last us a lifetime eh?" Karen nodded her agreement. This was indeed good news to hear; the shunt that had been fitted was working perfectly and there was no sign of hydrocephalus recurring. As far as we were concerned now our troubles were over, a few more post-operative recovery days in hospital and that was that; back to normality.

CHAPTER 8

Kaine's first Christmas.

The next couple of days went by uneventfully. On the third day following the operation on Kaine, I was at work when I had a phone call from Karen. I picked up the receiver to find Karen quite happy and excited on the other end of the line.

"The doctor's been round to see Kaine, and guess what?"

"What?" I said, expectantly.

"He said that Kaine is doing fine and he can't see any reason now why she can't be discharged."

"What-like-straightaway?"

"Yes, they want to see her again in a month just to check that everything is okay and that there are no problems."

"That's fantastic! You'd better get packing then just in case they change their minds."

"Mom's here with me and she's started packing my stuff. I've just got to go to the dispensary to pick up some medicine for Kaine and get the discharge note from the doctor, and that's it."

"Okay, looks like I'll see you at home tonight then," I said.

"Yes, you will, I'll see you later." Karen said, happily. I put down the receiver with my final words in my head. It seemed like an age from when we found that Kaine was ill at two weeks old, up until now; and those words I'd wished to say many times were now reality. A great weight, it seemed, had lifted off me, and Carol gave me a big hug when I told her that Kaine was at last going home and that it looked, at last, as if our troubles were indeed, now over.

I couldn't wait for the day to finish so that I could go home and see how she was. When it eventually did and I arrived at the flat, the aroma of a home-cooked meal greeted me as I walked through the door; it was only then that I realised how much I'd missed that. As I walked along the hallway I could see Karen in our living room holding our daughter who was quite content in her arms, it was then that a cheery 'hello' from the kitchen alerted me to my mother-in-law Pat's presence. She had stayed over to cook our tea on our first night back as a family.

"Don't expect this treatment all the time," she said, smiling to me. As Pat's cooking was a favourite of mine that statement was a bit disappointing.

"Thanks Pat, that's kind of you to do that,"

"Oh, think nothing of it Joe; it's the least I could do for you both, Roy is coming to pick me up soon so I'll be out of your way and you can settle in. I'm glad that Kaine's out of the hospital at last."

"Me too. I thought that the day would never come."

I walked into our living room and as I entered Karen said to Kaine,

"Oh look here's daddy." I felt an emotional surge at that because it seemed that we had fought a battle and won out against the odds, and I was happy.

"Right then, I'll ring Roy and tell him your back from work so he can come and get me," said Pat. I sat down next to Karen on the sofa and looked at Kaine. She was getting bigger, her eyes were bright and beautiful. The only tell-tale sign that anything untoward had happened to her was the little scar behind her ear and the bald patch where she had been shaved prior to the operation where her hair was beginning to re-grow. The shunt itself was just visible underneath the skin, but as soon as her hair had grown over it, that too would be out of sight. Karen passed Kaine to me and I sat back with her in my arms as she was looking at me with her enquiring mind studying my face as if to say 'who have we here?' I tickled her under her chin and she smiled at that. It was a moment of tranquillity to last with me forever.

Karen and her mom went off into the kitchen leaving Kaine and I

alone together; with all that had been going on over the weeks of her illness I think this was the first time that I had had Kaine to myself for a few moments in the comfort of our home without the worry of something being wrong with her.

"I think me an' you should get to know each other a lot better, don't you?" She smiled at me again.

"I'll take that as a yes." I smiled back at her and for that brief moment in time everything in the world was right.

Roy came to pick Pat up and after having a cup of tea and a chat we waved them off as they drove away from our flats At last the three of us were alone together. We sat down to have the evening meal that had been cooked for us and Karen put Kaine in her bouncy chair so she could be close by us as we ate. The chair had a metal frame with a material backing, slightly over horizontal, with a restraining strap in to keep baby secure. This was quite effective because she could see everything going on around her and kept her happy because if we had placed her in the Moses basket she would not have been able to, as she would have been lying flat. And of course we could talk and interact with her all the more.

After our meal I cleared the table and did the washing up whilst Karen tended to Kaine's needs. After that, all we had to do was relax for the evening quietly for a change as all our previous evenings had obviously been quite different until now.

"I'm so glad to be home," Karen said.

"Yeah, I'm glad it's all over. You said we've got to take her back to the hospital in a month for a check up, didn't you?"

"It's just routine apparently, to check that the shunt is working as it should be. They said we were to keep a close eye on her fontanel while it's still visible in case we see any signs of it bulging again."

"What happens though when her soft spot isn't there anymore, what then?"

"We need to keep an eye on her feeding and over drowsiness. The doctor said there would be clear signs that she would display if the shunt were to block but he told me they are effective and reliable. It's just something we need to be aware of really. They're hoping that she won't need the shunt at all as she gets older as the ventricles may unblock naturally anyway."

"Let's hope so." I said. For the moment though, we wanted to forget the hospital, the doctors, the nurses, and everything medical. We wanted to be a normal young couple with a baby having a night in front of the television, and that was precisely what we were going to do. The evening was as it should be; I put the telly on and we watched a video for a couple of hours. We went to bed around half-ten as I recall, both of us feeling drained and exhausted. Karen put Kaine to bed in her Moses basket right next to her side of the bed as this was convenient to her to feed her in the night. I didn't witness any of this as I was lights out as soon as my head hit the pillow.

The days that followed were happy ones as Kaine continued to recover from her ordeal, and both myself and Karen allowed ourselves to relax.

Soon it was time for Kaine's check up at the hospital, and for reasons of convenience to travel, her appointment was made with Doctor Mayne at Sandwell Hospital. I, of course, was at work but as everything was going well with Kaine, I had no reason to expect anything other than good news on my return home that evening, and it was to be so.

"How did you get on with Doctor Mayne?" I asked.

"She's delighted with Kaine and how she's doing; she really did fear the worst, she told, me when we had that meeting in her office, but now everything is fine. She's very happy."

"Well, she's not the only one, eh?"

"No, she certainly isn't." said Karen. In the month following her release from hospital, Kaine had gone from strength to strength. She had gained weight and was developing perfectly normally as regards cognition and awareness; those dark days when we feared brain damage were passing into an unpleasant memory for us and that suited me fine!

I was at work one day when one of my regular West Indian customers came to the counter holding a package; she was a middle-aged woman who lived alone and did her weekly shopping in the market and bought her weekly supply of meat from me.

"Hello Rose, how are you today and what can I do you for?" I asked with a smile and a wink.

"Stop ya nonsense buoy!" she laughingly said in her broad Jamaican patois dialect. She motioned for me to come closer to the counter, at the same time leaning forward herself as if to ask me something confidentially.

"What's up sweetheart? I can't lend you any money 'cos I'm skint," I said jokingly. She grasped my hand, leaned closer and said,

"How is your little daughter doing?"

"She's absolutely fine Rose; thank you for asking."

"Dat's good, now you take dis present back for dat little girl of yours. I prayed to Jah for her when I first found out about de meningitis; I wanted to give you dis earlier, but I thought it better to find out if she had de all clear first."

She thrust the package into my hand, blew me a kiss and off she went on her way. I felt a lump in my throat; here was a woman practically a stranger praying to God for the safety of my daughter. It shows that humanity transcends race and culture. Inside the package was a beautiful baby set for a girl three months old or more. Bless her.

The summer went on and everything remained fine with us then autumn came, the leaves fell and soon dispersed with the blowing of the winter winds; the days were growing shorter and the evenings and the nights colder. Soon it would be Christmas. This year would be our little girl's first, and so would be special; Karen and I were also busy preparing for our first Christmas as a family and Kaine was going to be spoilt rotten!

She was still having her checks at the hospital and with our G.P. who, it has to be said, was shame-faced on seeing Kaine and Karen for the first time after his completely missing her illness. He'd obviously had the letters informing him of Kaine's subsequent correct diagnosis and treatment from Doctor Mayne at Sandwell Hospital. Karen told me that it had given her great satisfaction to tell him to his face that we wanted to be attended to by another doctor at the surgery.

Kaine was a delightful little child who only kicked up a fuss when she needed feeding. Karen said in that sense she was very like me! Our happiness was growing as well as our little family for we had gained a four-legged addition to in the form of Karen's Staffordshire bull-terrier whose name was derived from the Greek god Zeus. Karen's mom had been keeping the dog at her house with their own dog Jessie throughout Karen's pregnancy and Kaine's illness, but now we felt that he could rejoin the family and be introduced to our newest addition Kaine.

He took a couple of curious sniffs at Kaine in her bouncy chair and waltzed off to play with his rubber ball. So much for introductions!

We were well into December and the climax to the year was fast approaching. The Christmas decorations went up throughout the city giving the time of year its stamp of uniqueness compared to the other eleven preceding months. We were busy at the shop, and it was a struggle to stay awake on the bus coming home in the evenings, a problem I relayed to Nobby who informed me that he had had a similar experience one Saturday night after ten pints, when he woke up on the upstairs deck of the bus at three o' clock Sunday morning in Birmingham Central bus Station garage in complete darkness, after the bus driver neglected to ensure all his passengers had disembarked before going home for the night.

Every evening I would get home, and Karen, enthusiastically, would have a catalogue open looking at children's toys choosing what presents we were going to buy for Kaine. That first Christmas it looked as though a small fortune would have to be set aside to accommodate the vast array she had in mind. Of course this was entirely understandable for only months earlier, the question of whether we would be celebrating Christmas at all with our daughter was not at all conclusive. Still, that was behind us now, and we wanted Christmas to be a magical time for us. We were keen to see the end of the year and looking forward to the new year of nineteen eighty nine and hoping that the challenges of the previous months were long gone and soon to be forgotten.

And so Karen was happily buying presents for Kaine and proudly showing me what she'd got before wrapping them and hiding them away. This was much to my amusement as I couldn't understand why she had to hide presents away from Kaine who had not learned to walk yet let alone open wardrobe doors and go mooching!

"It's what you do at Christmas," she said to me in answer to my bemused question, and laughing at the ridiculous notion of what she was doing.

"Are you sure you're not hiding 'em away from yourself? You know what you're like for opening presents," I said laughingly.

"I might be," she said, "so you had better make sure you hide mine away safe and sound."

"Don't you worry about that mate; even Zeus couldn't sniff out where I've hidden yours!"

"Good, 'cos I want to be surprised on Christmas morning."

"Don't worry; you will be," I said confidently, I'd been planning to make this Christmas a good one for Karen and Kaine but more especially for Karen, as the heartache she had endured during the time that Kaine had been ill had affected me deeply and I wanted to make sure she was happy.

The day all butchers long for and dread dawned for me as an extra early one. Christmas Eve, that was the make or break of the frenzied preparations made beginning in the second week in December. Thousands of pounds had been spent on extra stock. To say we had work to do was indeed an understatement! I arrived at work early, and fully aware of the hard day ahead, but looking forward also to the excitement the day itself generated within the market. I wasn't to be disappointed in any way that day. Our trade was fast and furious; our customers came thick and fast and were dealt with in the usual jovial manner they had come to expect. The day ended with Alan even selling half his own turkey to a late comer who was a little bit too full of the Christmas cheer. No-one was surprised at this, as Alan was a salesman unrivalled in his enthusiasm to sell his wares! The market hall doors finally closed at six on the dot. All was left now was to count the takings, store what little stock that was left, and clean up and go home. We all pitched in with what energy we could muster to complete our tasks and finally bade each other merry Christmas as we made our separate ways home that night.

It was late, and I was tired, and I still had a forty minute bus journey to do. I pulled my lapels of my coat tighter around my neck to keep out the freezing wind blowing directly at me as I made my journey to the bus stop. I got on the fifty one and slumped into the seat upstairs, the bus was half full of tired people finishing late as well from work and making their way home, also there were a couple of lads who were slightly merry as newts, singing Christmas songs. Nobody minded, it was Christmas after all. I sat in my seat and felt the thick brown packet in my pocket, it was my wages plus bonus from Alan and Paul for all the hard work that had been done over the preceding weeks, a feeling of pleased satisfaction came over me at the day's events. I had done well, all that building up of custom had paid off. I once again struggled to stay awake as the sound of the bus's engine had a hypnotic rhythm to it. Finally my stop came into view. I made my way downstairs and holding on to the rail I waited for the bus to come to a halt and I got off. It started to rain as I walked the final steps of my journey home, I opened the front door with my key and I was half-frozen, half-soaked by the rain that had fallen on my ten minute walk from the bus stop.

The contrast between the outside world and that just inside the door of my home couldn't have been greater. The warmth of the hallway reddened the cheeks of my face as I wearily took off my coat and went to hang it up on the coat hooks in the hall. It was then that Karen opened the living room door on hearing the front door being opened and closed again. She had Kaine sitting up on her left arm, her elbow crooked under Kaine's bum for support.

"Look who's finally decided to come home Kaine," Karen said to our daughter who, in turn, was looking at me with that heart-melting smile of hers. Framed in the doorway as they were, I could see the multi-coloured glow of the lights of our Christmas tree behind them. It was so warm and inviting; coupled with the aroma of my much-needed dinner, I doubt any man could have wished for a better homecoming.

"God, you look like a drowned rat!" exclaimed Karen, laughing at my dishevelled and rather damp appearance.

"Thanks, love you too," I replied jokingly at the same time bending down to take my boots off. I'd been standing in them for nigh on fifteen hours by this time. Foot odour was not a problem I ever really suffered from but the extended period of use that day was pushing the boundaries of foot hygiene.

The dog came rushing out of the living room on hearing my voice, no doubt in anticipation of the nightly treats he'd become accustomed to on my return from work, and was busily sniffing at everywhere about my person so as to discover its location.

"Get down hound!" I said laughing as he started to playfully push at me with his snout as if to say "come on, I know you've got me summat, so where the hell is it then?" I had indeed brought him his treat but he would have to wait until I was safely ensconced in the flat and reasonably comfortable before he could have his insatiable curiosity satisfied. Kaine found Zeus highly amusing and chuckled and giggled at the sight of me trying to fend off his boisterous antics.

"You need a bath, I'll run you one while you get changed." Karen said and went back into the living room to put Kaine into her little walker. This was a little frame with wheels and a material baby seat with a tray in front. This gave her the mobility she needed to follow her mom around the flat as it would be a while yet before she could master the fine art of walking; a problem I sometimes had myself after one too many. I went into the bedroom, got undressed, put my dressing gown on and slung my dirty washing in the laundry basket in the bathroom whilst Karen was running my bath for me.

"How was the day?" she asked.

"Chaotic, I've never seen so many people in all my life; we've almost completely sold out," I said in response to her enquiry.

"I bet Alan's pleased eh?"

"Yep, he was like a dog with two wotsits come the end of the day. I don't think I've ever seen him so happy; he even sold half his own turkey to some bloke at the end of the night!" I laughingly said, knowing Alan's penchant for making a few quid.

"Yeah, but how did you end up?" Karen asked, shaking her head in disbelief at the thought of Alan flogging half his own Christmas turkey.

"I dunno, my wages are in me pocket; I was too tired to even bother checkin' what's in there. It feels thick enough though unless he's filled it with cardboard to pad it out! I think we've come out okay."

I was in the warm inviting bath by this time and a little bump up the side of the tub signalled the arrival of

Kaine in her baby walker. Her little hands were grabbing at the side of the bathtub and she struggled to look over the edge, attracted as all young children are by the splashing of the water and soap bubbles from my bath foam. I gathered some of these in my hands and offered them to her so that she could feel the warm texture of the foam. This she did and I playfully put some on her nose and laughed as she wrinkled her little nose as the bubbles began to pop and make her sneeze a couple of times. Zeus put in yet another appearance and was up the side of the bath not wanting to miss out on all the fun. He copped a load of bubbles in the mush as well; and as dogs nose's are ultra sensitive, he retired from the proceedings sneezing violently as he retreated back along the hallway and into the living room. This Kaine found to be hilarious and chuckled even more at poor old Zeus's discomfort.

"You cruel sods;" laughed Karen. "You've upset 'im now."

"He'll be all right once he's got his chops around what I've brought him from work," I said.

"What you got him then?"

"A big fat juicy marrow bone for Christmas!" I laughed

"Oh! he loves them," Karen said.

"Yep, so I'm sure all's gonna be forgiven when he sees it." My stomach was dictating its own need now for sustenance and, so refreshed from my bath, I dried myself off and got into something more comfortable- namely my tracksuit bottoms and sweatshirt my favourite garb for relaxing in. When not being carried by either her mom or me Kaine used to wheel and bump her way around the flat taking paint off the door frames in the process but it didn't matter a fig; she was healthy and this was our first Christmas together and we were looking forward to many more.

I'd got to hand it to Karen, the living room looked spectacular. Candles adorned the shelves and window sills (out of Kaine's reach needless to say), the Christmas decorations shimmered and glittered in their warm comforting light, the large Christmas tree twinkled with flashing lights, and silver and gold coloured baubles sparkled, hanging from its branches. Underneath were placed a myriad of presents that heaped on top of each other, the vast majority for our little darling. The dining room table was set out with a candelabra as the centre piece and two bottles of wine, one red and the other white, reflecting back the flames of the illuminating candles burning so brightly. Karen had sprayed fake snow in the corners of the windows and the inclement weather beyond the glass complimented the layout of our living room perfectly.

"Wow! Look at this place." I said in deep admiration. "You two have been busy all day haven't you now?"

"Do you like it then?" asked Karen, knowing my response, and obviously proud of the look she'd achieved.

"Do I like it? It's absolutely fantastic!"

"Good I think you'll like your tea even more then. Sit down and I'll bring it in." I was indeed starving and the sight of a huge T-bone steak with chips, onion rings and mushrooms was a sight to behold. Homer Simpson wouldn't have stood a chance against me in an eating contest that night so voracious was my appetite!

My stomach satisfied after my long day we settled down for the evening to watch the telly. Zeus was curled up sleeping peacefully in his basket as we relaxed on the settee; Kaine had fallen asleep between us and looked like a little angel resting gently against her mother's thigh.

Our respective presents were under the tree ready to be unwrapped on the arrival of Christmas morning. The apartment was warm safe and cosy, the dog was sleeping peacefully in his bed, but the greatest gift of all that Christmas, was that Kaine was well and we would be celebrating the time with the magic of the day re-incarnated in the youth of our child, as our belief in Santa was a long-distant pleasant memory from both mine and Karen's childhoods.

So well satisfied with our life thus far and only too aware of the narrow escape we had had from tragedy earlier in the year we settled down and with a couple of drinks put a film on and relaxed in each others company for the night.

It must have been ten the next morning before my eyes opened and immediately the smell of the Christmas turkey cooking in the oven hit me. Karen had risen early in order to get it ready although we weren't having our dinner at our flat: instead, as was our Christmas tradition, we were to have dinner at Pat and Roy's house. Our turkey was being prepared for our own Boxing Day dinner. I got myself out of bed, and still yawning, I walked into the kitchen to find Karen busy with the rest of the chores to be done.

"Morning! sleepy head," she said as I walked in, "I thought you were never going to wake up; we're dying to open our presents." Kaine was bumping her way towards the kitchen by this point, as well as the dog, and I got the impression I was being ganged up on.

"Yeah, sorry, I must've really needed the kip," I said still trying to stifle a yawn.

"Tell me about it, there was no waking you. You were dead to the world. Go sit down and I'll make you a cup of tea, and then we're opening the presents! Ain't we Kaine?" Kaine laughed out loud at being included in this conversation and held out the rattle she had in her hands as she did, as if to say 'look what I've got!'

"Come on then, missus, let's get you back into that living room while mommy makes me a nice cuppa tea," I said, and proceeded to push Kaine in her walker out of the kitchen and along the hallway into the living room, where I picked her up under her arms lifting her out of her mobile paint remover and we sat down on the settee together. By this time in her life her front teeth had already come through and the rest were beginning to make an appearance, so her gums were a little sore. The rattle she had was one of the sort where the exterior was a latex rubber-type material, liquid filled which could be kept in the fridge to cool the liquid down; the idea being that the coolness of the rattle would sooth a baby's sore gums when teething as they have an insatiable urge to chew things whilst this is happening.

"Less 'ave a look at them liddle toothy pegs den." I said leaning towards her trying to see if any more teeth had penetrated her gums. All the reward I got was the saliva-coated rattle bashed off my nose by Kaine who thought this funny as well and squealed with delight at being exactly on target. "Ugh! Not exactly what I had in mind for breakfast but still, kids are kids," I said, trying to avoid the next swipe she took with that offensive little weapon. But more saliva broke free and hit me square in the eye. With that Karen entered the room with my cup of tea and matter of factly said.

"Oh, you're getting it now then. The poor old dog's been getting the dribble factory treatment all morning!"

Looking at Zeus who preferred the sanctuary of his basket to the no man's land of the living room at this point, I could see the remains of Kaine's spittle adorning his snout.

"I see what you mean," I said, swapping my rattle-waving little tempest of a daughter for the cup of tea Karen had made for me.

"As soon as I've drunk this we'll open the pressies eh?" I said.

"Ha ha! no chance mate." "We're opening ours now ain't we Kaine?" said Karen, positioning herself with Kaine next to her in her baby chair in front of the tree and the mountain of wrapped presents underneath it.

"Hang on a sec'! I'll get the camera so we can get her reaction to her presents." And off I went to the bedroom to get it. On my return to the living room Karen had re-positioned Kaine in the centre of the room and was busy piling the presents up around her in order to take the photograph. Kaine was looking a little confused as to this activity going on around her and was reaching over and touching the wrapped up boxes in turn and the look on her face was one that could be described as not really knowing what she was supposed to do. Suddenly she burst into tears and it was clear that she was completely overwhelmed with the array of goods before her.

"Ahh," said Karen as she picked Kaine up, realising the problem. "Is it all too much for my little baby?... Did you get the shot?" she asked.

"Yes, just before the waterworks appeared."

"That's good; I wanted one of her by her pressies for the album." As soon as Kaine had settled down again we sat down and busily unwrapped all our Christmas presents. As regards the amount Kaine had, it was a good job that the flat was large and the nursery was of a good size to accommodate everything that had been bought for her by us, and of course, by her grandparents and other family members. Baby toys of all sorts were there and little activity games for toddlers and many more too numerous to mention.

As regards myself and Karen, I had been saving hard for a number of months and in no small measure my monthly bonus had added to this. I had bought Karen a beautiful jewellery set consisting of bracelet, ring, and matching ear-rings as well as other more practical gifts. as she liked the rock pop band INXS, and more particularly Michael Hutchins the lead singer, I had felt obliged to get her the latest album.

With the unwrapping of the presents and the resulting paper mess cleared away we relaxed for an hour or two until it was time to make our way to my mother-in-law's for our dinner. The dog was busily chewing on his Christmas present from us and we were left in no doubt as to how much he was enjoying this, as to have tried to have taken it off him would have been to have risked losing several digits from one's hand.

The day was cold and damp after the rainfall of the previous evening and quite overcast, as December 25th tends to be; and so well wrapped up against the chill weather, we headed for Pat's house which was situated a couple of hundred yards away from our flat across the park. Upon our arrival the usual Christmas atmosphere pervaded the house with the cooking of the dinner in the kitchen being the main focal point, for the women at least. Karen's younger sister, Diane, was already there, with her husband Carl and their young daughter Sarah, who was a few months older than our Kaine.

Karen's younger brother Lee was excited about his Christmas gifts and being an eleven year old lad at the time he couldn't wait to show them to me.

"Joe, do wanna see what I've 'ad for chrimbo?" he asked me immediately upon our arrival.

"Hold on, let me get me coat off mate." I laughed. I could see he was fit to burst with excitement. And we made our way upstairs to his bedroom where an even bigger collection of presents than we had at our flat for Kaine took pride of place on his bed.

"Wow Lee! are these all yours?" I asked in mock surprise knowing that couldn't be for anybody else. Logic dictated that with just his mom and dad there, then, by process of elimination, he had to be the true owner.

"Yep," he said proudly, showing me the star present that all kids long for on the day.

"Well, you are a lucky lad having all these!" I wanted to get downstairs as soon as I could as I knew my brother-in-law Carl would be making short work of the cans of lager that had been set aside for the festivities and I didn't want to miss my share.

On entering the living room Roy was in his chair plonked in front of the television and Carl was on the settee, can in hand as I expected.

"Merry Christmas lads!" I said, the greeting was returned and a can was passed in my direction and gratefully accepted. The women had retired to the kitchen with the kids and were busy chatting away.

Roy and Carl were working in the construction industry; Roy being Carl's employer on a sub-contract basis as was the modus operandi of the building industry in those days and for a long time afterwards. They had been working in some other part of the country and were now finished up for the Christmas holidays,

"How's the littlun doin' Joe?" asked Carl in his broad Black Country accent, before gulping down the remainder of the can he was holding and reaching for another.

"She's fine thanks, mate," I said.

"That's good. Fancy goin' for a pint? We're off down the Foresters for a couple before dinner."

"Too right I do, what time we goin'?"

"Just finish this, an' we're off', eh Roy?" Roy, never a man who could be accused of verbosity, simply nodded in agreement. Karen came into the living room and heard the tail end of the conversation.

"Don't you lot come back legless!" she said laughing, knowing only to well what we were like once we got together for a drink.

"No, we're only going for a couple and straight back." I said unconvincingly. As she well knew I liked a pint at lunch time and due to the hours I worked this was a rare treat for me. And so off we went, with Pat shouting that dinner would be at three on the dot. At least it gave the women a bit of time together and they could talk about us in peace whilst we were out. Our time at the pub was a swift and short affair as the licensee also had designs on his Christmas dinner and so indeed we did only manage to get two or three down us and back we came sober as judges.

When we were back at the house everything was ready and looked fabulous. Pat, as ever, had done us all proud as it was her desire that we all had a big meal together that special day of the year. The two newest additions to the family, those being Sarah and Kaine, were both in their high chairs around the table as well, and unsuccessful attempts to place party hats on their heads for an impromptu photo shoot were thwarted by the children's taking them off as soon as they were put on.

"Looks like the kids don't like lookin' daft either," said Carl laughing. I had to agree as it was a pet hate of mine also being photographed in those silly paper hats that are the norm at Christmas, call it the vanity of the twenty some-things, but it was true.

Our dinner was indeed a sumptuous affair, and after the pudding was forced down into our already over-fed bellies, we all retired to the comfort of the living room for the afternoon to watch the obligatory annual re-run of the James Bond film.

Karen showed Diane where Kaine's shunt was inserted by delicately feeling behind her ear, you could feel the little bump under the skin. As this was now covered by Kaine's blonde hair it was completely unobtrusive. Her soft-spot had long since disappeared and as Kaine seemed completely healthy and lively, we hardly gave the shunt much thought any more. For all we knew it was redundant and the ventricles that had been compromised by the meningitis had unblocked or repaired themselves as the human body miraculously does. Kaine was, of course, still attending Sandwell Hospital for check-ups and was still under Doctor Mayne's care. Karen had got to know Doctor Mayne quite well from her frequent visits to the hospital; she had taken a keen interest in Kaine's on-going recovery and was as delighted with her progress as we were.

The afternoon gradually darkened and I wanted to get back home for the evening; and so we announced that we had better be going and got ready for the relatively short walk back to our flat. The dog would be needing a walk and I didn't fancy being out too long in the freezing December temperatures that evening. Kaine sat happily in her pushchair as we trundled along on the way home and was gazing about at the streetlights. They must've looked like giant orange stars to her little enquiring mind.

I was still feeling the effects of our extraordinary Christmas Eve marathon at the market and felt quite tired still. I was looking forward to Boxing Day as with the formalities of Christmas day being over, this was, for me, a more relaxed day. On getting back to the flat, we had left the heating on and it was lovely and warm on our return. We'd had a nice day so far and now all that remained was to have the Christmas Night at home, just the three of us again, not counting Zeus who couldn't wait to get back to his marrow bone. Boxing Day came and went; I had one more day off before the Market Hall opened again. As much as I loved my job I could have done with a longer break but however it would have to be back to the grindstone for us. I wasn't anticipating selling much meat as the amount we had shifted leading up to Christmas Eve and on the day itself would have led one to believe that our customers' freezers would have been full for the next six months at least. But the great British public had other ideas and it wasn't too long before the machine began to feed the monster again as the saying went.

All that was consumed was replaced and the few days leading up to New Year, although not being as busy as Christmas, were good none the less. And so the transition from nineteen eighty-eight to eighty-nine went off as smoothly as ever with the ringing of the bells at midnight and the echoes of Auld Lang Syne filling the early morning of the first of January of the new year. We waved good-bye to the old year never to come again, and my thoughts were a mixed review of the previous eight months since Kaine's birth, of worry and hope and ultimate triumph with Kaine being saved; and with that in mind I welcomed the new year which would bring my daughters first birthday in April. I wondered what the year would have in store for us as a family.

Of course I had no idea at the time of the tragic heartache and life changes that I would go through as would Karen, in the eleven months that were before us and were as yet in the future.....

CHAPTER 9.

Sowing the seeds of change.

On my return to work in the January the staff all wished each other happy a New Year as is the custom and everything returned to normal, but for me my days as a butcher were numbered. I didn't know it yet but events were about to take place that would alter what for me had been a nine year vocation and end with a falling out of sorts.

Kaine had had her all clear check up for January and we had put out of our minds any more interruptions to our lives and had begun to settle down into a comfortable complacency regarding the ongoing health of our daughter. Winter yet again gave way to spring and I'd started using my new Raleigh racer bicycle to get to and from work now that the weather was improving. The journey into work was ten miles exactly gauged by the mini computer that was attached to the frame and gave readouts on mileage, speed etc. I had bought it specifically for the purpose of getting fit as I used to see other bike users on the same route fly past my bus on a daily basis and I had thought it wouldn't be a bad idea to join the revolution.

A twenty mile daily round trip takes a little getting used to but it wasn't long before I was beating my bus into the city centre. Needless to say I was as fit as a fiddle after some weeks of this and felt like I could do the Tour de France at that rate.

Alan was a bit concerned that I was doing too much as I also worked on my afternoon off as well; but I was young, with a family and I was ambitious to get on and it didn't bother me in the slightest as I came from a family of workers. It was in my blood to graft and I felt proud as well to do so. The years 1988/89 were still part of the Margaret Thatcher era and the sifting and regeneration of the traditional labour markets of the late seventies and early eighties had given way to a new order, one in which I think I can say, (although not presuming to be an economist or political expert at all but merely a simple observer of events,) the seeds leading to today's present troubles were sown. (2009.time of writing.) New words entered the British vernacular such as 'Yuppie', 'Isas', 'Peps', and not so new such as 'greed' and 'gain'. The film 'Wall Street' proved a huge hit at the time; starring Michael Douglas, who, uttered the immortal line as the character Gordon Gecko, 'greed is good.' We didn't realise at the time how many future bank managers and financial suited and booted types were to adopt that saying as their permanent mantra. Mobile phones found their way into cars and for the ultra trendy, the prototypes of the tiny things we all use today. 'Be in when you're out' was the advertising slogan of the day.

Soap operas such as Eastenders reflected society's changing values in which market 'barrow boys' had swapped woolly hats and donkey jackets for pin stripes and now drunk champagne instead of bitter. 'Del boy' from 'Only fools and horse's' made us laugh as John Sullivan the writer epitomized the ridiculous aura of the times by casting Del as a yuppie director of Trotters Independent Trading co, who bought his council flat in Nelson Mandela House in Peckham South London as an investment in the burgeoning property market.

Times were speeding up, and for the first time people who previously hadn't been able to buy a property could now buy their council homes. This in turn gave rise to the property boom of the late eighties in which house prices were rising at the rate of hundreds of pounds per day. Not massive, by today's standards, but if you had plans to buy a house for the first time you didn't have to be a mathematician to work out that every fortnight a house was increasing in value by at least a thousand pounds or more. And as wages weren't accelerating at the same rate, at least not for the working class, the dream of owning your own home became a chase that was unequal in pace.

As I fell squarely into the category of the working class this fact along with my age and status as a newly-married man with wife and family meant that I could see the hope of owning my own house racing away from me if I didn't act soon and try to buy a property. Everyone was doing it thereby fuelling the fire of house-price inflation. Where would it end? Would I miss the bus?

So I worked every hour I could and even worked my holidays as well to put money aside for a deposit for a house, but the more I saved the higher the price went. I would never be able to close that gap I thought. One problem had vanished from my life only to be replaced by another, although I have to say that the problem of buying a house paled into insignificance compared to the life of my daughter. But it was for her and Karen and myself that I dreamt of owning our own home and more importantly one with a garden. It didn't have to be huge just a small house with an average sized garden where Kaine could play in the summers to come; It wasn't too much to ask for now, was it? Well in nineteen eighty-nine even small dreams were beginning to acquire large price tags and a conversation between myself and Alan whilst at work one day highlighted the growing trend.

"I went to look at a new car Sunday." Alan said to me whilst chopping a loin of pork chops up for his counter.

"Oh yeah? What sort you after Al'" I enquired.

"A new BMW seven series, beautiful car."

"Yeah nice motor, how much?"

"Twenty-three grand, the geezer at the garage says with trading in my old B'mer, plus a couple of grand, he can get me finance at three per cent."

"Is that good then?" I naively asked, as I'd never in my life bought anything on finance and was entirely ignorant as to how it worked.

"Good? That's excellent Joe; you can't borrow money anywhere for that rate." Alan replied a bit indignantly.

"Funny enough, me an' Karen went to have a look at a house on Sunday as well and they wanted twenty-three grand for that but it was a wreck!" I said.

"Who'd 'ave thought it, eh? That a car would cost the same price as a house." Alan said in reply, shaking his head at the thought.

"So what you gonna do then, are you 'avin' it?"

"I dunno Joe; I told him that I'd 'ave a think about it. It's a lot of money for a car."

"Yeah but what a car though eh? Well, you work hard enough, if you can afford it have it, that's my philosophy on it anyway Al'."

"Hmm, I'll see," mused Alan, somewhat pensively. A week later he answered the question unprompted and quite out-of-the-blue when he sidled up to me one day while I was working and said that he'd decided to give that car a miss.

"How come?" I asked, a bit surprised at his decision. For I knew that Alan could afford it and he did deserve it as the man was a worker and personally he also gave to charity and raised money for good causes as well. But he was no saint or Mother Theresa; he was just a normal guy.

"I thought about what you said that day when you mentioned you had been looking for a house and it was the same price as the motor, it sort of gave it a bit of perspective."

"I didn't mention it to put you off buying the motor Alan." I protested.

"I know you didn't Joe, it just took me back to when me and Angela were buying our first place and we didn't have tuppence to rub together that's all; no, my car will do me for now." he said contentedly, and that was that. Alan loved his golf, business, and car but not before his family and I saw the logic in his decision.

By this time a number of staff changes had also taken place. We'd lost Mark and Rodney who had both gone off to pastures new and also Ian had left to work with a mate of his outside of the butchering trade. I enquired of Nobby if he'd miss his favourite sparring partner.

"I won't miss the bulls**t." came the reply. Short, and as ever, to the point. In their places we had acquired

Daniel who was Alan's son and who immediately acquired the nickname 'Desperate' after the comic book character Desperate Dan. A nice lad who I liked. There was also Dustin added to the fold who was Paul's son and finally we had gained another Mark whose Christian name had been dispensed with immediately and hence forth became known as Red, due to the shock of ginger hair carved into the 'flat top' style of the day. The rest of the staff remained the same but as I said events were beginning to shape themselves in a way quite unknown to me that would see my own exit from the clan.

At night I would get home more and more exhausted after the days work and the ten mile cycle ride. I was beginning to lose weight and looked pale as I was constantly indoors apart from Sundays when, invariably, I was finding myself too tired to venture out much. Kaine was still doing well and was growing into a gorgeous child. She had little dimples on both cheeks when she smiled, and her blonde hair was beginning to thicken and set off her blue eyes. She was out of her walker and beginning to crawl about and this was something we had to be wary of in case she bumped her head and damaged the shunt, but as Doctor Mayne had pointed out to us that due to the location of the shunt behind her ear this would be unlikely to happen even when she became a toddler.

Karen's maternity pay had long since expired and it was a mutual decision by us both that she was not to return to work given that Kaine was still at risk of being shunt dependant. This meant that my wages alone had to keep us, Karen's sister Diane and husband Carl had managed to buy a house in Oldbury near West Bromwich and so I felt the increasing pressure to provide for my family a residence of our own rather than a rented council flat. My wages after tax amounted to £130.00. A meat allowance of approximately £20.00 at the end of the week boosted it a little more, and of course there also was my monthly bonus of £50.00. That gave me a total of £160.00 plus change, a week for sixty-five hours.

Money was never my god and as long as I had enough I was satisfied with what I got. But as I've alluded to previously, the times were changing rapidly and the gathering pace was dictating that you either kept up or got left behind. I certainly didn't want to be left behind. Buying a house was a subject that was constantly being talked about in the media and by people who were our friends and of course at work. I began to feel frustrated that my modest income was inadequate to secure even the purchase of a normal terraced house as each day saw bricks and mortar rising in value in the feverish scramble of the property world for 'bigger' and 'better'.

Then, as today, if you wanted to live in a decent area it cost money, I had a wife and child and was the sole earner of my family; it was my duty to provide the best that I could and that was what I was determined to do. As I've said I came from a family of workers and my ethic from when I started school was 'work hard and rewards will follow'. In the burgeoning yuppie culture of the day, dictionary defined as, 'young educated city-dwelling and materialistic', the mantra of 'work smarter not harder' was beginning to replace the traditional values of the normal working man who now saw his previously uninteresting and relatively simple home as an asset to be exploited in the growing housing market. This was fine if you were fortunate enough to own one but not so good if you were in the position of trying to get your foot on that elusive first rung of the so called property ladder (as I was).

Wages became the crucial focal point of life in this atmosphere of expansion; everybody needed more money to keep pace, myself included and the length of time I was spending to earn it was not lost on me. I was working five and a half days a week and taking no holidays; Saturday alone was a twelve hour shift not including travel to and from work. In short I needed a rise and I thought I had a case for receiving one. We were busier than ever at the shop and my counter was bringing in a lot of trade. My customers were loyal and the good relations we enjoyed through being friendly and helpful ensured return trade and of course the quality of our produce was important as well. Of course the increase in trade was good business and profitable as always. I had good custom across the board and we had out of town customers once a month from the city of Coventry and as far away as London taking advantage of the cheaper prices Birmingham offered in comparison to their home towns and as always we were busy.

Alan had moved house from Coleshill to Solihull, a much more up-market area of the city; Paul also had moved and they were obviously enjoying the rewards of the business. However the gap I perceived between my circumstances and those of my bosses was growing ever wider and so I decided to ask Alan for a rise, one day when it was quiet, usually this would be on a Monday morning.

"Alan I need to have a word." I began. Now Alan was not a stupid man and for a time now our conversations at work had centered on the huge changes we were beginning to see around us as society and the economy were changing shape.

"This is about money, isn't it?" I felt that he had anticipated the situation and was responding accordingly.

"'Afraid so, Al'. I'm struggling to keep up with all this crap that's goin' on with houses an' all that."

"Yes Joe, I know times have changed. So you want a bit more dough."

This he said without humour and I could tell that he had expected this, but wasn't pleased to be confronted with the prospect of sorting it out. I think in hindsight that Alan was very aware of the pressures of life as his own background was working class and he had fought his way up through hard graft and, as he readily admitted, he wasn't 'a man who spent money'.

"You're under pressure from Karen and I know what it feels like." This was only half true. As I have said I was ambitious myself to improve my lot and that of my family by honest means; nothing wrong with that. I differed from the other lads at the shop by being the only one married and with a child and this had obviously increased my outgoings and had changed my outlook on the future. As for Nobby and Red, who were of the same age as me, they both lived at home and apart from board and lodging, their cash was theirs to spend as they liked. The furthest point in the future that had any bearing on their thoughts was where they were likely to end up next Saturday night and, more importantly, who with. But that was their business and they were happy. The other lads were too young for any of this to have any bearing on them and so I was in the unique position of having to ask for a rise outside of the annual increase I'd been accustomed to up until that point.

"You'll have to leave it with me Joe," Alan said, and the usual friendliness in his manner wasn't there as he said it. I had the distinctly uneasy feeling that I had done something wrong and a bit of an atmosphere pervaded the remainder of the day.

Obviously I had discussed with Karen my intentions of asking for a rise and on my return home that evening Karen was anxious to know the outcome.

"How did you get on then?" she asked me, expectantly.

"I don't know." I replied.

"What do you mean you don't know?" Karen seemed surprised by my answer.

"Exactly what I just said, I didn't really get an answer, all's he said was that I was to leave it with him, I s'pose he's gonna think about it."

"What if he says 'no', what will you do?"

"He won't say 'no', he knows how hard I've worked on my side of the pitch and how busy we are, and he knows the situation we're in." I said reassuringly to Karen. However the distinct lack of conversation between Alan and myself that day led my gut instinct elsewhere than the optimistic side of town.

We normally had the choice of being paid on Thursday or Friday in the shop and, as ever human nature went for the earliest opportunity for our remuneration. The week went on as per usual and on the Thursday evening Alan was in his usual position of cashing up the till and putting the wages up for us while we put everything away and the hygiene of the shop was being implemented. One by one he called the lads over for their wages and as soon as they got their reward for the week they were off. Nobby had, earlier in the day, asked me if I fancied a quick pint after work as was his custom and that day I had said 'yes' as it had been a while since we had had a drink together.

Nobby was called for his wages and as he went past he gave me a wink and said he'd see me in the pub and he would get the beer in. After the other lads had gone it was my turn and Alan called me over but his demeanour was somehow different; he looked serious and troubled and wore the sort of look that one would wear having upset a friend's feelings.

"I've put you some extra dough in your wages Joe, you'll get that every week from now on." Without looking at me he just handed me the sealed packet.

"Thanks Alan, I appreciate that." I said.

"That's okay." But I could feel that something wasn't right somehow. I then said goodnight and that I would see him in the morning. Paul who, it has to be said, didn't take much interest in the wages side and was happy to leave that task to Alan, playfully tripped me up as I was leaving, somewhat relieving the tension I had sensed from Alan. I made my way to the goods lift and when inside decided to see what the extra 'dough' in my wages amounted to and if my drink with Nobby was to be a celebratory one. I felt sure that Alan would have appreciated my efforts in building the business to the level that I had achieved and that I was a valued member of the team, and as such deserving a fair increase in my wage. I opened the packet and counted my money. Disappointment was an understatement. He had given me an extra ten quid a week. Not enough. Not nearly enough. At a stroke I felt undervalued and unappreciated and the feelings that had been welling up within me until that point were now coming to a head. I made my way to the pub where I found Nobby waiting for me with a pint in his hand and one sitting on the bar waiting for me. Nobby was my mate and I had earlier confided in him that I had asked for a rise.

"How'd you get on mate?" he enquired of me after slurping a mouthful of lager.

"He's give me an extra tenner a week." I replied, raising my own glass to my lips.

"A tenner!" Nobby squeaked indignantly in his high pitched voice. "I told you he was a tight bar steward. It's not as if 'e don't know where the next box of golf balls is comin' from," he added, pointing his finger for emphasis.

"Yeah, I'm not too happy mate. A few rounds of drinks and that's gone eh?"

"I bet you won't be gettin' your conjugal rights tonight when you tell Karen how you got on," laughed Nobby at my predicament.

"Shurrup ya pillock," I laughed in response to his good-natured jibe. In all seriousness though, I felt well 'put out', it was Alan's business but we all played a major part in the success of it. The majority was indeed down to Alan but my own contribution far outweighed the paltry sum he had deemed fit to give me for a raise and I felt that it would have been better if he had not given me anything at all instead of a token gesture of appeasement. There was absolutely no way the rise I had just got would compete with the increasing costs going on around us.

I decided to stay for more than two quick drinks with Nobby and ended up leaving my trusty bike at the market and catching the bus back as the safer option; probably a good idea as the alternative of cycling ten miles after eight pints didn't appeal to me. I got in late and Karen wasn't too pleased but her displeasure was directed more towards Alan when I told her how much my extra efforts were actually worth. She was eye witness to the amount of hours I spent there, and my fatigue at the end of the week was becoming more evident. I was doing way too much even for my age, and the pressure was beginning to show.

"Your dinner's not looking too good," she told me as I sat at the table. We didn't own a microwave and the only way Karen could keep my meal for me was on a low gas in the oven; consequently it was a bit dry but I was tired, a bit drunk, hungry and more than slightly annoyed at my day.

"I'm gonna have a word with mom for you," she suddenly announced.

"How do you mean?" I asked puzzled as to what her mom had to do with my work situation.

"She can ask Roy if he's got work for you," she said, determinedly. And I could tell that she wasn't at all pleased at the turn of events.

"I don't know the first thing about Roy's work!" I protested.

"Well neither did Carl when he started, and him and Diane have got a house," said Karen indignantly.

"Point taken; okay then, see what she says and we'll take it from there then," I said wearily. The only thing I wanted now was bed and I satisfied my desire for rest very shortly thereafter.

Kaine was in bed and sleeping peacefully and it wasn't too long before I was in a similar condition. Karen stayed up for a while obviously thinking things over and came to bed later.

The next morning the alarm went as usual and as soon as I opened my eyes my mind focused on what Karen had said the night before. I was still happy in my job but the peripherals were changing and a seed of change had now been sown in my mind. On the bus into work I thought of little else and my feeling of being undervalued grew in me with the thought that I needed to get my family into a better place. I wasn't too happy with the flats any more as a few undesirables had moved in and on a few occasions someone had urinated in the lifts. This wasn't what I had had in mind for my wife and child particularly as Karen had to use the lift for getting the pushchair up and down from the flat.

On my arrival at work I had decided not to say anything or challenge the amount Alan had decided to up my wages by; I thought it was obvious what I was worth and it didn't need clarifying. Nobby wasn't too far behind me and I could hear his cheerful whistle and the slap of his morning paper against his thigh as he had the habit of doing as he approached the shop.

"Morning Nobby, how you doing mate?" I asked cheerfully as he entered the shop.

"Mornin'" came the high pitched reply from my friend.

"'Ave you seen the paper?" he enquired as always after some news item or other had caught his attention.

"Nah, never mind that. Listen, I ain't too happy and Karen wasn't either as you predicted," I began.

"Toldja you wouldn't get your conjugals didn'I. Ha! ha!"

"Yeah, yeah, funny guy, no, listen mate, I might end up workin' for her old man."

"What! you finkin' of leavin'?" Nobby blurted out loudly just as I could hear the sound of Alan and Paul's voices approaching.

"Sshush. I'll talk to you later." Alan and Paul both entered the shop and said their 'good mornings' as usual. They hadn't heard Nobby as they were talking to each other while approaching the shop.

Nothing untoward was mentioned by Alan and the tense atmosphere of the previous few days was gone. I think Alan thought that my increase in wages was acceptable and he would hear no more of it. That part at least was true for the time being. The weekend was on us again and the functions of the shop and the needs of the customers took precedence.

When I got home that evening I was sitting with Kaine on my knee while Karen was making dinner when I asked if she had mentioned to her mom about my working with Roy.

"Yes, he's back tonight from Wales and she's gonna ask him after he's had his tea and he's in a good mood. Oh and we're going over Sunday for dinner so you might have an answer by then."

In the space of a few days I had gone from being content in my work to totally discouraged, and so the seed of change had germinated and was beginning to take root.

"Don't get your hopes up too much in case he hasn't got anything for you though." Karen added cautiously.

My hopes were up though; I had already being thinking that we would never be able to buy a place of our own on my money and that this might just be the opportunity I needed. I was to be disappointed however.

Roy explained to me on the Sunday that the job he was doing was coming to an end and the next one didn't require any more men and the obvious truth of my inexperience didn't help, and so that was that. I put my disappointment behind me and soldiered on for now.

Chapter 10.

Happy birthday baby Kaine.

It wasn't too long before events were to take a new twist though, and the consequences would be far reaching as far as I was concerned.

Weeks later Kaine's first birthday arrived and it was a happy celebration for the family. We had a little party and a cake for Kaine with her single candle placed proudly in the centre. Karen had invited some of the other young mums who were her friends with their babies, and the whole thing went better than expected; with the place awash with babies and toddlers the flat resembled a kindergarten.

Work for myself carried on as usual, I settled back down, and put the thoughts of leaving from my mind. It was great now that Kaine was making a total recovery and that she was happy, and in like fashion so was I, and more obviously her mom. Despite our personal triumphs though, the economy and its inflationary drive continued, and I'd resigned myself to living in the flats for the time being. The way forward would be to put our names on the housing list, and hope a suitable property came available, and after the expiration of time, take advantage of the discount being offered by the council. And that was our plan.

One Sunday a few weeks later was to change all our plans though and set the pattern for a chain of events that changed things forever for our little family. It started as usual with breakfast and taking Zeus for his morning run. It was a fine day, the summer would be approaching its zenith in the next few weeks, and as I walked the dog through the fields at the back of the flats, the sun shone down warmly. I had been out for around and hour or so and decided that the dog had enough exercise by now and so headed back home, deciding what to do with the rest of the Sunday. I had no idea that this was a choice that was no longer in my control at this point; this became clear as soon as I entered the flat and saw the worried look on Karen's face.

"Something's not right with Kaine's shunt," she said. I looked at Kaine who was lying on the settee and looked absolutely fine.

"What? How do you mean?" I asked, troubled by this.

"Look here," she said, and sat down next to Kaine, raised her to a sitting position and manoeuvred her head so as to show me what she meant. She brushed Kaine's hair to one side with her hand and delicately pointed to where the shunt's position was when it was first inserted.

"I think it's slipped out of its position where it's supposed to be."

With her fingers she felt an area further down from Kaine's ear and said,

"It's here look, feel it." This I did and it HAD moved from being directly behind her ear to a position about an inch further down. I looked at our daughter who didn't seem to be displaying any signs of discomfort or the tell-tale signs that pressure was beginning to build if indeed, the shunt was malfunctioning.

"We'd better phone the hospital straight away," I said. Karen immediately rang the Children's Hospital was put straight through to the Paediatric Ward and was soon talking to one of the duty doctors. She explained to her what the problem was and was answering the doctor's questions relating to Kaine's present condition, who despite the fuss surrounding this development with her shunt seemed perfectly fine and was her normal self.

"You'd better bring her in for us to take a look at her," the doctor told Karen.

And so the day changed immediately from a normal Sunday into the memories of the months before when the hospital was the largest thing in our lives. I was just hoping, as Karen was, that it wouldn't be again. When we arrived at the hospital, we were shown to a waiting room and told by one of the staff that a doctor would be with us as soon as practicable. We didn't have to wait long as a young blonde woman in her mid-twenties entered the room after twenty minutes or so and introduced herself as the doctor to whom Karen had spoken to on the telephone earlier.

"Hello, who have we here then?" addressing Kaine, whose face immediately lit up with a smile. Kaine was on Karen's lap and the doctor had a look at the positioning of her shunt and was feeling with her fingers the location to which it now had moved.

"Hmm, it looks as though it has slipped down a little, but it still appears to be functioning properly as I can see no sign of hydrocephalus at the moment. However it may be too soon to tell." she said to us.

"Do you mean that the pressure hasn't built up sufficiently yet to be noticeable?" I asked her.

"Yes, that's quite correct. But in any event the shunt will have to be revised as soon as we can. I don't want any increase in pressure in her brain occurring and causing a set back to her recovery and development."

"How soon can this be done?" Karen asked her.

"Well, I'm afraid she will have to stay in for observation. I see here that Kaine is still under Mr Hamilton's care," she said, looking at Kaine's notes. "He'll be in tomorrow morning and he'll be able to say exactly when the shunt can be replaced."

Karen and I both looked at each other; we really had thought that our hospital days were finished with. Now it looked like another operation was needed. But still what had to be done, had to be done. Kaine, of course, was unaware of the events surrounding her immediate future; still too young to understand still too innocent.

We had to wait for a bed to be sorted out for Kaine on the ward and also for Karen as well. Even though she was now a little older, the thought of Kaine being without her mom was not an option. So we resigned ourselves to another bout of hospitalisation hoping that it wouldn't be for long. We weren't too happy that Kaine had yet another dose of pain and discomfort to endure, this was made all the more poignant by the fact that she was now older and that bit more aware, but as of yet would be unable to understand why she had to go through what she had to.

Eventually we were ushered to the ward and a bed with side rails was found for Kaine. She continued to be her normal self and was looking around her in total curiosity as I carried her along. We had taken the precaution of taking some things with us in case our fears were confirmed, as indeed, they now were.

The fact that Kaine seemed totally well was a matter of frustration to us and to her, as she was now confined to the bed and lacking the freedom she had become so accustomed to at home. But we as her parents knew that this was necessary, and we did our best to keep her amused by carrying her to the window and letting her look out periodically.

Karen had phoned her mom who was shocked when she had explained that we were back at the hospital with Kaine but reassured to find that she was okay for now but obviously concerned that an operation would have to take place. The dog was still at the flat and Karen asked Pat if she could go and get him as we would be there for some hours. Obviously the same arrangements as before would have to take place with Zeus staying at Karen's mom's house. although the dog was the least of our worries, he did matter. The routine of our lives, and this included poor Zeus, was rent asunder again by these unforeseen occurrences. It couldn't be helped though, so the best thing was to knuckle down; we'd been through this before and so we could do it again.

An all-too-familiar pattern was beginning to develop. The day turned into evening and I made my way home, leaving the car for Karen in case it was needed. And so I got home to an empty flat once again and the comforting noises of Kaine there were now missing. But disappointed as I was, I was also confident in the abilities of the medical staff to do their jobs properly as they had done before. I chided myself for thinking negatively and that this was but a temporary setback.

I arrived at work as normal and on time but in spite of my own optimism that everything would be okay I couldn't shake the mood that had overtaken me. Not even Nobby's irrepressible humour could do anything to lift the feelings of unfairness that I felt. Normally my persona is the chatty type and I try not to dwell on things that bring me down; but this time, I remained pretty sullen and just got on with what I was doing and waited for an opportunity to ring Karen at the hospital to find out what developments had occurred.

I took this time when the preparations for the shop were at an end and I spoke to Karen on the hospital phone that had the advantage of being plugged into a line installed by Kaine's bed. I knew the routine by now; the doctor would be doing his rounds at ten o' clock or thereabouts and no new information would be available until then. My reason for ringing was to enquire how Karen and Kaine's night had gone, and of course to see whether she was displaying any signs that the shunt had malfunctioned and hydrocephalus had set in.

Karen told me that Kaine was fine and I could hear her calling 'momma' in the background as she spoke. The consultant, Mr Hamilton, was due to come to the ward later to see Kaine; we had not met this man, as you may recall; he had been on leave when Kaine was first brought to the hospital and had been seen by his partner Mr Hockley, instead. It was obvious that Kaine's shunt had not failed as by now she would be displaying signs to that effect; this gave rise to the hope in me that, although it had slipped from it's designated position and might not be working properly, maybe she didn't need the shunt anymore or not one hundred per cent as she had done. But we would have to wait and see about that as tests would have to be done to determine whether this was the case or not. In the meantime all that remained to do was sit tight and wait. Karen told me that she would be taking Kaine into the playroom where there were children around the same age or just a little older to let her have a little inter-action with them. These kids were either convalescing or waiting for an operation to be performed and their parents, as Karen was, were glad of the break from the tediousness of the hospital ward.

We signed off with Karen saying she would ring me as soon as Mr Hamilton had seen Kaine and let me know what was going on. I felt a little happier that Kaine wasn't displaying any symptoms that would hasten her to the operating table and I clung to the hope that the shunt was either partly or one hundred per cent redundant and so could be removed and that she would function as normally as anyone else without the aid of the artificial valve in place.

Around eleven o' clock that morning a phone call came through for me from Karen. She told me that the consultant had been to see Kaine and mentioned that she did not like him as he was an older man in appearance to Mr Hockley and much more abrupt in manner and business-like in his dealings with Kaine in that she appeared more like an object that he was examining than a young child. And this hadn't pleased Karen in the slightest. She went on to relate to me that upon his examination, the shunt would be replaced and that a scan would be done first to determine the condition of the ventricles blocked by the virus. If they had repaired or unblocked then the shunt could be removed and dispensed with. If, on the other hand, the ventricles had only partly unblocked, then the shunt would still have to be employed as a relief to the fluid build up in the central chamber. Obviously the former situation was the more desirable but even if it was the latter then that at least would be an improvement as Kaine was completely shunt dependant; if a blockage occurred in the valve the build up of fluid would not be drained by any natural means resulting in an emergency operation to replace the blocked valve. But the only time that we would know that the shunt had partially or fully failed was when the pressure inside her cranium had already built up and caused dilating of the pupils, drowsiness and resulting lethargy in Kaine. And this was dangerous and hence produced the constant worry that lurked in the background of our lives.

The scan was scheduled for later in the day and we would know how things would go from there. It was completely possible for a child with a shunt fitted to grow to adulthood and live a perfectly normal life providing that the shunt functioned as it was supposed to. Even if a blockage were to occur though, upon the replacement of the valve, normal recovery was probable and expected. But as I have said and I'm sure the reader can appreciate, it would be better by far not to have to rely on artificial means to maintain health.

If the shunt hadn't slipped from its position and natural drainage had commenced then the valve would have been redundant and would have remained where it was for the rest of Kaine's natural life, being completely unobtrusive, and providing no other problem arose to prompt its removal. This was what we had hoped for but now things had changed.

My day continued pretty normally, and had the function of distracting me from the thoughts of the hospital, although automatically they would just pop in my mind periodically during the course of the day. I kept the information to myself mostly as to what was to happen to Kaine, as the rest of the staff already knew the story behind Kaine, and, I wanted to keep it in low profile as much as I could, save obviously the essentials that needed to be told. I was halfway through my day when the phone call I had been expecting came from Karen for me.

The scan had been done on Kaine and Mr Hamilton had been back to explain in his unsympathetic manner that the ventricles within Kaine's brain remained blocked and that it was unlikely now that they would ever function normally. The result would be that Kaine would be completely shunt-dependant for the remainder of her life.

Karen was obviously as upset by this news as I was. He had told Karen that the operation would most likely be the Wednesday morning surgery that week. So that was that. I would be going straight to the hospital as soon as I finished work anyway and so get the details first hand.

"What's happening then Joe?" enquired Alan as I got off the phone.

"Kaine is most likely having an operation Wednesday morning, so I'll need to be there." I said.

"But Karen's there though isn't she?" he said in slightly surprised manner. I knew what he was implying, but I decided that as I was giving one hundred per cent commitment to the shop anyway, then that Wednesday morning they could do without me. Even though Wednesday was one of the busiest days of the week for us, it was half day closing at the market hall at two o' clock and so I thought that a half day off to be with my child in her hour of need wasn't to much to ask!

Alan was a decent man, but one of his faults was that he hated staff being off. I was slightly angered that, he being a father himself couldn't see that this was a necessary thing for me to do, and Karen being there, had no bearing on the matter whatsoever. Carol overhearing his reaction to this just gave me a knowing look as I resumed my position at the counter.

The day's end saw me make my way to the hospital again and on arriving on the ward I found Karen in the playroom with Kaine, leading her by the hand as she was still a little unsteady with the walking business. She gave a little shriek of delight when she saw me, Kaine that was, not Karen; for she was used to my sudden appearances. As I bent down on one knee and gestured for her to come to me, I held out my arms and Karen then led her to me I picked her up and said 'hello' to my little girl by way of a kiss.

"How has she been?" I enquired of Karen.

"She's been her usual self. I think she's been enjoying the company of the other kids in here. Glad somebody's having a good time at least," Karen said, smiling at Kaine and tickling her cheek at the same time.

"Is the operation definitely this Wednesday morning then?"

"Yes, it's definitely Wednesday; did you tell Alan that you wouldn't be in?"

"No, he knows I won't be in." I said with what must have been a different inflection in my voice as Karen picked up on this immediately. Karen knew Alan well and liked him, but she also knew that it was a problem for him to not have me there.

"Oh, is he being a bit funny about you being off?" she asked.

"Well I think that having been through this before I get the impression that this is all old news to him and a bit routine so anything to get in the way of business is a problem, but this is different." I said.

"Too right," answered Karen.

On Tuesday evening as I was putting my jacket on, Alan had said to me,

"So, are you in tomorrow morning?"

"No, I'm not Alan." I answered. On the way home on the bus that night, I was preoccupied by the events of the next day, I was still put out at Alan not fully realising that the operation that Kaine was to have was, although not major brain surgery, it was still serious enough to warrant just concern by both myself and Karen as her parents. Given the choice of having a healthy child at home and going to work the next day was a far better prospect to the events that had to take place that following morning. Did he actually think I was looking forward to having a day off, and not even a full one under those circumstances?

I got up around seven Wednesday morning that was usually the time that I would be starting to lay out my window display and I was thinking that Alan wouldn't be pleased that I wasn't there. This in turn gave rise to a feeling within me that I should be more worried about what was to happen later on in the hospital than the feelings of other people, particularly as I hadn't asked for any of this and more importantly neither had Kaine asked to be born with the affliction that now continued to have an impact on her life. And so I was angry. I was angry at the insensitivity of other people as to how I felt, the worry that pervaded my waking thoughts and had even penetrated as far as to disturb my dreams when I slept. But what can you do? You can't make others feel what you feel; you can only rely on empathy of others to get some sense of what you are going through.

I arrived at the hospital an hour before Kaine was due to go to theatre. Of course being too young to realise what was to take place, she had no understanding as to why her hunger wasn't being satisfied as it always was in the mornings, and so her resulting hunger pangs gave rise to a little crankiness; of course this was understandable but unfortunately totally necessary for her to go through.

We tried to distract her as best we could from this by playing with her and taking her for little walks, but to no avail. She cried all the more and this was a stressful experience for both myself and Karen to have to go through on top of the worry already present within us.

The time came for Kaine's operation to be done, the parting this time made all the more heart-rending in that Kaine was aware of being separated from us and screamed and cried as she was being taken away, the attendant nurse's comforts to her having no effect on our daughter. We listened as her cries got fainter and fainter as she went away into the elevator to take her to the operating theatre.

And so the wait. Two hours later Kaine was back on the ward and being lifted onto her bed by one of the staff.

She wasn't conscious and from where we stood we could see that her hair had been cut back and shaved to expose the area where the shunt was; the tell-tale iodine stain around the fresh scar an indication that the operation had been recently done.

The post operative procedure was almost identical to the last time I had witnessed when Kaine was much younger. I felt a sense of relief again now that it was over, but the nagging thought that Kaine was dependant on this valve to maintain her health, particularly now that it had moved and had needed to be replaced, sat uncomfortably in my mind. But I pushed that thought away for now; I was simply glad that Kaine was back from theatre and the well of optimism for the future would surely spring forth and banish any negative thoughts remaining within me.

Karen attended to Kaine as was needed and I for my part decided to phone our parents and let them know that everything had gone well and that Kaine was once again out of danger. I would normally have called work to inform them that all was well and that I would be in the next day, but something changed in my thought processes as I was contemplating this. No I wouldn't be in the next day either; I was going to have the time to give to my wife and daughter. For once my priorities were now going to take precedence, the anger I felt previously was now more inflamed due to the sight of Kaine in her helpless condition on her return from surgery.

All that we had to do was to await Kaine's revival from the anaesthetic. When this happened, we had to keep her from pulling at the dressing now covering the stitches to where the shunt had been replaced. Our poor darling had obviously not known what had taken place and was thirsty, and still a little 'out of it' from the operation. This, however, was minor and we knew that the next day, apart from maybe experiencing some localised pain in the area of the shunt, that she would be as right as we could possibly expect and we were hoping that within a day or more so that Kaine would be able to go home.

I spent the next day at the hospital where, as we expected, Kaine was awake and her usual self. She kept feeling for the dressing area of her operation and it was a constant vigil to prevent her from pulling it off and at the same time doing damage to the stitches. But this was a good sign; that she was aware of everything, and as soon as the slight discomfort that she had felt behind her ear went away then the likelihood was that she would not pay much attention to the area.

We didn't see Mr Hamilton after the operation. I as yet had not met the man at all and was reliant on Karen's observations of him. My concern was that despite his manner, were his skills as a neurosurgeon up to the mark? Apparently so. Kaine was attended to by some of his junior staff who were obviously qualified to make the decision as to when Kaine was to be released. This was to be on Saturday. Kaine had been through her second operation in under a year and we hoped again that this was to be the last. We were given no explanation as to why the first shunt had slipped out of position, significantly it hadn't failed or blocked and so my faith in the technology was not dented too much.

Karen was a little upset as Kaine had blonde hair and she was letting it grow so that she could put it into pigtails with pink ribbons on, but now half of her hair had been shorn off. This was a small set back however, and this was not in the least a great concern to her; merely a reminder that the operation had taken place, and as she knew, her hair would soon grow back. The pigtails and ribbons would have to wait for now.

CHAPTER 11.

"I imagined Kaine older now, Walking the beach with us."

My return to work on the Friday morning was one that I thought would bring me a slightly frosty reception. This I was more than prepared for as I felt I held the moral high ground in attending to my daughters needs. I was entitled to two afternoons off per week, one being on the Wednesday half-day closing of the market hall and the other being Thursday, the latter I had forfeited in favour of the extra money this brought in and I hadn't taken that time off for months now. The total time therefore that I had taken off amounted to one full day, and I wasn't going to get all bent out of shape for that. After all it wasn't as though I'd taken a 'sickie' or had a day off for any other reason than one which I thought was right and proper.

Nobby as always was first on the scene.

"How's the nipper mate?" were his first words.

"Okay Nobby ta, she's making a good recovery again, we're hoping she'll be home tomorrow." I said in return for his concern.

"How was the captain's mood yesterday with my no show?" I asked, the 'captain' being Alan's nickname. I thought I'd get a feel for what awaited me on his arrival at the shop. Alan wasn't the type to go screaming and shouting, in fact, as I have said he was a good man to work for and ninety-eight per cent of the time a good laugh, but if upset he could get as moody as the next bloke.

Nobby grimaced in reply pulling a face we all used to use in silent recognition that Alan had descended into a mood. We both laughed at that.

"Take no notice mate; if 'e starts just tell 'im to kiss this."

Nobby bent over and slapped a cheek of his backside by way of indication as to what he thought.

"Ha! ha! shall I say you told me to tell 'im that then?" I asked jokingly of my mate who I knew that even if I did, it wouldn't bother him in the slightest. I could hear footsteps approaching and through time I knew who those footfalls belonged to. Alan entered the shop.

"Morning lads," he said as he put his briefcase on the counter. Nobby used to joke that all he kept in there were his sandwiches which was untrue, but gave us a good giggle nonetheless.

"How's Kaine Joe?" were his next words and he looked to be as he always did.

"Err, she's fine thanks Al', she's making a good comeback and should be home tomorrow." I was a little surprised at his light mood and had been expecting him to fire off about my absence, but to be fair he was concerned for Kaine and the atmosphere to my relief, bore no signs of the moodiness I was expecting and we had just picked up where we had left off.

"His missus must've seen 'im alright last night, ha! ha!" whispered Nobby in my ear at an opportune moment.

"What you pair sniggerin' at?" asked Alan, probably guessing that he was the butt of Nobby's humour once again.

"Nuffin' mate," said Nobby knowingly using the 'M' word with a little smirk.

"Don't start," said Alan with an all-too-familiar air of resignation signifying that Nobby had indeed got the upper hand in the mickey taking department. But to be fair to Alan he could give and take, and when he used to take the mickey out of Nobby's high pitched voice he had us all in stitches.

And so it was business as usual; the rest of the staff were arriving on time and the comforting sounds of the kettle being filled and switched on made me glad that I was back at work instead of at the hospital facing what I had in the days previously. I was looking forward to Kaine's coming home and looked upon this latest incident as a temporary setback and tried as best I could not to dwell on any more of that sort of thinking as they were still other problems in our daily lives to be tackled and one of these was that we were no longer happy living in the flats and I had decided that somehow I was going to have to buy a house.

Kaine was duly released from hospital on the Saturday morning as expected and that was a nice homecoming for me on the Saturday evening, though Zeus would have to spend a few more weeks at my mother-in-law's in case he licked Kaine as he was inclined to do. We didn't want to run the risk of any infection occurring in her wound, just a simple precaution that we felt was prudent at the time.

A week later we were having our Sunday lunch at Karen's mom's house as Cath and Stan (those being Karen's aunt and uncle) were over for dinner. They lived near the border of Wales; we had been to their house a couple of times in the past as they lived in the country they were in a bit of a remote area and could get snowed in the winter months. Stan was a heavy goods vehicle driver who delivered to meat companies up and down the country and he was also keen to try and start up a little business of his own breeding pigs for the local abattoirs in the area.

Stan was a little eccentric. He was also a musician, but a top bloke who I liked very much, and over dinner he liked to chat away with me about the butcher's trade as he was attached to it by driving and was soon hoping to have a vested interest of his own in the trade. The topic turned to house prices and I was saying that, at the moment, due to my wages, it was unlikely that I could afford to buy in the present climate.

"I might be able to help you out there boyo," said Stan munching away on a chicken leg.

"How's that then Stan?" I asked.

"I delivers to a company on the island of Anglesey, a big abattoir they are see, and they's lookin' for butchers who can speed bone."

"Depends on what sort of money they're payin' though Stan, and by the way mate where is Anglesey anyway?" I asked realising that I had absolutely no clue as to where he was talking about was. Roy chimed in as to where the location of Anglesey was.

"Just off the coast of North Wales, me an' Wilf worked there a few years ago, it's a nice place."

(Wilf being Roy's cousin and partner in business.)

"Three 'undred and fifty squids a week they's takin' 'ome out of there," Stan said completing the first part of my enquiry. I almost choked on my dinner!

"Three hundred and fifty quid a week take home pay?" I asked incredulously.

"Yep, that's what I's hearin', you gotta be quick mind cos they's workin' piecework an' it's 'ard graft."

"Tell me you ain't pullin' my leg Stan?" I asked, not able to believe that amount of money.

"No, I ain't pullin' your leg boyo, I's too busy pullin' at this leg for that." he said laughing and waving his chicken leg around slightly.

This was too much. If we hadn't gone for dinner then there would have been no way in the world that I'd have heard of this opportunity. The speed boning piecework was no problem as way back in nineteen eighty-four I had been working at a local abattoir in Great Bridge called Barrat and Bairds, one of the Midlands biggest suppliers of meat. They had contracts with the likes of Waitrose Supermarkets and supplied the beef to McDonalds for their beef burgers amongst other large consumer companies. I'd spent a year there working on the night shift doing the job that Stan was talking about but for a lot less money. I was even younger then and had just turned twenty-one and so the night shift, which was permanent, had been a real drawback to my social life and so I left in eighty-five to resume shop work. The experience was good for me though as I had retained the skill and the speed required in such an environment.

So far I ticked all the right boxes to do the job, only one snag remained. It would mean, assuming of course that I got the position, relocating to Wales and on an island to boot! Plus first and foremost I would have to discuss this with Karen, but from the look on her face I could see straightaway that that was unlikely to be a problem.

"I can take you there if you like Joe, I's got a delivery there next week, I'll arrange for you to speak to the right man so's you can sit down in front of him and tell 'im what you knows."

This was too good to be true; I was going right to the front door to see the guy who was hiring who happened to know my uncle-in-law well! Plus I'd got the skills for the job. This had got to be fate and I wasn't going to look this gift horse in the mouth I could tell you.

The following day I was back at work in the market having arranged with Stan that I would ring him later in the day. This gave him the time to speak with the guy in question and arrange an interview and, I assumed, a block test which was a pretty standard bit of practice in the trade for assessing the skills of a likely employee. All I had to do was approach Alan and ask him for a few days holiday in order for me to make the trip to Anglesey, do the necessary, have a look around and get back. Karen and I had discussed this at home the night before and as for Karen the thought of moving to a different part of the country and in particular by the sea had posed no problems at all. In fact a concern that we both had was that the air content around where we lived was poor as we lived in fairly close proximity to the M6 motorway at its busiest section, that being between junctions nine and ten. Frequent users will testify to the jams there almost on a daily basis. And so we reasoned that a move by the sea would be good for us and more particularly for Kaine as a young child and still, as yet convalescing from her recent operation.

I had a week's holiday left from my annual entitlement but although I only needed a few days it was a bit short notice to ask. The 'phone call to Stan had furnished me with the number of the man I was to be seeing in the abattoir and the resulting conversation with him had been constructive. He had enquired of my experience as Stan had told him that I was qualified to do the job; he had said that he was reluctant to take on 'shop' butchers as they tended to be too slow for the demand that was put on them, but as my track record included factory butchering then he was willing to grant me an interview and block test. This had been arranged for the Wednesday afternoon to coincide with Stan's delivery there. And so it was all going to plan. I was fired up with the thought of a massive increase in my wage the result of that being that we could buy the house that had so far remained so tantalisingly out of my reach. My only regret was that I had become so fond of the market where I worked. I wished that it was possible to achieve the goal I was aiming for without the huge change that this would bring. But at the same time I was sick and tired of hearing how all our friends had managed to buy property yet we seemed to be stuck in the same old rut; if a change would alter the circumstances then a change it would have to be.

I picked my moment to speak to Alan, but what was I to say? He knew I didn't take holidays and I respected the man to much to lie to him. Would he be suspicious of my motives for requesting time off at such short notice? In the event I was correct, we both knew each other too well by now for any shenanigans to take place.

"Al', can I 'ave a quick word?" I asked, feeling my stomach turn over slightly.

"What about Joe?" enquired Alan with a slight air of suspicion, as I had been off to the 'toilet' for a long time earlier on. This of course had been my subterfuge for making my 'phone call to the abattoir in Wales.

"I need a few days off at short notice, a family problem has come up that I need to deal with." I said, praying that the warmth I was feeling in my reddening cheeks wasn't turning into two flashing neon signs screaming out the words 'liar liar'.

"Oh, that's a bit sudden ain't it, when do you need the time off?"

"Yeah, well these things happen like that, you know. I could do with Wednesday Thursday and Friday off."

"Hmm well I suppose so Joe; if you need the time, you need the time." part of me was wishing that he had put up his usual resistance to taking time off and I was feeling ashamed of myself for fibbing to a man I considered a friend as well as my boss, but I had my family's interests at heart and so I thanked him and carried on with my normal duties. The other thing that bothered me was that Alan had given in rather meekly to my request as he would normally have probed a bit further than he did regarding my sudden request for leave of absence; however I couldn't detect any real change in his mood and put the thought out of my mind for the remainder of the day. On arriving home later that night Karen was eager to hear if I'd managed to get the time off and the result of my 'phone call to Wales.

"Well, how did you get on?"

"Okay, I've got an interview arranged for Wednesday afternoon; I gotta ring Stan later to arrange for him to pick me up on the morning."

"What's up? You don't look too happy at the prospect, I thought you'd be pleased, don't you think you'll get the job?" Karen enquired of me, picking up on my mood which, surprisingly, was a bit deflated. I had been thinking on my way home of how I had deceived Alan and it was weighing on me; as I said I considered him a friend and I felt bad for the lie that I had told him.

"I'm feeling like crap for lying to Alan." I told her.

"I can imagine you do, but you couldn't really tell 'im the truth though could you? He'd go mad," said Karen by way of assurance that I had done the right thing. She was right I couldn't just say that I needed a week off at such short notice and three days sudden holiday were an unlikely event so it would seem that I had had little choice in the matter or any alternative other than to lie about the reason for my absence at the shop. The happiness I felt at being in a position to alter our living arrangements was tempered by these stabs of conscience.

"I still don't feel too happy about it though," I said as I was getting out of my work gear.

Kaine was in the living room and I could hear her giggling at whatever toy she was playing with and the reminder of why I was actually doing what I was about to do became evident to me there and then.

"Come and have your tea," Karen said. I think deep down she knew how unhappy I was to be in a situation where I felt deceitful to Alan as in all the time we'd known each other some of the topics of our conversation while courting had been centred on that mad house shop in the market, and many a time we had been in stitches when I recounted some of the antics of the boys who worked there.

After my evening meal we just went about our normal family routine. I was spending a little time with Kaine, her wound was healing well and the check ups at the hospital gave no rise for concern. Her hair was slowly starting to regrow over the area that had been shaved off. This couldn't happen quickly enough for Karen as she had her heart set on those pigtails and ribbons.

I rang Stan and gave him a quick rundown on the conversation I had had with his friend at the abattoir; Stan saying how property in that area of Wales was still much cheaper than the Midlands and that fact, coupled with the increase in wages if I secured the job, would certainly ensure our ascent onto the property ladder. I was still unhappy about the circumstances that had led me to be devious with Alan and after a while I couldn't come to terms with how I felt any longer; so around nine o' clock I decided to give him a ring at home and be up-front as to why I needed the time off. I was feeling nervous as I depressed the buttons on the phone dialling Alan's number. As the dial tone turned into the ring tone I thought about putting the receiver back in its place.

"Hello?" Alan's voice was on the other end of the line.

"Hello?"

"Hello Alan, it's Joe."

"Hello Joe, what's up?"

"Alan, regarding today, about the reason for me having the time off I've asked for."

"Yeah?" he said, in a tone that told he half knew what I was going to say.

"Well, I wasn't being straight with you why I need the time."

"Thought not, Joe." As I've said before Alan was no mug and, being older and hence wiser, had put two and two together and come up with four. He knew me too well as we were similar characters.

"Alan, I've got a job interview lined up in Wales."

"Wales!" he exclaimed. "I thought you were going for another job Joe as I could recognise the signs but what threw me was why you needed three days though. So, how come Wales and what's the job?" I went on to explain about the position and the reasons why I was going for it. Our many conversations at work regarding the state of house prices and his knowing that I was as keen to advance as he had been at my age had given him an insight into the future behaviour of the young Joe; and knowing I had been somewhat disappointed in the rise I had received he now thought that this might be my next move, and of course he was right.

Business was business, and I think Alan adopted the position whereby he wasn't keen to have a run on wage rises if it got out that he was a soft touch. Alan wasn't a mean boss but it is fair to say he was careful. Many was the time when reminiscing on his youth he would say loudly, pointing his index finger skywards, "nobody gave me sod all, what I've got I've had to work for." This of course was perfectly true. Nobby and Ian would both yawn loudly as he said this. As for my own case, I'd hardly been brought up with a silver spoon hanging from my gob. I had been raised by my Grandmother in Ireland, I couldn't even say that I was of 'working class proper' as my Nan had been on what meagre benefits the Irish government were giving to a woman who was widowed and with a young child to bring up. The rest of the family had chipped in with what they could and thankfully I had never felt the sting of abject poverty or what it had felt like to go hungry. My Nan was a proud old bird who had instilled in me a strong, honest work ethic and saw education as the road to success, and more importantly had taught me to never expect anything in life without having to work for it.

And so my options were open and limited at the same time. Alan was more than aware that I wanted to advance in life, and not being slow on the uptake, if a better position arose then I was going to go for it. What really surprised him though was the money on offer at the abattoir in Wales; there was no way that any shop butcher could earn that kind of money. Butchers wages were notoriously bad and the long hours worked due to cleaning the shop diluted the hourly rate to below average, but it had other compensations, particularly if you were, as I was, in a good shop. Having had the experience of working in a meat factory previously I knew what to expect; as jobs go it was indeed 'hard collar' and pretty relentless in supplying to the ever hungry consumers food for the table. This I was prepared for. Alan wasn't too pleased at this turn of events and his strategy thus far had been to see what job I'd go for and what my reaction to the offer was before committing himself to any counter measures. Of course he didn't tell me this but as personalities go, the door can swing both ways and I knew him pretty well as much as he knew me.

The conversation remained very civilised and my fears that Alan would feel betrayed were allayed somewhat when he told me that he understood perfectly why I was making the decision to go for this job, and that he was pleased that I'd been up front with him rather than sneaking behind his back. This was also something that I was pleased to have done. I liked Alan immensely, and if I was to take the other job then it would be a major regret having to leave my friends with whom I had worked for the last two years and who had been the source of so much laughter in my life. Alan and I had worked together in another shop in the market even before then, he as the manager and myself as a cutter. Nobby went back even further having worked with Alan as a Saturday lad in some shop years before that.

So far the hand that life had dealt Karen and myself, particularly with regards to Kaine's health had not been good, but maybe this was the change in fortune that everyone wishes would take place; the proverbial ship docking, to recall an old saying. I was full of excitement and expectation at the thought of heading up to Anglesey and seeing what exactly lay before me. The next day at work was a peculiar one. I was full of beans and my inflated humour and confidence ensured that the day was full of wisecracking with the customers. One guy in particular to whom I had managed to sell some meat as he was passing through the market came to the counter and, in front of Alan gave me high praise saying how he had enjoyed being 'forced' to part with his coinage in return for some very nice meat and handed me a freezer order in the vicinity of one hundred and fifty pounds. A big order by any standard. I remembered the guy as he had been in building site clothes and he still was; it turned out that he owned his own building firm and had a bit of cash and wanted to spend it with me. Alan looked and acted pretty much the same as any other day, except that I could tell that at times he was deep in thought about something. I dared to presume that it was about my impending interview but maybe not. As it was no longer a secret the other lads at the shop got to know about my prospective job in Wales, a fact I don't think Alan was pleased about. At the end of day I said the usual 'good-byes' as I was leaving and I said to Alan that I would be back on Saturday.

"Okay then Joe, I hope it goes well for you."

"Thanks Alan, that's a nice thing to say," I said in return, I was glad he knew the full story as I felt I was being honourable with him as a man. It turned out that unknowingly my honesty had done me a big favour as I was later to learn.

I hardly slept that night as I was nervous about the coming tomorrow, how would the interview and block test go? What if I went all that way and I didn't get the job? What if the guy didn't like my face? These thoughts and more were racing through my mind. moreover if I didn't get the job I would have to go back to the market with my tail between my legs and this I was sure would weaken my credibility with Alan as he would be in the stronger position, knowing that I had nowhere else to go. I was beginning to regret my act of forthrightness, for if I had just gone off on three days leave for my 'family problem' on my return no one would have been any the wiser. Alan would have had his suspicions but those would have been unsubstantiated and would have faded in time. Everything was riding on this horse so it seemed. However the dye was now cast there was no turning back so I would have to give a good account of myself.

I was up bright and early at five o' clock, I had prearranged to meet our Stan by the flats. He was making a special detour to pick me up in his articulated lorry and he was duly waiting for me at the end of the road leading to our block. The whole trip had been pre-programmed like a military manoeuvre. Stan was to drive us up to Anglesey, drop his load, pick another up and continue on his rounds country-wide. I was to spend Wednesday evening and all day Thursday in Anglesey and he was to make the return trip to the abattoir on the Friday afternoon and pick me back up again. We would then make the journey to the Welsh-English border where he had arranged with a mate of his to take me the rest of the way home as far as West Bromwich where this chap would be dropping off his load. A complicated business but it worked well.

I had decided to take my bike with me having first cleared it with Stan as I thought that if I was to have a couple of days on the isle of Anglesey I would do a little touring about to pass the time. The weather would be good and it seemed like a good idea. I'd packed a change of clothing and some money for bed and breakfast and food in my rucksack and I looked more like a tourist than a guy going for a job interview in these strangest of circumstances. However 'nothing ventured nothing gained' was to be my motto and 'he who dares wins' as good ol' Del boy would say.

"Mornin' Joe, how's you doin' matey?" said Stan all bright and consistently cheerful as his personality was.

"I'm okay Stan, where do we sling the bike?" I enquired of him. In this huge articulated lorry one would have thought that there would have been tons of room but instead when Stan opened the back door it was rammed to the roof with boxes for prepacking the vacuum packed produce at the factory where we were going. We struggled to find space and when we had made a little niche for my bike, we climbed into the cab and we were off heading for our destination.

I was relaxed in Stan's company and looking forward to the drive through the countryside. I thought that even if nothing came of this then at least I had proven to myself and others that I was willing to go the whole nine yards to give it a go. I would be able to ring Karen en route by means of Stan's cab phone; no-one could accuse Stan of being a 'yuppie' even though he was equipped with the latest technology. As the time approached seven I wondered what Alan was thinking; that would be when my presence in the market hall would be missed as a man down when getting the shop up and running, no matter who he was, was a vital missing link, and put pressure on the others there. However I was determined to enjoy these few days I had and viewed them as a holiday with an interview chucked in for good measure.

Our journey time to Anglesey would be around five hours as the route we were taking involved some motorway travel but was mainly country roads. The miles roared by beneath this huge transport system we take for granted, and the closer we got to Anglesey the tighter my stomach muscles became. Stan must have picked up on this because he reminded me that I had nothing to worry about, and was just to enjoy the few days break that had been enforced on me. To be honest I was looking forward to having the time off, as it seemed all I had done these past months, apart from the time spent at the hospital, was work and worry. I'd called Karen to tell her we were nearing our destination and to enquire how Kaine was, this reminded me also why I was doing this, as I was, and still am a creature of habit, and I don't like too much change; but what I was about to take on was as different as night is to day in terms of my previous daily routine. The hurdles I had to clear were the interview and block test looming as near now as were the gates to the abattoir as we turned off to the left and headed down this road at the end of which I would soon get to see what my immediate future had in store for me.

The air brakes of the huge truck hissed as Stan brought us to a standstill outside the gatehouse window, wherein a disinterested security guard barely looked at us as he pretended to write something important on a clipboard.

"Afternoon," said Stan to the guy. He didn't answer, just passed Stan an entry form to sign in; the routine was obvious and I myself was no stranger to the workings of an abattoir having witnessed this procedure countless times at Barrat and Bairds. We drove off down a road leading to where Stan was to be unloaded; he skilfully reversed into a docking bay where the forklifts operated and we dismounted the cab and went in through a door to gain access to the back doors of the trailer in order to first get my mode of transport out and secondly to let the fork truck drivers do the work of unloading.

"We'll give my mate a ring in a minute Joe and get you sorted out eh?" Stan said to me as he was unlocking the substantial padlock securing the doors to the trailer.

"Whatever you say Stan," I answered, feeling even more isolated now than ever and a thought ran through my head of a man walking the plank and very nearly reaching the end of it. However I was here and had a task to do and I was determined not to be found wanting in front of all these Welshmen; I was after all of Celtic stock myself and had a reputation to protect.

If I had thought the first person I would speak to would be a Welshman however I was to be mistaken, for as I unloaded my bike from the back of the trailer, a dark-haired man exited from a small office on the loading bay, he looked about thirty and was of average height. He was looking intently at my bike as he was approaching me. He was dressed in a white coat and white Wellington boots and had on a white hat with a hairnet attached. I noticed though that he wore a shirt and tie which identified him to me as one of the managers there. His counterparts at Barrat and Bairds in the Midlands wore blue plastic helmets and were called obviously enough the 'bluehats' and were hated by the rest of the workforce as they behaved more like concentration camp kapos than work colleagues, using the power of instant dismissal over the track butchers (as we were known) for the slightest infraction of health and safety rules.

I immediately thought we were deep in the brown stuff for having a bicycle on the loading bay; although we were far enough away from any food production in my experience it didn't take to much to get these mini Hitlers jumping up and down on the spot screaming abuse at the offender. However my expectations couldn't have been more wrong as a broad smile appeared across his face on nearing myself and Stan.

"Whose isa da bike?" A thick Italian accent confirmed that the man wasn't a local.

"It's mine." I said in answer to his query.

"Dasa nice bike," he continued. He was interested in the small computer fixed to the crossbar and was curious as to its function. I explained to him what it was for and it turned out the guy was seriously into bike racing and was impressed with my bike with the bit of technology attached. He couldn't have been more different to the 'bluehats' I had come to know and hate in the old days; he was friendliness personified and enquired as to why I had a bike in the back of a delivery truck. I told him I'd got a lift here for a job interview and I think he assumed that Stan and I didn't know each other at all and was very impressed that I'd made my way all the way from Birmingham to Anglesey for a job. I didn't feel any need to correct him in his assumption as essentially he had got the gist of the story as I had indeed made my way all the way from Birmingham but not the way he thought, and who was I to shatter my new mates impressions? Stan too had picked up on this and acted pretty nonchalantly towards me as if we were new acquaintances.

It turned out that it was a good stroke of unexpected luck taking my bike with me as the man took me under his wing and knew exactly who I was to see and where he was to be found. As we walked off in the direction of this man's office I looked back at Stan who gave me the thumbs up. I'd be seeing him in two days again by the gatehouse on his return journey from wherever he was bound.

My new best friend was the chatty type and worked in the same capacity as the man who was to interview me that, being the role of general manager. So far things were looking good; my nerves were still with me but the friendly disposition of my companion put me at ease as we walked closer to where I was to have my interview.

My new best friend was from Milan and worked for a major importer of British meat there. His company had sent him to Anglesey for a year to oversee the new contract between the two companies and he had bought a bicycle of his own while he was here to tour the island. I liked the man immediately and thought that if he was typical of the management here then I shouldn't have many problems. We entered the office and the man I was to meet was sitting behind a desk; he was dressed in similar garb to my Italian friend who introduced me as, "disa guy has a cycled all da way from Birmingham for a job, I tinka dat you shoulda give him a job no?" He laughed as he said this in his friendly manner and obviously knew the guy at the desk well enough to joke with him.

"Well now, that's very impressive boyo, but there's more to getting a job yere than bein' a good cyclist see!" came the reply good-naturedly enough in the first real Welsh accent I'd heard since arriving. We shook hands and I introduced myself as the person he'd spoken to some days earlier in Birmingham.

"I will leavea you to sort da business with my friend," said my new best Italian friend and he left the office with a cheery "see you again."

"Well don't just stand there boyo, sit yourself down," came the compelling order from the general manager. This I did and tried to get my thoughts in order ready for the barrage of questions which based on my previous experience, I was expecting.

"So, tell me, you've worked at a big plant like this in the Midlands you were saying?"

"Yes sir, I was employed at Barrat and Bairds meat processing plant and abattoir for twelve months in 1984."

"And what exactly did you do there?"

"Well, I was a track butcher on the beef line; my role was as a cutter boner for the vacuum packers at the end of the line."

"Why did you leave?"

"I was on a permanent night shift, I was only twenty one and I felt I was too young to work constant nights at that age, but I enjoyed the work. It was a good experience for me there."

"So why do you want to work for me?"

"Well sir to be honest, I was happy in my job and it's purely for economic reasons, better pay, and that's why I'm here."

"Fair enough. Well you seem okay to me. But we'd need to see what your like with a knife in your hand before I can give you a decision."

"I was expecting that anyway."

"So you won't mind giving us a demonstration of your skills then?"

"Not at all."

"Good, I'll sort that out straightaway and we can get you on-to our production line."

That seemed to be the end of the talking; obviously the emphasis would now be on whether I was capable of doing the job rather than my sparkling wit and personality, which was fair enough. He reached for the 'phone and told whoever was on the other end of the line to come to his office as he had a candidate, namely me, for a block test. This was the easy part for me, I had plenty of experience in the trade and I was quite fast at de-boning meat as the twelve months factory work had honed it into me.

Within a few minutes a guy walked in who, it seemed, was the track foreman. he had on a white overall with a butcher's apron over that, white Wellington footwear and a hat with the obligatory hair net. I could see that he had his chain-mail anti-stab protection apron on underneath his butchers apron and on his left hand he wore a chain mail anti-slash glove which was the standard protection worn by butchers in this environment. Around his waist he wore a chain belt with an aluminium scabbard that contained three boning knives and a longer steak knife; not the sort you would get in a restaurant as part of your eating utensils for steak, this knife would be about nine or ten inches in length and was used for cutting down larger pieces of meat and resembled a small sword with a rounded curved business end. Attached to the other side of his chain belt on a smaller chain was sharpening steel for his knifes. So far all familiar gear that I myself had worn on the production line.

"This young man yere is going to impress us with his skills, see that he gets the opportunity to do so," the manager said. The guy just nodded and bade for me to follow him.

"Right we'll see you in an hour then young man," he added and returned to his paper work on the desk in front of him.

I followed my so far silent guide towards the changing rooms where I assumed I would be kitted out in my hygiene and protective gear for the test. Most factory butchers regard shop men with distain as they tend to be slow by comparison and overwhelmed by the factory environment. When we got to the changing rooms my guide hadn't so far uttered a single word to me and I got the impression that he assumed I was just another shop butcher who fancied his chances at a big boy's job. He opened a locker and pulled out a 'one size fits all' set of overalls and apron. Pointing to my feet he uttered the only word so far in our five minute acquaintanceship.

"Size?"

"eight."

He then opened another locker and pulled out the chain mail apron and glove along with scabbard and chain and a brand new set of knives with sharpening steel.

His attitude immediately changed towards me as I clipped my chain mail apron into place with the familiarity of an old hand and attached my scabbard and knives to my belt with none of the confusion that unfamiliar handling of these items bring to the uninitiated.

"Oh, have you come from another factory then?" he asked.

"Yeah," I answered, surprised that he could actually attach words of more than one syllable together to form a sentence.

"Good, you'll know the score then an' I won't have to stand over you in case you cut your hand off!" he said.

"Don't worry 'bout me just show me what you want done." I said. I pulled my boots on, and fixed my hat in position and was ready to do what was required of me. We went through a couple of doors and as we did so I could hear the all too familiar sounds of a busy track, with the pneumatic circular saws of the track breakdown butcher whirring away as he broke down the fore-quarter and hind-quarter sections of beef into the smaller components to be de-boned and trimmed by the men on the production line track. I was led to a space on the track and positioned between two other butchers who were busy working away.

"What do you want me to start on?" I asked raising my voice to counter the elevated noise levels in there.

"Process every piece that comes down the track doesn't matter what, you've got an hour and I want to see how you tackle all the different cuts," my now more talkative guide instructed.

"Okay!" I said and took my position next to the two other strangers in the place. I felt the familiar feel of the knife in my hand and I grabbed a spare hook and pulled the first thing that came my way which happened to be a brisket and got stuck in.

The time went by quickly for me and a tap on my shoulder from the foreman signified the end of the test. We walked back toward the changing rooms and I took off my gear. My companion remained silent again throughout and I wondered if he had been sufficiently impressed with me to give me the thumbs up.

We back-tracked our way to the manager's office and on entry found him at his desk writing away. He merely looked up at my companion and uttered one word.

"Well?" A nod was the answer and my silent guide left us to it without a word.

"Talkative isn't he?" the manager said with smile.

"Strong silent type eh?" I answered.

"Well it would appear you have what it takes to join us Mr. Lawlor, all we have to do now is give you a start date. When would you like this? I assume you would have to give notice to your old employer?"

A sudden wave of euphoria came over me and all of a sudden a hundred and one things ran through my head.

All my energies and thoughts had been focused on getting the job so I hadn't given much thought at all to what I would say should I acquire the position.

"Well, er, yes, of course I would have to give two weeks notice, which would be ideal if I could, and that would give me time to find a place to stay as well."

"Two weeks it is then. Go through to the next office and I'll get my secretary to take all your details from you." He pointed to an adjacent door. I thanked him for his time and for giving me the job and did as he had asked of me.

On entering the room adjacent, a lady of about fortyish sat at a desk.

"Can I help you?" she asked.

"Er I've been told to give you my details as I'm due to start work here in two weeks time."

"Oh right, you'd best come in and sit down and I'll get the forms. This won't take long." And so the next twenty minutes were spent with me giving my name and address and also my tax details etc to her. When all this was completed I had to find my way back out to where I'd left my bike chained up, I met my new Italian best friend on the way back again and he asked me how I got on. I told him I'd got the job and would be getting my start date and confirmation of the job by post in the next few days. He was extremely helpful to me in that he gave me directions to a bed and breakfast and a good place to get something to eat and also the names of a few places to tour around if I'd got the time. I thanked him for his kind help and got my bike and made my way towards the gate-house where I would be meeting Stan in a couple of days. My mood was euphoric now and I felt relief beyond belief. I'd done what I'd set out to do and that was to improve our financial situation and give Karen and Kaine a better standard of life than that in the flats we were now living in.

A few things had to be checked out though. First and foremost, was how far we were from the nearest hospital, and what was the standard of healthcare like there in case anything went wrong with Kaine in the future. That was something I intended to discover in the next two days but for now I had to find the bed and breakfast in the town that my new Italian best friend had recommended to me. I also wanted to find a 'phone box so that I could let Karen know that I'd got the job.

The weather was fine if a little windy as I set off back down the long road that had brought us in, the sky was blue with a few clouds about, but as far as I was concerned the horizon was cloudless!

I turned right at the top of the road and reversed my course down the main road now following the directions I had been given. We had passed a small town about six or seven miles further along earlier, and this was where I would find the bed and breakfast. It was a nice ride along with the wind at my back and taking it steady I covered the distance in about twenty minutes or so. On arriving in the town I dismounted from my bike and decided to follow the directions I had been given on foot. The 'town' was a charming little Welsh village with a few nice pubs that I made plans to visit later and some nice little restaurants as well. I eventually found the bed and breakfast and walked up the path and rang the bell; the time was around five o' clock now and I had been on the road a long time and due to the stress of the day I felt both tired and hungry. I was hoping to get a room and grab a shower before I went out exploring the place a bit later on. The door opened and a plump middle-aged lady greeted me with a typical Welsh accent.

"Hallow, what can I do for you?" she asked.

"Oh, hello. I was given directions to your bed and breakfast by one of the chaps who works at the abattoir. He recommended you, and I was wondering if you had a room for two nights?" I replied.

"Well, the only room I've got left is a shared room, I've just this second let it to a young chap around your age. If you don't mind sharing your welcome to that."

This wasn't ideal but I didn't fancy a jaunt back through the village or even a bike ride to the mainland, and so I thought that if I didn't like it I could stay tonight and move the next day. I'd be going to the pub later on and so figured by ten o' clock I'd be too drunk to care about sharing a room with a stranger anyway, and so I agreed.

"I'll just ask him the same question then." It hadn't occurred to me that the guy who was in the room first might not agree to this arrangement and that I might have found myself 'on my bike' again sooner than I'd planned.

I waited in the hallway for the lady of the house to make her enquiry with the occupant of the room and mentally I could see myself having to look further a-field for accommodation that evening. To my surprise though, when she re-appeared after five minutes or so, she was smiling and told me that the chap in the room didn't mind in the slightest that he was to share with a total stranger as well. I was grateful for that and hoped that if the situation were ever reversed that I would show the same graciousness as he had.

"You can bring your bicycle through to the back if you like, it will be quite safe there," said the plump lady beckoning me to follow her lead.

"Thank you." I said. We went through the long bright hallway through to the kitchen and a door led into the back garden of the spacious property. A little covered entryway was where she had in mind for me to store my bike and that's where it resided for the evening.

"Right then, let's get you to your room and I'll introduce you to your room-mate." I followed her back through the house and I was amazed at the number of rooms we passed. This place reminded me of the Doctor Who Tardis, in that it didn't look all that big from the outside. We came to the room and she politely knocked on the door before entering. I followed her in.

"This is the chap who will be sharing with you for a couple of nights," she announced to the guy who was unpacking his gear from an army kit bag. He stuck out his hand and in a broad Australian accent said,

"G'day mate, pleased to meet ya, oi'm Andy."

"Hello Andy, I'm Joe, very pleased to meet you, and thanks for sharing the room with me."

"Aw, think nothin' of it mate, if ya can't help a fellow Bruce in schtuck what can you do eh?" his handshake was firm, he was around my age and I could tell that he was a military type not only from the kit bag but from his over-all appearance and manner. He seemed the archetypical Aussie, friendly and down to earth and I immediately felt comfortable with the guy.

The landlady left us to it and Andy pointed to the other bed,

"That's your bunk there if you like we can swap, I'm not fussy."

"No mate, this'll do me fine; it's just a flop so I'm easy enough," I said.

"No worries then." he answered. He was the first Australian I'd so far had any extended kind of face-to-face conversation with and it struck me how typical of his race that he was, my other only real reference I had of Aussies was what I'd seen on television and film, but if he was anything like his fellow countrymen I'd seen in that capacity and it certainly seemed like it, then I could see 'no worries' was the standing order of the day.

I stowed my kit on my bed and had a quick look around the room, it was a fairly big room with two medium sized beds in and an ensuite shower and bathroom attached. The décor was bright and homely and a large window flooded the spacious room full of light.

"What brings you to Wales then mate, you touring?"

"Well, I'll be having a tour round in the next couple of days, but the real reason I'm here is for a job."

"Oh right, have you got one then?" he asked whilst hanging his clothing up in one of the wardrobes.

"Yeah, I've just been told I can start at the local abattoir not far from here. How about yourself then Andy, I take it you're on holiday, you touring around as well?

"Yeh, I'm on leave from the army for a month, saved up me dollars and decided to see the old country. Me folks are originally from Blighty so I had to come and see the place didn't I?" Andy replied shutting the wardrobe door and then bodily throwing himself onto his bed.

"I thought you looked the army type when I saw you, I was in the Irish FCA, a branch of the Irish army;

so I could tell by the way you looked, the hair cut gave it away."

"May as well have it stamped on me forehead!" he laughed, vigorously rubbing the top of his crew cut.

"What branch of the army are you in?"

"Bloody paratroopers! The only ones nuts enough to jump out of a bloody plane with no engine trouble!"

We both laughed at that, and I could tell me and Andy were going to be fine. I thought how ironic it was to come to Wales in a lorry and get a job on an island first meet an Italian and then meet an Australian from the other side of the world and end up sharing a laugh and a room with him, and all in the space of a few hours. Just goes to show you never know where life will take you!

"Hey d'ya fancy a few jars at the local watering hole a bit later?" he asked in that enthusiastic way, like the thought had just come to him.

"Sure do Andy, I'm up for that, I've just got to find a 'phone box to ring the 'Sheila' and let her know how I got on today."

"Cool mate, I fancy headin' out around eight if that's alright?"

"Fine by me bud." And so off I went to find the nearest call box. Which I did indeed locate about a hundred yards or so from the guest house. I dialled our home number and after two or three rings Karen answered the phone.

"Hello?"

"Hello, it's me, you okay?"

"Fine, fine, come on then, how did you get on?"

"How do you think I got on?" I teased.

"Come on don't keep me in suspense, you got it didn't you?"

"Yes, piece of cake." I said, trying to make out that the butterflies I had had in my stomach before the event were imagined.

"Fantastic! So we'll be moving to Wales then?" Karen asked excitedly.

"It looks that way, I'll check out the area properly tomorrow and go and see any estate agents in the area to see what the house prices are running at. And also see where the local hospital is, shouldn't be too hard to find out, I'll ask the locals.

"Good, have you found somewhere to stay yet?"

"Yeah, I've ended up at a nice guest house; have to share the room though with an Australian paratrooper of all people! Ha! ha!"

"An Australian paratrooper? Are you having me on?"

"No honest, he's a really nice bloke, we're gonna go for a drink together later on tonight." "Don't end up blind drunk then the two of you."

"No I won't, how's Kaine?"

"She's ok; we've been over at mom's today to see Zeus and took him for a walk."

"That's good, look the money's goin', I'll call you tomorrow; love you."

"Love you too." I put the receiver back in place and headed back to the guest house. I was going to grab a shower and relax on my bed for a bit before my now new Australian best friend and I hit the town. When I got back to the guest house Andy had already taken his shower and was ready to go out to have a look around. I was glad of the privacy as I could unpack and have a shower myself. We arranged to meet at the pub on the end of the road called the Red Lion at eight o' clock so that I could have an hour or so to sort myself out and grab a bite to eat.

175

Later I met Andy at eight in the pub as arranged; he was sitting at the bar and had already got himself a pint of lager sitting in front of him when I arrived,

"How you doin' mate, wotcher 'avin'?"

"I think I'll try one of those you got mate thanks."

"Good health and happiness," said Andy as he took a long swig from his glass.

"Same to you mate." I said doing the same. The cold lager tasted like heaven after such a day, I had no doubt that we would be having quite a few more that evening judging from the way my new mate emptied his glass in two more gulps. I did the same and ordered two more replacements or reinforcements as Andy liked to call them. He was an easy guy to chat with and although the same age as me, his experience in travel made his conversation all the more fascinating and mine by comparison dull and boring as my life had revolved around the market where I'd laid my hat for the last two years. However it was my life and I suppose not everyone is cut out to be Marco Polo.

Andy was a single guy, he'd got a girlfriend or two back in Oz, but I really got the impression that here was a young chap who loved adventure whose job gave him all that and more. We sat and chatted away all night like old mates and come drinking up time we were well acquainted. The next day for me would be busy as I was to be out doing a bit of exploring of my own. If this land was to be our new home then I would have to find a place for us to live, the plan being that I would get lodgings at first and buy a house when something suitable became available.

The next day brought the hangover from hell as I opened my eyes, and within seconds it felt as if a military marching band was parading through the middle of my head.

The groan from the other side of the room indicated that my Oz pal could hear the same band as me, we must have had a few too many the evening before; ah well, it was allowed.

"Mornin'," Andy croaked as he struggled to sit up.

"Strewth, how many beers did we have? Me noggin feels like crap." He was rubbing his head as he spoke.

"If it's any consolation mate, I'm feeling the same." However a shower and hearty breakfast took care of most of the headache I was feeling and the fresh air would take care of the rest. After breakfast Andy and I went our separate ways, we would have a repeat performance later on when we'd both rendezvous back at the Red Lion. I got my bike and headed off into town looking for an estate agent. The day was a glorious one and my headache soon disappeared as I cycled my way along the country lane, the fresh, clean air so different to the bus and car fumes I was used to in Birmingham city centre.

I soon found an estate agent and looking at the properties listed on the board in the front window I could see that a lot of the houses

advertised were sea-front homes with sea-front price tags; not really for me I thought, perhaps in a hundred years or so when I could afford it. However, the kind of house that I was looking for was also on the market; two and three bed roomed properties and I was pleased to see that the madness of the Midlands hadn't quite reached this area, and that even on my wage from the market I could afford to buy, with my wage at the abattoir it would be a cinch.

I went in and spoke to one of the guys who worked there. I explained that I had just landed a job locally and would be looking to rent for a while and buy as soon as I could. The chap I spoke to was helpful and said that they could help me out on both accounts.

"We've got exactly what you're looking for in terms of buying a few miles from here, if you'd like to go and take a look?"

"Yes I would." He pulled out a folder and showed me a list of houses that had just been built five or six miles away; it was a small brand-new housing estate of two and three beds twenty two thousand pounds each for the two beds and three grand more for the three beds.

I couldn't believe it; brand new houses for that sort of money! By now in the Midlands the asking price for a fixer upper of the same ilk would be in the thirty to thirty-five thousand mark.

I became more and more convinced that my long journey here had been exactly the right thing for me to have done. And so I took the directions from the estate agent and headed off to have a closer look at these houses and the surrounding area.

I found myself heading off out through the countryside again, taking in the pleasantness of the surroundings as I rode along the quite roads. I was wishing that Karen was with me so that she could see how nice it was and the thought of the houses I was to go and look at excited me as I could see an end to living in the flats.

I came to a small village, stopped and asked directions at a local paper shop as I bought a drink. I was only a mile from my destination and on hearing my accent the woman behind the counter asked me if I was looking at the new houses with a view to buying one. I told her that that was my intention and she said that how nice they were and that in this location we were only three miles from some sandy beaches if I was interested in taking a look around the area. I was indeed as the phone call I was going to make to Karen later on after I had viewed the estate would be all the more welcoming if I could tell her that I had located a house and not only that but one three miles from a sandy beach!

I cycled further along and eventually came to the housing estate itself.

It was so new that the building workers were still there finishing off; so having asked if I could go into one of the houses to have a quick look and being told that this was no problem I managed to have a look at the two and three bed houses. The estate was tiny in comparison to the large housing estates I was used to back in the Midlands, it consisted of about twenty houses built in a horse shoe configuration, and from the upstairs bedroom windows the sea was clearly visible in the distance. My report back to base camp would indeed be a good one.

I left the housing estate full of excitement and couldn't wait to check out those beaches I had been told about, and so off I set in the direction of the sea that I had earlier observed from the bedroom window. Ten minutes or so saw me arriving at the edge of Anglesey Island, the Irish Sea lapped gently on the shores of Wales and my former homeland lay out to the west beyond the horizon.

The beach itself was lovely; I dismounted from my bike and walked down onto the golden-brown coloured sand. I had the whole beach almost to myself; the only other people there being an older couple walking hand in hand along the sea shore with their jeans rolled up and footwear held in their other hands as they walked. A dog ran ahead of them, clearly excited and barking at the breaking waves coming onto the beach. It was so peaceful; it seemed I had found paradise. I walked further along until I came to a sand dune and decided to take a rest there for a while and let this atmosphere soak in. I pulled my drink from my rucksack and sat there staring out at the sea. I let my mind go back to the time when I was at school and had been taught that the Irish pagan warriors had used to send raiding parties across the sea to Wales to pillage the Welsh coastal villages and take captive as slaves any they could find. This was how we had gotten our very own Saint Patrick I was told, as he had been unwillingly taken to Ireland by such means and he was later then responsible for eventually spreading Christianity throughout our island. The Guinness family must have raised many a glass at their mansion to that raiding party for their fortuitous find that day as they saw the profits from the national drink soar on the seventeenth day of March every year the day set aside for our Patron Saint. As I sat and pondered on past history, my mind I also allowed to wander into the as yet un-fulfilled future and I imagined myself and Karen in the years to come with Kaine older now walking along the same beach; and maybe Zeus happily running on in front of us barking at the waves as I had observed earlier on with that older couple's dog.

The sun was warm and I lay back to soak up some of its rays. I had by now been indoors so long that I feared that it would take a month of lying on a beach to put the colour back in my cheeks. After a while I decided to move on as I only had today and a part of the following day to see the rest of the island and a bit of the mainland. I went further up the expansive beach pushing my bike along by my side and eventually came to an exit a mile or two further along where I found a main road and decided to set off and see where the road took me to. I'd figured on a few hours cycling and then stopping off at a pub for something to eat, yes that seemed like a plan and that was what I was going to do. The road I followed had some road signs along its way and I came to a T- junction after a few miles. I decided to take the route signposting the Menai Bridge, which was the link bridge to the mainland that lay ten miles or so to the east and I'd worked out by the time I'd cycled the distance and had had a bite to eat at a nice pub I had in mind it would be time to take a quick run over the bridge and check out the main hospital that the landlady at the guest house had told me about at breakfast; an unusual request from a seemingly fit and healthy young man enquiring the whereabouts of the nearest main hospital, but I had assured her that my hangover from the previous evenings fun didn't require hospital treatment.

I arrived in the town and stopped off to have lunch at this nice place I had spotted earlier the day before when Stan and I had crossed the bridge to get onto the island. The main hospital lay only a few miles further inland and so by car from where the houses I'd looked at were we could be there In around forty minutes or less. The hospital itself was on a par to the rest of the facilities anywhere else in the country that I could observe from my limited perspective and so all the necessary requirements that I needed to cover and satisfy both myself and Karen with regards to Kaine's future health issues were in place for me to tell Karen about when I rang her later that evening.

The day was getting on now after my jaunt over the Straits of Menai and my return journey across the bridge was hampered by the strong winds that are very often commonplace over exposed stretches of water; so much so that I had to dismount and walk across using the pedestrian footpath adjacent to the roadway.

Safely across to the island side of the bridge I set off back to the guest house with the intention of ringing Karen and letting her know how I had got on with my exploration of the area. I was happy with everything that I had seen so far and if time would allow, I was going to go back to the estate agent I'd been to earlier and tell him that, as soon as I could, I would be interested in buying one of the houses I had looked at. Alas this wasn't possible as they had shut up shop for the day and gone home; no matter I thought to myself, first thing in the morning would suffice for the task. The next thing for me to do would be to get back and have a shower; that was if my mate Andy wasn't back before me and already using it.

I got back and saw that Andy's car wasn't on the car park and so assuming he was still out and about I put my faithful iron steed away again for the night and went up to the room for a shower and have an hour or so before I went out for the night. Andy returned within the next hour. I was flat out on my bed watching the telly when he arrived,

"Wotcha mate, how you doin'?"

"How you doin' Andy, had a good day?"

"Yeh, not bad mate, oi've been everywhere today think I must've done two hundred kilometers!"

"Kilometers? Andy, you really are goin' to 'ave to speak the queens English here old son, its miles in blighty not bleedin' kilometres!"

"Oh yeh, I forgot; you poms only work in imperial not metric."

"Never mind all that jazz matey, what time d'you fancy goin' for a pint? Or is that kind of imperial measurement too much for an Aussie to get his head around?"

"Nah mate, not me head, it's me mouth I want 'round a pint, ha! ha!"

"Now yer talkin'."

"I'll hop in the shower and get me strides on and we'll be off if you like eh?"

"Right, while you're in the shower, I'm gonna ring Karen and let her know how I got on today. I'll tell you about it over a pint mate."

"Okey dokey mate, I'll see you in a while." I headed off to the 'phone box which would also allow Andy a bit of privacy with the shower and to get himself ready. For both of us it was our last night in this part of Wales; Andy had two weeks of his leave left and was off to another part of the country and for myself I had my rendezvous with Stan the next afternoon and I'd be homeward bound.

I rang Karen and told her all about the houses and their prices, she could barely contain her excitement on the other end of the phone as I described how they were not far from the beach and the hospital was close in case we needed it. I didn't like to think that we ever would again but it was something that as a responsible parent that I had to take into consideration and especially with Kaine being dependant now on the shunt.

Everything it seemed was perfect for us to move here. I had secured the job with good money, houses were still cheap enough to buy on my old wage and so we would be able to save as well. The island of Anglesey was picturesque, and the medical facilities close by. The one thing more we had to consider was that we would be on this island miles from family and friends and so we still had to weigh up the whole package. But for now I was going to leave that for when I got home as I still had to deal with the very real problem for me of telling Alan that I'd got the job and was intent on leaving if everything when weighed in the balances was in favour of that happening. When I went back to the guest house Andy was ready and waiting; we headed off to the pub full of good cheer and if you had seen us together you could have been forgiven for thinking that we'd been mates for years.

The night went pretty much as the night previous with us having a good old drink, swapping stories and just general chit-chat. I felt slightly envious of Andy's lifestyle as two days from now I would be back at my job in Birmingham in pretty much the same hum drum routine whereas Andy still had two weeks of adventure in this country ahead of him and then back home to Australia and the paratroopers. His next posting was in Singapore or somewhere exotic like that. No matter that was his life and this was mine; together we drank in the Red Lion in Wales, toasting my new job and life to come and his safe journey home and his new posting. The next morning saw a repeat of the marching bands of the morning before for us both and the same cure was the order of the day. We were both leaving for different destinations and I have got to say that rarely in my life have I met a total stranger such as Andy and had such a good laugh together. After breakfast I got my bike and was ready to push off, my new Australian paratrooper mate was waiting to see me off and we shook hands warmly and wished each other well for the future; we were unlikely to meet again but it had been good getting to know the guy. I had nearly the whole day to fill before I met Stan later. I headed for the estate agent's office and spoke to the man I had seen the day before. I expressed my interest in buying one of the houses on the estate, most likely one of the two beds to begin with. He gave me an A4 print off with all the details required, with his business card attached for me to show Karen when I got back home. I thanked him for his time and set off to see what I could see in the last few hours remaining to me on the island.

The day was nice and pleasant and the views were good as I made my way around. I stopped off to ring Karen and have lunch and decided in the early afternoon to head back toward the abattoir where I found Stan parked up waiting for me, having arrived half an hour ahead of his own schedule.

"How you doin' Joe?" he asked when I cycled up to where he was parked up.

"Fine Stan, how are you, and have you been here long?"

"No matey, half hour in front of meself so no problems. I hears you got good news."

Obviously Stan had spoken to his mate prior to my arrival and been informed of my impending start date there.

"Yes Stan, I got it mate and I can't thank you enough for giving me the tip off."

"Think nothin' of it Joe. Now then we got to get goin' if we're to make the meetin' with my mate to get you 'ome." He said and we put my trusty bike in the now empty trailer and got in the cab. I was looking forward to getting home now to see Karen and Kaine. I felt satisfied having accomplished what I'd set out to do two days earlier and I'd had a good break and a bit of a laugh to boot. Yes, job done!

CHAPTER 12.
Pandora's Box.

The journey back was as uneventful as when we came through; of course this was a well travelled route for Stan. We chatted away and I told him of the house I had seen and he said that when he was at the abattoir that he'd pop in for a cup of tea with Karen as I'd be at work; of course he would have been more than welcome to do so. There was, however, a lot to be sorted out between now and that happening and this was only the first leg of the journey. I'd thought that by the time I got back home and got some sleep there would be very little time to gather my thoughts and prepare myself for telling Alan of my plans, as in an all too short a time I would be back behind the counter in the market, which wouldn't have given me much time to talk to Karen, and I wanted to do so before making any major decisions about our future.

We were to meet Stan's buddy somewhere by the border of England and Wales at a truck stop; Stan would then complete his journey home to Cath and the kids and his pal was to take me on to West Bromwich where he was to load up with more boxes for the abattoir. We met at the truck stop around eight in the evening; Stan's pal was there before us drinking a mug of tea when we arrived.

"Hello Stan you old dog," he said as we sat down at the table.

"Hullo Terry, this is Joe my nephew who yous are goin' to make sure 'e gets 'ome safe 'n' sound, aren't ya?" said Stan to the guy.

"Hello Joe mate, pleased to meet you, I'm Terry just call me Tezza."

Terry held out his hand by way of introducing himself.

"Hello Tezza, pleased to meet you. Stan and Terry worked for the same haulage firm and while I got the teas in they chatted away about work and such-like. Three steaming mugs of tea down us later and it was time for me and Stan to part company again until the next time we saw each other; it would transpire that our next meeting would turn out to be under very different circumstances, but as yet this was still future and of course not known to either of us.

"Right young fella me lad, are you ready for the last leg home?" Tezza asked me as we prepared to leave.

"Am I ever, I just got to get my bike out of the back of Stan's truck and I'll be with you."

"No problem." answered Terry. We proceeded to get my bike from Stan's wagon and put it in Terry's truck. I shook hands with Stan and climbed into Terry's cab and within a few minutes we were to be on our way. The route home was not a straight forward one and Terry had a couple of drops to do on the way which meant that my arrival time in West Bromwich town would be well after midnight. In the event, it was just after one in the morning when we pulled into West Bromwich town centre. I thanked Terry for his kind favour to me and got the bike from the back. It had been raining earlier on but had now stopped; there was no wind, and the roads were completely deserted as I peddled home; a journey that took twenty minutes, good going for the distance involved.

I was tired when I got in; Karen had heard the key go in the lock and came to meet me as I entered our flat.

"God your late aren't you, are you going to work later?" she asked.

"I'd better, I'm going to cause enough upset without not turning up for a Saturday shift!" I said, Saturday being the busiest day of the week and where the absence of one of the staff either on holiday or off sick is most keenly felt.

Karen put the kettle on to make a cup of tea, Kaine was sleeping soundly and in a few hours I would be back where I was three days previously, except that this time my whole out look on the future was to be of a different tone and colour. But for now my bed was calling me, I would be taking the car to work to give me an extra hour in bed and I needed it I can tell you. Life was to get very interesting in the next few days and some serious decisions would have to be made.

It seemed like only five minutes had passed between closing my eyes and the alarm going off, forcing me out of my comfort zone and go and to turn the darned thing off. For a second I stood there contemplating whether or not to give the day a miss; I could say I was delayed getting back from Anglesey couldn't I? After all what had

I to fear? I already had another job in the bag and there was nothing Alan could do about it. I quickly dismissed those thoughts from my head. I didn't operate that way and in spite of the tiredness I was feeling, the right and honourable thing to do was to fulfil my word to Alan. I had promised him that I would be back on Saturday and come what may when I got there, that was what was going to happen; at least then no-one could say that I had let anyone down. I got myself ready for work and whilst I was getting dressed I was trying to arrange my thoughts in order as the last three days had been a bit of a whirlwind and myself and Karen hadn't even had time to discuss even the basics of such a gigantic move and all it would entail. I was, however, in a better position than if I had gone to Anglesey and come back empty handed, and knowing Alan as well as I did I knew that he couldn't fail to feel a bit sore as to what he perceived as my shift in loyalties towards him. As in all cases though there are two sides to every story; my perception of what I had done was that I had shown loyalty towards my wife and child. I felt I'd been dealt a pretty bad hand with everything we had been through over the last year since Kaine's illness struck, and anything I could do to improve our circumstances then I was going to do. I wasn't asking for something for nothing and was quite prepared to work for it and indeed go and get it.

As I passed my bike on the way out I thought that it was having a well deserved rest from the twenty mile round trip in and out of Birmingham and wished that I could do the same. I wasn't going to relish the atmosphere when I got in but bolstered myself with the thoughts that I had been upfront and honest about my intentions and hadn't sneaked around and I wasn't doing anything Alan wouldn't have done himself to improve his lot in life as well, and surely he couldn't blame me for that?

I arrived at work customarily early and found Nobby there before me. To my surprise both counters were half-full. I immediately sensed that all was not well as this was a most unusual thing to see and I got the impression that Alan had engineered this for a reason.

"Morning Nobby, how's it going mate?" I asked with more than the normal enquiry that the simple question would imply.

"Morning," replied Nobby, but in a subdued voice and his eyes told me that all wasn't well. Just at that point, Alan emerged from the back fridge carrying a tray of meat in each hand. The air turned icy and I wasn't talking about the cold air emerging through the open walk-in fridge door and I felt as if I'd just been found guilty of murdering a ninety-year old pensioner.

"Morning Alan," I said.

"Morning," came the single word reply with none of the customary humour.

It was obvious to a blind man what the intentions of the very early morning start were, the rest of the lads were in as well and it became clear that the topic of conversation regarding my absence was hot news when Red suddenly appeared out of the goods lifts with the trolleys of meat for the floats ready to put in place. Effectively my job was being done in front of my eyes; the implication being that I wasn't needed. This bad atmosphere was confirmed when Red caught sight of me and, obviously sore as well at having been dragged in early (as Red was habitually late and been warned on many occasions by Alan), he decided to vent his displeasure in a sarcastic way.

"Here's the three-hundred quid a week man!" he quipped.

"If you've got summat to say Red just say it!" I could feel my colour coming up now.

"That's enough Red!" said Alan sharply. But it wasn't for my benefit that this was said; Alan preferred the silent protest designed to both make me feel guilty and at the same time demonstrate that they could get along fine without me. I was beginning to wish I had stuck to my original story. It was obvious that what I had told Alan regarding the other job and its remuneration hadn't stayed a secret for very long, as though he couldn't believe that that sort of money was being offered by anyone as wages. But it was, and I'd got it. Despite Red's mocking tone implying that I thought that I was better than everyone else for even daring to think that I could improve my lot, I had no reason to feel guilty, or that my efforts in the shop were not needed because if they weren't then he could have his notice right then and there.

Nobby stayed well out of this brewing tornado. The man that I am now is the older, more mature version of the young hot-tempered Celt that I was then, and the frustration of the preceding months had just found an outlet in the form of Red sticking his nose now firmly where it didn't belong and being in serious and very real danger of having it broken.

"Did you get the big job then? Red was goading me now.

"Why don't I tell you downstairs in the car park tosspot, if you're that eager to find out I'd be happy to explain how I got on!" I said, removing my jacket and leaving no doubt by my tone what 'explain' meant, had Red taken me up.

"Now that's enough out of the pair of you!" shouted Alan, who could now see that due to Red's indescrectionary mouth not being fully connected to his brain was derailing his peaceful protest at one of the family. He decided to step in which was probably just as well as I doubt either myself or Red would've reached the underground car park before the fists had started flying.

"Red, get back downstairs and carry on with what you're supposed to do!" ordered Alan, trying to remain calm as the atmosphere suddenly threatened to turn very nasty.

"Yeah, get back downstairs under your bridge ya troll!" I shouted, deciding not to let Red get away lightly for his comments. I wouldn't have minded a go on the car park or anywhere else for that matter as I was considering following him down.

"Enough Joe! Come on get your gear on and go to work!" I could feel things starting to diffuse, it would have been better had Red, (being the blundering type that he was and not known for his alert mind) not said a dickey bird as Alan's strategy of the cold-shoulder and being sent to Coventry type of punishment would have borne fruit; but you can't beat a good fight or even the threat of one to clear the air.

"Oh you're sure you want me to?" I asked, now going on the offensive.

"Yes Joe, why wouldn't I?" countered Alan to my heated question.

"All this crap, the counters nearly on at half six and all that with Red!" I was getting hot under the collar; Alan knew it and decided to play it cool.

"We weren't sure if you'd be in that's what the counters are nearly on for."

"Yeah right, I told you I'd be in; when have I let you down in the past then Alan? And I suppose the atmosphere is typical of Saturday morning eh?" Alan knew I was right; we both left it there and I got my coat and apron on and carried on with what was left to do. Twenty minutes later and the shop was ready, nearly two hours before the market was open! Myself and Red were kept well apart for the remainder of the day. The subject of whether or not I had even got the job wasn't raised that day, not by Alan, and I didn't volunteer the information, not even to Nobby. I was in a bad mood with the lot of them; fair enough, Alan had the right to be in a huff and I could understand that, even-though I had the right to improve things for my wife and child, but what the hell had it got to do with the rest? If any of them had gone off and got a better job with improved pay such as Ian had done months earlier, then I would have done to them as I had done with Ian and wished them all the best of luck.

The day couldn't have finished quickly enough for me that Saturday and if any doubts had remained in me about leaving the market when I got there that morning then they were truly dispelled by end of play that night; I even turned down Nobby's offer of a pint when we finished, such was my mood on finishing.

When I arrived home the little girl I hadn't seen for nearly four days now banished any violent thoughts I still had towards poor old Red,

as I picked her up in my arms she squealed with delight at seeing her old man.

"Hello my liddle princess," I said lifting her high into the air and swinging her around as she laughed loudly.

"How did you get on at work today?" asked Karen when I had put Kaine down and was getting out of my gear.

194

"Don't ask!" Which always means 'yes do ask'.

"Me and Red nearly ended up having a scrap this mornin'." I volunteered the rest anyway.

"How come you and Red?" she asked, surprised.

"Cos he's got a big gob and stuck his beak where it wasn't wanted!"

I explained everything that had happened that morning which I had felt was completely out of order, as though I'd committed a crime of some sort; and that Alan didn't even know how my quest had gone; in any case we had lots to talk about, and my misgivings about how I would have felt had I come back without the job would have been fully justified judging by the events of the day. Carol and Anne had remained as they always were toward me, but as for the rest you would have thought that I had brought back the plague with me from Wales. Fine by me I'd thought, if that was how it was to be, then it would make the whole process of giving notice easier, if the feelings between myself and the rest of the shop staff were still running high.

Unbeknown to me, I wasn't the only one with a lot to think about that weekend; that would be revealed to me on Monday morning when I got to work and after the weekend had passed, cooling our heated feelings and allowing calm reason to take it's place.

Karen wanted to hear all about Anglesey and the beach and the house and so, after tea, we had a sit down with a drink to relax; my neck muscles felt tighter than a suspension cable to a bridge and I needed the rest and relaxation of home to unwind. These last few days, coupled with today had been rare ones indeed, and never in a month of Sundays would I have ever imagined myself so close to having a scrap in the shop that I had come to regard as part of my life, and the staff as close as workmates could get. In all fairness Red used to rub me up the wrong way as I'm sure I did to him as well but it had before never got to the point of violence.

Karen and I sat and discussed everything from moving the furniture to Kaine's schooling and what had even come into my mind was that if Kaine was educated in Wales she would be taught to speak Welsh as I was taught to speak Gaelic Irish as part of our school curriculum. I joked with Karen that she would be able to talk about us with her schoolmates in front of us and we wouldn't be able to understand a word of it! We also discussed having Kaine's medical records transferred to the doctor that would become our local G.P., depending on where we moved. We still had a lot to discuss and both our families' feelings and considerations had to be weighed as well; ultimately though, the final decision was ours alone to make, after all it was for our benefit that we would be moving to a house where we had a garden for Kaine (and not forgetting the dog).

The events of the day troubled me though, the people I had thought were friends I now saw in a different light, I felt hurt by this, I had felt held back by the situation of my life and had wanted to move forward not only for myself, but also because we had come so very close to losing our daughter. I felt that this had been a personal wake up call as to how fleeting and fragile life could be, and it had awoke in me a desire to do better for Karen and for Kaine. I was a husband and a father and it was my God-given duty to provide the best that I could. But the spirit of the human condition is such that each will seek his own advantage. I had felt that my seeking the best for us had been the right thing to do, and no doubt Alan to preserve the fine balance of his business had thought and felt he had been right to do as he had done, and that my leaving for my own benefit would be a disadvantage to the business with the custom I had built up. My being there was by no means the glue that held it all together. I was merely a link in a chain, it was Alan's business after all and he had built it. He was a hard worker and a nice man but for now we were in conflict and, as in family situations (such as the kinship at the shop made it feel like), if one or two members of a family fall out then it sends ripples through the rest. That was my analysis of the situation, if the truth be known. But for now I was tired and all I wanted was to sleep. We could discuss the rest of what we needed to talk about the next day.

In the morning I awoke. My body still felt physically tired though and the uneasiness I felt now made me wish that all this had never occurred, that the stirring in me for change had somehow remained dormant, but it hadn't and Pandora's box was well and truly open. For the first time in my life I wasn't looking forward to the following week. I had been fortunate enough never to have suffered from the Monday morning 'blues'; being an irrepressible optimist had always fostered in me a longing for what the next day would bring. In my mind I knew what the next day had in store for me and this tainted the day for me now. The dye was cast and the compass set, nothing would change my course, or would it?

CHAPTER 13.
Deal done.

Monday. While shaving and getting ready for work, regret crept into my thoughts, the people whom with I had worked and laughed for the last two years (and I had known Alan even longer than that), were no longer going to be part of my daily life.

When I arrived at the ramp which led down to the market car park and where we caught the lifts up to the higher levels, I met Red on his way in.

"Morning' Joe," he said.

"Morning' Red, how you doin' mate?"

"Sound, drunk all weekend!"

He laughed, so did I; old Red liked his grog. We walked to the lifts chatting away not even mentioning Saturday which was quite clearly forgotten now.

"See you in a bit Red, I'll stick the kettle on." I said.

"Right ho!" came the reply. I carried on up to the market hall level. As I walked in Alan was there before me, again.

"Morning' Joe." He said to me, I knew he wanted to talk.

"Morning' Al', sorry about Saturday, with all that with Red."

"I want you two to sort it out between you later on Joe and I don't mean kill each other."

"No need, I just came up in the lift with 'im, it's forgotten, you know what Red's like; a few beers all weekend with his fweinds and he's as happy as a pig in shite!" I said, laughing. Alan shook his head smiling; he knew what Red was like.

"Is he in then?" asked Alan looking at his watch and laughing. "He must've crapped the bed to be here at this time."

"Knowin' Red he probably ain't even been to bed."

"Joe we need to have a chat," Alan said, more seriously now.

"Yeah I know."

"Wait until we got the shop sorted out and then we can have a talk with no ears listening."

I wondered what he had in mind. In all honesty I could guess he didn't want me to leave and, in spite of what Anglesey had to offer, I didn't either. There was nothing the matter with the job nor my workmates and Alan was a good boss; but my personal situation had to change. I wasn't prepared to bring Kaine up amidst degradation and wanted more than that for her.

At least we were talking now and with discussion comes progress, we would see what became of it. Nobby arrived and on seeing Alan in before him stopped momentarily like a rabbit caught in the headlights and furtively looked at both of us, trying to gauge the atmosphere before proceeding. I looked at him and laughed as I could tell exactly what he was thinking, and on seeing me do this he carried on as if nothing untoward had occurred.

"I seen the lights on downstairs, is coppertop in then?" Nobby almost shrieked in surprise in his high-pitched tone.

"Yeah, I know we reckon he ain't been to bed yet." Alan said. Nobby took his coat off and gathered the cups together in anticipation of the rest of the staff arriving to start yet another week.

Paul, throughout all this had, remained pretty much in the neutral position; although he was in equal shares with the business with Alan he always seemed to be like one of the lads. I could tell though that he had felt a bit put out as well by the turn of events and he hadn't really spoken to me in the same way as he always had done prior to me going off to Anglesey. Paul had worked at the Longbridge car plant in Birmingham for years and was more in tune with the effects of low wages than Alan was, so for the time being he had kept out of the fray.

The shop was ready and the decks cleared in good time; everyone disappeared downstairs for the deliveries of meat to replenish our depleted stocks. Monday was a busy day for the lads down-stairs in the cutting rooms and it was less so for us on the counters upstairs. Anne was off that day which left just myself and Alan on the pitch. Carol would be coming in around ten and so if Alan wanted to talk to me well now was the perfect time to do so.

"How did you get on up there then Joe?" eventually came the inevitable question.

"I got on okay Al' I did the block test and the interview and they gave me the job."

"I thought as much." Alan said, he was fully aware of my background with the big abattoir of the West

Midlands and knew my cutting skills were more than adequate to do the job, but my employment for Alan was ninety percent sales whereas cutting was hard work, breaking down sides of beef, lamb, and pork. I was young and that didn't bother me; my main requirement was not the relatively easy life of sales with a guaranteed wage but an increase in pay to address my immediate problems.

"So, is the dough what they said it was?" he asked.

"Yes, its piecework so the more weight you cut the more you earn."

"So what do you think?" I could feel a game of brinksmanship starting to develop.

"Well, what I think is this; I like working here and I like working for you, but things have changed, Nobby and Red are the same age as me and both single and we're on roughly the same wage. Whatever the lads do with their money is entirely their business. As for me, I've a wife and, until recently, a sick child to support and Kaine's ongoing health issues make a return to work for Karen impossible and so my money goes nowhere near what we need to progress like others are doing, and I ain't goin' to bring my kid up in a poxy block of flats with Friday and Saturdays curry and beer up the walls and all over the floors Alan. That's what I think!" I thought the direct approach more appropriate. Alan, though, was ready for this.

"Yeah, but Joe, it ain't my fault that your married and unfortunately Kaine got sick yet you're asking me to solve your problems for you," he countered.

"That's where your wrong Alan, I solved me own problems. Getting that job has given me the financial aid I need so Karen can look after Kaine and I can put some decent housing around us as well. And I know it was my choice to get married and have Kaine but I feel it is my right the same as yours to have children if I want and that choice shouldn't be dictated to me by what's in my wages at the end of the week. In short I'm not asking for anything I haven't worked for, I instituted the second knockout on my side of the pitch and our sales went through the roof with the Caribbean's and the Irish so you know I've put my shoulder to the wheel with you!"

"I know all that, so what's it gonna be then? Are you going to leave?"

"That's up to you persuading me to stay."

"I can't afford to match those wages you're talking about Joe."

"Alan, I ain't trying to bleed you dry; a fair wage for a good effort is what I want, and you know I need to get a house so the ball is in your court."

"I'll 'ave to think about it."

This was a cooling tactic and I knew it. I wanted the whole thing resolved now, not at the end of my notice.

"No dice Alan, I told you what I was going to do, I didn't hide it and spring it on you in one big surprise at the last minute, you've had a week to mull this over so what's your proposal?"

"Can't operate like that Joe, you're gonna have to leave it with me," replied Alan, trying to keep the upper hand by steering the conversation into the parking area.

"If you can't decide after five days then you leave me with little choice then, I'm going to take the job."

This wasn't a tactic on my part. I disliked beating around the bush and genuinely wanted the dispute resolved one way or the other and dragging the negative atmosphere on in our work environment wouldn't accomplish much; plus, I needed to make plans.

"I can't do this with a knife to me throat," Alan said and I could hear a little desperation creeping into his tone.

"What knife? It's a clear choice in my eyes, I need a rise, the job in Anglesey has given me that. If there's now't else on the table then that's that really isn't it?" I wasn't negotiating now, I saw clearly what I was going to do, and I knew that Alan was trying to wait me out.

"Right then," he began, "you said that the job in Wales was piecework, yes?"

"Yes?" I answered, wondering which way this was going to go.

"So some weeks will be better than others and some weeks not so good, correct?"

"Yes, that's the nature of piece work."

"Why don't you work for me in the same vein?"

"How do you mean, I'm not a cutter now, I'm on the counters."

"The more you sell the more you earn!"

"I already sell loads, are you saying I got to increase my sales even more then, to up my wages?

"LOOK I'll up your money by forty quid a week, that puts you on two hundred notes. I'll up your meat allowance to fifty quid a week and increase your bonus to come in line with the shops profits, meself and Paul are going to buy another shop and want you to manage it for us. All in all Joe, you won't be far off what you want, plus I've got a mate of mine called Pete Worthington who handled mine and Paul's mortgage and even got one for our old man at his age. I'll get him to do you a deal, he'll get you a mortgage, I can't do better than that Joe."

"You don't have to, that's good enough,"

I didn't even think about it, we shook hands on it there and then; deal done, crisis over, and no upheavals to be made. Karen would be a bit disappointed not to move to Wales by the beach, but with my increase now in wages and impending promotion, I could afford to take us to other beaches. Besides, the most important thing was getting out of those flats and now I saw that we could accomplish our task. Alan, the fox, had probably already made up his mind to do what he did but the business man in him had been trying to fathom me out to see what I would settle for.

"Well, you certainly called my bluff Joe, you should play poker!" Alan laughed now, obviously relieved that the tension had passed.

"I wasn't bluffing Al' honestly, you know I needed to sort it out and I was prepared to leave."

I said this because I wanted him to know that this hadn't been some elaborate scheme to force an increase in my money. I was intent on improving our circumstances and if it had meant moving half-way across England and into Wales then that's what it would have taken.

"No matter, it's sorted now."

"Yes it is," were mine and Alan's final words on the subject; both of us glad to close the book on it.

Alan called downstairs on the telephone link to order up some loins of pork for our counters, and, surprise Nobby brought the gear up instead of the young lads, who by nature of age and status did all the donkey work. Alan had protected his interests and had told me our deal was strictly confidential, which it was, but I thought that he must now be wishing that he hadn't told Red and Nobby that I was off chasing a three hundred quid plus a week job and got it, my remaining presence there would seem to indicate logically that a deal must have been struck along similar lines. This was a conclusion that would have had to have the aid of a trampoline to jump high enough to catch Red's attention, but as for Nobby, he was as sharp as his own butchers boning knife.

Nobby manhandled the loins of pork onto the block nearest the entrance to the shop; he immediately found an excuse to come over to my end of the shop by way of collecting some empty trays left over from earlier.

"What's the story mate? are you stayin' with us?" he whispered to me out of the corner of his mouth.

"Joe's stayin' Nobby!" called out Alan, as ever anticipating that Nobby's good deed of bringing the loins of pork up himself and collecting the trays for me had been a means to find out if the shop crisis had been resolved.

"Oh right Al' I was only askin' 'cos I'm makin' the tea and I have to count the cups out, mate," replied Nobby, quick as ever and sticking the 'mate' word in response to Alan's sarcasm. Alan winced at this 'mate' word and as Nobby disappeared downstairs to wash the cups he muttered, "Little rat."

I was glad not to be leaving. I smiled to myself and thought how much I'd have missed all this if I had been forced to head for Wales. When I arrived home that night Karen was eager to find out what the days events would mean for us both. As I expected she was disappointed not to be moving to Anglesey but then later confessed that the move away from her mom and the support that she had was something that she wouldn't have been one hundred percent comfortable doing. The other factor that weighed on her mind was that all her friends and mine lived in the West Midlands and therefore while I was at work she would effectively have been stranded with no one to talk to bar the dog and, of course, Kaine. The more that she had thought about it the more the initial buzz of moving near the sea had begun to lose it's shine but would have remained a valid alternative to staying at the flats. However, the extra money and my promotion to manager was the solution to our personal crisis and when I also explained that Alan's financial adviser would get us a mortgage and thus 'get us the hell out of Dodge City' then she accepted that this was the better way out. Just one question remained for her.

"What are we gonna do with all that meat?" she laughed, referring to the huge increase in my meat allowance that Alan had given me.

"Buy a bigger freezer." I replied laughing as well. Kaine laughed at us laughing, she couldn't know what we were talking about but as far as I was concerned now her future was to be in better circumstances than the ones we were in right now. I was glad that I'd made the effort to go to Wales and the result that came from this made me feel like a hunter of old returning with enough provisions to satisfy the tribe. Yes, we were on the move, although, Kaine's health was still to be the catalyst for changes which couldn't be helped and altered my life forever. Kaine was doing well as regards recovering from her operation; her mom had taken her to the local hairdressers and had had her hair cut to even it up and to try and match both sides so as to take the unevenness out when it was shaved off at the hospital. They had had to cut it quite short and now she looked more like a very pretty little boy than a girl. Karen wanted to have her ears pierced to get ear rings but I asked her to leave that until she was a bit older and she agreed. She would have to wait a little longer for Kaine's hair to grow back before she could put her hair into the pigtails and ribbons that she had sct her heart on. Things at the shop returned to the normality I was used to, my rise in bonus and wage was honoured I had been to see Peter Worthington as Alan had promised and a mortgage was arranged in principle in anticipation of us finding a house, and the extra meat we incurred and couldn't possibly consume Karen gave to her mom and my own mom benefited from this too. Alan was on the lookout for another shop as he had said, and I looked forward to running this as soon as one became available. Ideally he wanted another pitch in the market hall in Birmingham but my experience of working in other shops elsewhere notably in West Bromwich town prompted discussions that we could open one further a field. In the end these considerations were to be academic as one hot Thursday in July ended my aspirations as a manager, my friendship with Alan, and set a course for consequences that had far reaching implications into the unseen distant future.....

CHAPTER 14.
"Joe, what can you do?"

The night before, I came home as usual and had a bath and my tea; the only notable difference to this night than any other was that Kaine was really 'cranky;' we assumed she 'had one on her' and eventually she went to bed at her usual time and looked as though she would sleep peacefully. When I got up for work the next day, I could see out of the living room window that the day was going to be a very warm one. We had fields at the back of the flat where I took the dog for a walk; I noticed a heat mist lying just over the top of the grass and it was warm at even that early hour of the morning.

"We're gonna have our work cut out today flogging meat," I said to myself under my breath, knowing full well the temperatures in the indoor market rose rapidly as the day went on. I left the flat quietly so as not to disturb Kaine and Karen who slept on.

The market opened on time, and the trickle of early morning customers gave an indication that we would have to fight for every sale that day. Alan looked pretty tense.

I'd managed to shift a few trays of meat when the phone rang; I took the call thinking little of it.

"Joe, Kaine's just been really sick when I got her up; she ain't well at all, I think her shunt might have blocked." She sounded pretty scared.

"Have you phoned the doctor? How is she?" I asked Karen, feeling panic in my stomach.

"She's awake but not herself. She wants to go back to sleep all the time and her eyes don't look right. I'm taking her straight to the Children's Hospital myself; I don't want to be fobbed off like we were the first time." I knew what she meant as she and I had little trust in the staff operating the telephone lines.

"Okay, well you'd best get going and drive carefully, I'll have a word with Alan and when you know exactly what's happening, ring me here and I'll come straight to the hospital."

"Okay, I'll speak to you in a while then." I put the phone back in its place and walked around to the front of the shop. where Alan was working, as we were aware you could always tell when he was in a mood as he had his 'face' on, and he definitely had his 'face' on today.

"Alan that was Karen." I began.

"Yes Joe, I heard." Alan said without looking at me, he carried on with what he was doing.

"Kaine's not well; Karen is taking her to the hospital."

"Is she goin' to let you know how Kaine is when she gets there?" he asked. but I could tell from his demeanour that he really wasn't interested at all in this turn of events.

"Yeah, she'll ring me." I said.

"Well, you'll find out then won't you?" he said in a matter of fact way that wasn't his style.

"Right then I suppose I will." I was starting to feel annoyed with myself, I knew we were under pressure at the shop but this was different. My entitlement still stood that I could have Thursday afternoons off, but since my rise I'd worked them and I think Alan pretty much figured that he'd bought them off me with such a rise in one go. However I left it for now as the tension was a little high, as was the temperature. My thinking was that when Karen got to the hospital and Kaine saw a doctor then I'd know more; after all it might not be a blockage to the shunt, there might be a dozen reasons why Kaine hadn't felt well and had been sick, upset tummy and so forth; but the drowsiness bothered me and her 'crankiness' the evening before had bothered me also, as Kaine was a pleasant little thing in general. I carried on with what I was doing trying to keep my mind focused on being polite to the customers that were coming through the market, sales were slow but I was making progress in shifting what we'd got.

My mind shifted between what I was doing and wondering how Karen was getting on. As she would be at the hospital by now, and knowing the routine inside-out, I figured that Kaine would either have been seen by one of the doctors or was going through the process of being examined. As these thoughts were going through my mind the phone rang; it was Karen for me again.

"Hello?" I said.

"Joe, I was right, they think Kaine has got a blocked shunt because her eyes aren't responding to light properly and she's getting more and more sleepy and lethargic," Karen told me straight away.

"What's happening now then?"

"They're waiting for Mr Hamilton to get here, and they're getting Kaine ready for surgery because they are going to have to do an emergency shunt replacement. How long do you think it'll be before you can get here?"

"I'll go and tell Alan what's happening; he's in a right mood though so I might have a bit of trouble getting away."

"Joe, this is serious! Don't let him keep you for very long," Karen said and from the way she said it I could tell that she was starting to get scared, as indeed, I was.

"What time do you think they'll be ready to operate?" I asked.

"They said an hour and a half most like by the time they get everything ready." I looked at my watch, it was five minutes to twelve. If I left at one o'clock that would give me twenty minutes to get there and I'd just be in time to see her before she went down for her operation.

"I'll be there for around quarter past one or so."

"Okay, hurry up though." Karen said to me as I put the phone back on the receiver. I knew that Alan probably knew now that the news wasn't good.

"Alan, I need to have my afternoon off." I said.

"Paul's off this afternoon Joe, so I can't have the two of you off,"

"Kaine's having an emergency operation in an hour and a half Alan," I said, puzzled slightly at his answer.

"I know Joe but in all honesty, what can you do?" Stunned into silence, I looked at him for a few seconds.

"Are you sayin' you're not letting me go to the hospital?" I eventually asked, somewhat incredulously.

"Well, what can you do Joe? All you can do is be there," he said.

"Some people might think that's enough," I said, my tone hardening as I felt the rise of anger build within me now.

"Alan there won't be a soul in the market this afternoon on a day like this. And I'm sure Paul wouldn't mind working to let me go." I said now getting to the point of his objections. Paul was a cutter not a salesman, I could guess that Alan's reluctance to let me go that afternoon had it's foundation in the fact that if I went, then my counter would be manned by someone who couldn't sell at the rate I could. This mattered little to me now as my priority was Kaine, and she was being prepared for surgery for a brain operation.

"We'll see how it goes," he said, rather flippantly. I went over to my counter and Carol gave me that knowing look again. As I bent over to attend to something she whispered in my ear.

"Sod him, Joe, just get your coat and go!"

"I'll wait." I said to her in return.

I could see very clearly why he didn't want me to go, I'd not long since negotiated a hefty rise in wages and Alan wanted his money's worth. Well as sympathetic as I was to his frustrations at the day's trade, it didn't hold a candle compared to my daughter. Paul was totally unaware of all this as he was downstairs in the cutting room and I fully expected Alan to come to his normal senses and ask Paul if he would work the afternoon, it was after all half his business and thus he shared half the problem. I was to be disappointed however; as one o' clock came, Paul came up from the lower rooms, put his coat on and with a cheery 'good-bye' left for the afternoon. Alan never said a word, and neither did I. Underneath I was fuming that he put money over this crisis that had arrived on me out-of-the-blue. So far in spite of the day being warm I managed to sell a fair bit. But as Paul left the market I stopped selling. We sold by out-cry and so I stood in silent protest to Alan's handling of the situation. I would do nothing more that day. I looked at my watch and the time for Kaine to be taken down for surgery came and went. Karen rang again and I just told her to expect me as soon as I could get there. Alan picked up on my silence as you would imagine.

"What's goin' on Joe?"

"Well if all I could do at the hospital was to be there, and you thought that wasn't worthwhile, I figured all I can do here is the same." He caught my drift.

Half an hour later he went to the till, pulled out a bundle of notes and counted them out in front of me like the thirty pieces of silver to Judas Iscariot.

"Here's your money you might as well go." I picked my wages up knowing full well the symbolic meaning of counting them out in front of me. It was clear that the wage I was now on was, in my bosses mind, supposed to supercede any of my personal woes; and I had broken the unwritten contract. Little did Alan realise he couldn't ever find enough money to keep that contract's integrity. I then removed my apron and hung it up. As I was leaving Alan pointed to the two counters full of meat and asked,

"Would you like my problems?"

"I'll swap you in a heartbeat," I said. As I walked away I knew that was the last time I would work for him. I was angry at Alan; it wasn't his fault that Kaine was ill again but in my mind there was no excuse to put financial loss or gain over what was quite clearly a serious matter. If that fact was lost to him, then so was I. I decided the fastest way to the hospital now was by taxi, I ran to the exits into the glorious sunshine that flooded the day outside, there was a black cab taxi rank situated by Saint Martin's church and I jumped into the first one in the queue.

"Where to mate?" asked the driver.

"Children's Hospital please pal, quick as you can." I answered. I was desperate to get there to find out how things were going. Karen wasn't happy that I wasn't there when Kaine was being taken to theatre and neither was I.

When I finally reached the hospital having paid the taxi fare, I ran to the lifts to take me up to the ward where Karen and Kaine both were. I arrived just as Kaine was being brought back from surgery. She looked so ill; her face and lips were white, her hair shaved off on one side yet again and a white dressing covered the re-opened area where the previous shunt had been fitted. A little trickle of her blood ran from this and tracked down her neck. Karen was in attendance with two nurses and she was passing water to Kaine again by way of the sponges mentioned before. We had gone to bed the night before not knowing what today was to bring and woke up to the day that altered the course of our lives. The anger within me simmered at the thought of my being deliberately kept at work while Kaine was being operated on. I wished Alan could have seen the pitiable sight of my daughter now to make him ashamed of his actions; but most of all I was angry at providence. Why did this keep happening? As soon as we began to think everything was fine with Kaine, and we wanted to keep believing so; then wham! we were back where we started. Tears welled in my eyes at the sight of Kaine so sick and helpless and Karen's face was etched with worry as well. The shunt was replaced and working again but now we were left with the uncomfortable question in our minds as to when, not if, this was to happen again.

Yes, that was the day when we realised fully that we were at the mercy of chance. The shunt was artificial, a crude method to take care of a small but vital function of the most sophisticated and complex organ in the human body, and every time Kaine was exposed to surgery, anything could go wrong. For all I knew, back at the shop, the night before could well have been the last time I was to see Kaine alive. Yes I was angry but I held my emotions in check. Stuff the job and house and every-thing, for that's all they were, things, replaceable, unimportant, expendable things, Kaine wasn't.

I took my place by Karen's side now and she looked at me, not saying anything she didn't have to; something in her eyes told me what I was beginning to fear already, that this scene was one we would never escape from. How many more operations and how long would Kaine be able to take them for? Questions thought but remained unsaid. We had both made Kaine, and the look between us that day with the words unsaid, told that what time we had with Kaine we would have to make count.

"What happened at work?" she asked quietly.

"Doesn't matter, its unimportant now." I answered. I just knew it was the end for me there; Karen knew me well enough to know what was the likely outcome of my not being allowed to be at the hospital.

"Yes, you're right, it's unimportant; she is." Karen said quietly again whilst giving Kaine some water. She was unconscious but the reflex action of licking at the wet sponge to quench her thirst galvanized within me the thought that my little girl was completely dependant upon us, and not a single person on the planet would ever stand in my way again from being by her side in her time of need.

But for now the important thing was to tend to Kaine's needs; it would be awhile yet before she was fully conscious and still being so young she would not know why she was in this position and would still feel the pain of the operation. Any parent who has seen their child go through pain will empathise with the feelings of helplessness; in that you can't bear it for them, or take it away. We wanted to take the pain away and if it were possible, remove the chances of this ever occurring again. But this was wishful thinking on our part. All we could do was hope that this operation would be as successful as the last one, and that in a few days time we'd be going home with Kaine again.

For now Kaine slept on with the effects of the anaesthetic in her system; rest was what she required. The nurses attended every twenty minutes to monitor her gradual return to full consciousness and logged her progress in the clipboard hanging from the end of Kaine's hospital bed.

Karen would be staying that night and I would go back to the flat. There were things to be sorted out that Karen had left unattended to as she had rushed out earlier that morning, washing up and clothes in the washing machine, nothing important, just needed putting away.

"What are you going to do about work?" Karen asked me.

"What do you think I should do?" I asked her, I knew my mind but I wanted her opinion.

"Pack it in." she said without hesitation. She was very angry at the days events and didn't think much now of my relationship with the market.

"What about the extra cash and the house?"

"I don't care." I agreed, but I had cooled down now not that this was going to change my mind; I had never left one job without getting another position first. It was too late to think about Anglesey again as that ship had sailed, I would have to think of something else.

"I'll go in tomorrow and come straight here after work again." I said.

"What you going to tell Alan and Paul?"

"Nothing." A few hours went by, and towards the middle of the evening Kaine suddenly opened her eyes and immediately sought out the most familiar faces in her life. Her eyes rested on Karen and myself and she cried immediately on seeing us both. Karen picked her up being careful with the drip tube that was attached to Kaine's arm and calmed her down a little. If she had any memory of the night or day before it would be that she had been feeling normal and today she woken up in hospital with no understanding of why. And this was evident in her eyes as she looked around her in fearful remembrance of the last visit there. And this is for me the hardest part writing this; I couldn't explain to her why she was in hospital or the reasons for that, she was too young to understand.

Having made sure that Kaine was okay and settled with her mom for the evening, I went home. It was quite late so I decided to take a taxi. I sat in the back of the black cab pondering on the future; one thing I knew was that my days behind the counter at the market had ended, I felt wounded and I was going elsewhere. Deep down

217

inside I knew that this situation with Kaine would arise again and I wasn't going to be put in the situation that had just developed by anyone ever again......

CHAPTER 15.

Hang up your butcher's apron.

When I arrived home the evidence that Karen had had to rush from the flat was everywhere, notably the towel that she had used to clean up Kaine's vomit was in the bath. Looking at this, I could almost feel the panic that Karen must have felt when this had happened. Also the blanket from her cot was stained from this too; the bed remained unmade and clothing was scattered about. Some half-eaten toast on a plate was left on the kitchen side, most likely what Karen had been eating just before she got Kaine up and discovered then that she was not right.

I tidied up as best as I could. I was exhausted and hadn't even eaten, but that could wait. My mood was subdued and overcast with the renewed worry that this latest turn had presented; surveying the scene of Kaine's illness that morning did nothing to dispel my gloomy thoughts. The next day brought nothing for me to be cheerful about, I caught the bus to work as I had left my bike there the day before. When I got there the place was quiet as usual with just the faint whistles and noises usually heard at that time of day. I was not myself; I remained pretty quiet even when the others arrived. Nobby was my mate, he knew me best and having heard about the previous day's goings on was on my side of the argument. I didn't wish to hear much regarding all that now, though it was the larger picture that was emerging from the whole scene that interested me more, that being of course my daughter's recovery and well being. This was foremost on my mind; not some petty argument. I opened the walk in fridge doors to see what we had left from the day before, not as bad as was thought. This revelation though, would be of no consequence to my newly formed way of thinking. Alan arrived and seemed in a better mood than the previous day, I couldn't have cared less though if his mood was such that he had cart wheeled all the way into work.

"We had a good knockout yesterday Joe in the end," he said deliberately avoiding asking me how Kaine was.

"That's nice," I said in return.

"How did you get on?" he now asked, and I could tell that he was feeling his way around to see how I responded.

"When Kaine comes out of hospital I'm taking the week off," I said curtly.

"I'll have check the holiday rota first."

"Alan, I don't care, mate, if you've an appointment to see the Pope. I won't be here on Monday. And this isn't a holiday, mate, so don't fret. I won't expect you to cough up for it." I had chosen my words and tone very carefully and nothing more was said on the subject. Kaine would be allowed home on the Sunday as her recovery was, as expected, fairly rapid from her unexpected visit to the surgeons table. We arrived home on Sunday morning with Kaine, who was happy to be back to her toys and the familiarity of home. Karen's mom and step-father Roy came to the flat to see Kaine and we sat down and had some tea. Karen was still upset that Alan hadn't let me get to the hospital on time and told her mom that as soon as I could I would get another job.

"I'll give you work Joe if you're lookin' to change jobs," said Roy suddenly.

"Eh?" I said surprised at this, as the last time this subject had been mentioned it was my inexperience in construction that had been the issue.

"I've had two lads go off on their own so I'm short of men."

"What if I'm no good?"

"This week off that you've got, come with me and you can see how you get on,"

"He will," said Karen suddenly, and the deal was done. Monday morning was to be the beginning of a new job for me one that was completely different from all I'd known before. I could feel that it was time to hang up my butcher's coat and apron for good providing the next week was the new beginning I was hoping it would be and I could prove that I could handle working the heights called for in the construction of the type of buildings in which Roy specialised. The first pleasant surprise in store for me that evening was not having to set the alarm clock for five a.m., as Roy was working in Cannock, an area of the West Midlands only six or seven miles away from where we lived. The other surprise was that I wouldn't even have to make my own way to work as I'd been used to doing. Roy used to pick his guys up from their front doors, a concept completely alien to the routine to which I had become accustomed.

221

Through habit I was up early and sat watching TV AM, another new experience in my life that I previously had no time for. Seven o' clock came and my mind turned to events going on in the market. By now I would have already had to cycle ten miles and around this time I would have been opening up the fridges and starting to get the first of the meat trays and tubs ready and sorting out what had to be done. Nobby my mate, would have been there by now and the familiar click of the kettle switch wouldn't have been far off. Instead, now here I was sitting in the comfort of my own living room, drinking a cup of tea, waiting for a lift to arrive to take me to work! If this was any indication of the life ahead for me then I was all for it!

Karen was up and made me some sandwiches to see me off to work on my first day as a builder instead of a butcher. I felt a great deal of trepidation at the thought of being on a construction site with all these tough, experienced building workers and me with very little experience of anything of that ilk. My woodwork skills, the only offering I could make to the building trade, went back to my days at school in Mr. Le Blanc's woodwork class and these had long since faded in my memory, and in those days the transition from imperial measurements to metric had just come into vogue, and this had caused a great deal of confusion amongst those unfortunate enough to be in the position educationally wise that is, to have to change step half-way through the dance.

"You'll be okay, don't worry," she said, picking up on my anxiety.

"Well I just hope I don't make a prat of meself in front of all Roy's lads."

"If Carl can do it then I'm sure you can," she said, reassuringly. Carl, my brother-in-law had started with Roy in much the same circumstances, those being that he was off on holiday for two weeks from his job in a poultry processing plant in Bilston, one of Roy's men had let him down and Carl had been shanghaied as a replacement and had remained ever since.

"I s'pose you're right." I was aware though of the ribbing Carl had used to get from Wilf, Roy's cousin and partner, regarding his status as 'son-in-law'; and as I was in the same category I wondered how I would be received not that this bothered me for in my working life up to that date, mickey-taking had been part of the norm and it was obligatory to be able to take a bit of stick. Kaine had woken early that day and I was sitting with my daughter on my lap before I went off to work, yet another previously unknown concept for me. So far all this was new and good. I knew also that if all went well and both myself and Roy were happy with the arrangements that if there were any medical emergencies in the future that I was with family and no problems would arise in my needing time to tend to my daughter's needs as had recently been the case and had in fact shaped the situation in which I now pleasantly found myself. At twenty minutes past seven I heard the sound of Roy's Volvo car horn from down on the car park, and in a minute flat, I was down the stairs and sitting beside him in the passenger seat.

"Mornin'," he said, and drove off. Roy wasn't the greatest of conversationalists and we didn't say too much as we headed off pick the other lads up.

"Mornin' Roy," I said thinking how this was a strange turn of events. The man who was my step father-in-law, through marriage to Karen's mom, was, if everything worked out okay, going to be my new boss.

We had two lads to pick up, the first being Rob Kelly. Rob didn't actually work for Roy. He worked for another set of contractors, who worked on this particular site. Roy was merely doing Rob a courtesy by giving him a lift to work throughout the duration of this job. Ironically enough, it was Rob's brother Chris who had previously worked for Roy and had left to work for himself taking with him a guy called Darren Sly who had been with Roy since leaving school. Both these lads were very experienced in the trade and I felt that I couldn't come anywhere near them in terms of being a replacement. However I was given the opportunity to do the job and I had no intentions of letting myself or anyone else down.

The second man we had to pick up was Rob's cousin Dickey Day, who did work for Roy and he was surprised to be greeted by a new face when he climbed into the car. Dickey was a natural born comedian and was cracking jokes from the moment he got in the car until we got to site.

On arriving it was clear to me that the job itself was well along and that there was only a matter of a few weeks at most left in it. We parked next to Wilf's white Renault van which doubled as a canteen as it was equipped with a small gas cooker fed by a Calor Gas cylinder. It also served as the office as well as the tool store. All this was completely new to me, and I felt as I had done on my first day at school, when I hadn't known anyone, and, hadn't known where to go or what to do. I had the advantage of course of knowing Carl and Wilf fairly well which eased the 'new guy' feeling. The other member of the crew was

Johnny Vaines otherwise known as Vana; he was an old mucker of Wilf and Roy's from youth, he was a genial type of man from Tipton as were Roy and Wilf. He was down-to-earth and a good laugh. So there were six of us in total, Roy and Wilf the bosses and the rest the workers. The discussions as to which jobs needed doing that day were begun and the terms used relating to that trade might just as well have been in Greek for all I knew. However this was an opportunity to change trades completely and learn a whole new set of skills. Ordinarily I would never have been given the opportunity to change jobs so completely as I knew nothing of the trade, and all my friends and contacts so far were in the meat business.

Two of the main advantages to doing this job were, one the aspect of working outside in the fresh air, and two not working Saturdays, as had been my lot for the best part of ten years now. So I was determined that this was going to be my future, I had been a big fan of the television series 'Aufwiedersehen Pet' from a few years previously. I used to watch it when I worked in a different shop at the market and had envied the lifestyle of the characters in it, with the freedom they had 'workin' in the sun drinkin' schnapps havin' fun, that's livin' all right' as the theme song went. It seemed that my new work mates also had the freedom to choose that the building trade in general offered as a whole back then. So, here I was part of my own magnificent six, (soon to be seven, made possible by the return of the prodigal son, Darren, who was unhappy at his choice of working partnership with Chris.) This was my first day in a job that would last twenty years, and would bring many adventures, some funny others not so. I would miss Nobby and the lads at the market, I was still sore at Alan and I wanted no more to do with being pleasant to customers on the days when inside, worry for Kaine was tearing me apart. This week was going to count I would make sure of that!

"How did you get on?" asked Karen upon my arrival home.

"Great! I loved it, what a change, and look at the time!" I was overwhelmed by the fact that I was at home so early. Having had the opportunity of seeing my daughter in the morning and having more time to spend with her in the evening was the icing on the cake for me. It really highlighted the difference in the hours I spent at the market and showed me how much of my life that it had been eating up in time. I felt as if I had been imprisoned and suddenly been set free.

"So you don't think you'll change your mind and go back to the shop?" Karen asked me. I think she was wanting to confirm to herself that I would be happy doing a different kind of work as she was aware that I had enjoyed my life in the market hall, leaving out recent events. But now being exposed to this kind of freedom with less hours and proper breaks with my wage equal to what I earned at the market for twenty-five hours of my time less per week; I think that the answer was obvious.

"As soon as this week is over I'm handing in my notice." I said emphatically.

"Good! I don't want you working there any more!" said Karen. The fact that profit had been placed higher than her daughter's welfare had burned her, and a woman scorned is an enemy to be reckoned with. Myself and Alan were to have a showdown....

CHAPTER 16
auf Weidersehen Alan.

My week with Roy had come to an end, my mind was fully made up. I had enjoyed both being outdoors and the thrill of working at heights; although it had been a scary prospect at first, I never shrank from a challenge, and if roofing and steel erecting were to be my future vocation then the mastery of vertigo was a definite advantage. Thrilled as I was to have a new and exciting job with less hours and breaks galore, I didn't relish the thought of breaking the news to Alan on Monday morning; picking my moment was going to be the hardest part. When I got there as I felt nervous at the prospect. Part of me wanted to vent my feelings and tell him how disgusted I had felt that day he wouldn't let me go to the hospital, but it is not my nature to embarrass people and I didn't want to do this to Alan as I knew him to be a decent man. Most likely on the day in question he had felt the stress of that day's problems which had clouded his judgment. He arrived at his usual time. I decided to grasp the nettle and approached him after about fifteen minutes or so.

"Alan, can I have a word?"

"Yes Joe, what is it?" he responded.

"Alan I'm sorry, I'm gonna have to give you notice. I'm leaving." I heard myself say.

"I knew it! Just go Joe, go on leave now, we don't need you!" he shouted. I was shocked at his reaction and hurt by this, I thought about letting fly with my reasons but by now everyone had been alerted by Alan shouting at me. I decided to get my coat and leave; I would let him ponder my reasons for going and see if he arrived at the correct answer for himself. My arrival back home was as big a surprise to Karen. It didn't matter as the next day I was to be at work in my new vocation and happy to do so, but very sad that Alan and I had parted company on such a sour note.

CHAPTER 17.
Home sweet home at last.

And so to a new beginning; I threw myself into my new job with gusto, there was a lot for me to learn and I was keen to do so. I loved being outdoors even when the rain came it didn't bother me in the slightest. Of course I missed my friends in particular Nobby, but the crew I was with was equally as funny in antics and laughs just in different ways was all.

Kaine had recovered well again now from the replacement shunt and we dared to hope that if it failed again, if at all, it would be a long time coming so as to give her time to recover properly and also give her that little bit more understanding as she grew older. She was walking well, but her speech was slow in developing fully. It was explained to us that each time the shunt failed, the pressure on the wall of her brain created a setback in her development. But, she was coming along and apart from that she was developing quite normally. Her mom cared for her so well and took a very keen interest in developing health issues. When we had saved enough money to go abroad, she had a concern about Kaine's shunt when we flew. She wondered if the difference in air pressure at high altitudes would have any effect on the operation of the shunt as it worked on pressure. This was a valid concern, as anyone who has experienced flying can testify to the feeling one has in the ears as the aircraft descends. We were assured that this was not a problem encountered or logged in any medical journal by any other person who had had a shunt fitted and had flown; and so this put our minds at ease, and we looked forward to a break in Mahon on the island of Menorca.

We had saved every penny we could to find a deposit for a house and it was fortunate that the construction trade was busy and we worked weekends typically Saturday and Sunday mornings until dinner times, which suited me absolutely. We also earned bonuses for how quickly we completed contracts as the majority of our jobs were 'pricework'; speed being the key.

However the rise in house prices continued unabated and even with the extra money I was earning, the pace of the increases threatened the deposit we were saving on a weekly basis. We were still looking at houses, and went far and wide to buy, but in a lot of cases the houses on offer for the price were just totally inadequate, and so we kept on looking as the weeks turned into months.

I was enjoying my new job even as the weather started to turn colder, there was something about construction that satisfied in me a feeling I never had in the market.

However one Friday I arrived home from work to find that I'd had an unexpected phone call from an old friend I thought I'd lost.

"Alan phoned today for you." Karen said.

"Alan Doherty?" I exclaimed, very surprised. "What did he want?"

"He wanted to talk to you, but I think he was sounding me out first."

"What about?" I asked, curious now.

"Well, he said that what he had to say to you might make you to go back to being a butcher again."

"Right. How do you mean he was sounding you out, though?"

"He was asking how you were getting on in your new job, and whether or not you liked it now that the weather had changed."

"Ha! ha! good old Alan, always lookin' for a sales angle," I said with genuine affection for the man.

"He wants you to ring him later on at home." Karen said to me.

"Hmm, I wonder what this is all about, what did you tell him?"

"I told him that you loved bein' outdoors and loved the job too. You ain't thinking of goin' back are you?" she asked me, now with a note of concern in her voice.

"No, but the least I can do is give him the courtesy of a call to see what he has in mind." I said.

I didn't ring Alan until around eight o' clock to give him a little time to have his evening meal and settle down. I picked the receiver up with a bit of trepidation; the last time we spoke you will recall it had ended acrimoniously. I thought however that, knowing Alan as I did that with the expiration of some time, he would be okay with me as I felt I was with him. I dialled his number.

"Hello?" Alan's voice was on the other end of the line.

"Hello Alan, its Joe, you okay?"

"Yes Joe, I'm fine thanks, and thanks for ringing."

"Think nothin' of it, what's up anyway? Karen said you wanted me to call you."

"How are you getting on in your new job?" he asked.

"I gotta be honest with you Al', I love it, I'm gettin' on well." I said.

"How you coping with the weather?" I wondered where he was going with the line of questions he was posing.

"The weather ain't an issue with me Alan, come on spit it out, what's on your mind?" I said, cutting straight to the point.

"Well Joe, a pitch is comin' up in the market, one you'll know well, its old man Bridges old pitch," he said. He was of course referring to the shop where we had both worked a few years before.

"I'm gonna need a good pair of hands to put it in and your name is top of the list of the guys I could think of running it," he said.

"Well I'm really flattered at that Al', and to be honest I don't know what to say."

"That's easy Joe, just say yes! Look, I know things didn't go well last time, but I think we're both big enough to overlook past problems, don't you?"

"Oh absolutely Alan, that's all forgotten. It's just there's a lot to consider right now and I'm still tryin' to get the cash together for a deposit on a house; it's lookin' as though we're goin' to have to find more money."

"Well I can offer you weekend work if you're up for that; it might help you out?" Alan now asked.

"Well I could do with the extra money Alan, that's for sure,"

"Just come in on Saturdays for now then Joe, and we can try and work summat out where we're all happy; you never know you might just wanna be a butcher again."

"What, shall I come in next Saturday then?" I asked.

"Soon as you like Joe," he answered. We chatted on for a bit about the lads and left it at that.

Karen was more cautious about what my plans were. She thought that as soon as I was back in the market, Alan would work his charm and persuade me to give up construction. I knew for certain that was not an option for me, I liked the idea of having two trades under my belt and I was learning the building trade fast.

I was by now working away from home, this obviously gave me less time to be with Karen and Kaine. I was about to shorten it by another whole day, but I viewed this as a sacrifice well-worth making if it was to speed up our buying a house and leaving the flats.

While I was away Karen was looking at houses and when I called her, as I did every evening, she told me that she had spotted a nice bungalow in Willenhall just outside Wolverhampton. It was a brand-new house on a new estate and she set her heart on it. The only problem was, it cost forty-three thousand pounds; nothing in today's terms but then it was the most expensive so far that we, or rather she, had looked at. We worked out our money and phoned our mortgage advisor to get some idea of how much the monthly mortgage payments would cost us. With the deposit we had it was just outside our comfort zone. He suggested that if we were able to put a bigger deposit then this would bring the payments within what we could afford fairly comfortably. He worked out that a figure of an extra fifteen hundred pounds would be sufficient to do this. The advantage to buying this bungalow was that there was no chain and no chance of being gazumped, as it was being sold directly by the builder. I had to come up with the extra money somehow. Roy was out of the question as he had to settle a large tax bill otherwise he would have helped us out. I thought of Alan, and so I rang him as I was about to start work for him again albeit on a part-time basis. I explained the situation I was in and to his credit, and my eternal gratitude, he had no hesitation.

"No problem Joe, I'll help you." Alan had saved the day. In spite of all the searching about for a better job it was Alan who ultimately enabled me to buy our house for Karen and Kaine.

"When you come in next week the money will be there for you," he said.

"Alan, I can't thank you enough,"

"Don't worry, I'll think of something!" he said, laughing. He was as good as his word and the following Saturday I was back behind the familiar counter of Alan's shop.

With the money we had saved plus the loan Alan had made me, Karen went to the builder's office on the Monday morning and finally the first rung of the elusive property ladder was within our grasp. I finally felt that things were beginning to move in the direction that I had for so long laboured towards. I spoke with Karen that evening and she told me that the wheels had now been set in motion to buy the house that we had dreamed of. Things looked to be going well; the only cloud on the horizon for us was the ever-present fear of the problems Kaine had experienced with the shunt recurring again.

This we had to live with as there was no way of knowing when, or if ever, there was likely to be a blockage. In the meantime I continued to do the two jobs; I was in my main job of construction juxtaposed with my part time butchers job, Nobby referred to me as the oldest Saturday lad in Britain. Good old Nobby, some things just didn't change.

The weeks passed and finally the day we had been hoping for arrived, the completion of the purchase of our bungalow. We moved in a single weekend using the works van, no more graffiti on the landings, no more urine in the lifts.

For the first time in Kaine's life she would have a garden to play in; the only problem was that we hadn't enough money to put the fence up yet to separate us from our neighbours, and we had to lay our own lawn and patio. This would have to wait; although the garden was small, all our money went on the mortgage and things we needed to buy for the house. Shortly after our move, my working away stint came to an end. as the job came to completion. We had other contracts to do and I found myself on a series of smaller jobs in and around the West Midlands, due to this I was getting a little pressure to give up my Saturday work with Alan and work the weekends in construction. To be honest, half a day on Saturday and Sunday was more appealing and yielded much more money which was what I needed in order to keep up with our increased mortgage payments. I spoke to Alan regarding this and thankfully we didn't have the same parting of ways that we had had when I first left Alan's full-time employment. And so I had left completely my old life in the market and was feeling more a part of a

construction team fulfilling a greater satisfaction in me....
....I will always be grateful to Alan Doherty though, for giving me a job and enabling me to take my family from those horrible flats. They don't exist anymore I'm happy to say, but they were part of my life, and that whole period in particular, especially Alan, and the other lads in the market I will look back on with fond memories.

Thank you again Alan, you always were, and still are, a gentleman.

CHAPTER 18.

I could see by the look in her eyes.

Winter was beginning to take on it's cold grey appearance now and the realities of working outside in freezing temperatures replaced the days of working on the roofs clad only in shorts and t-shirts, if that. But I was the happiest I think I had ever been in those days and never thought that they would end.

One cold day in October though my happiness ceased to exist.

Roy had dropped me off at the top of my road, we had finished early that day for some reason or another. I walked down the street leading towards our house and encountered Karen as she had came in the other direction. She had been into the town to do a little shopping. Kaine was with her in her pushchair; as I got closer to her I could see that all was not well.

"Thank God your back; I was wondering how I was going to get in touch with you," she said, I recognised the look of panic in her eyes and my own fell upon Kaine who was lying down in the pushchair. I could tell from her appearance what was wrong; her face was a sickly, sallow yellow colour and the cover of the pushchair retained the traces of her having recently been sick.

Karen confirmed that whilst walking through the town Kaine had regurgitated her food for no apparent reason and that on the short walk back from the town she had lost consciousness and her colour had changed to how she looked now. We wasted no time getting into the house and I immediately phoned for an ambulance. This arrived within ten minutes and we were taken to the local Manor Hospital in Walsall. We knew that Kaine's shunt had blocked again and equally knew that unless they had the facilities at the Manor to replace the shunt that our ultimate destination would be the Children's Hospital in Birmingham.

Kaine was displaying all the symptoms which we had observed before when her shunt had failed to work and so we were able to tell the examining doctor the likely cause of the problem on our arrival at the hospital. With no facility at Manor Hospital or expert to perform the procedure Kaine needed, our assumption that we were to be transferred to the Children's Hospital turned out to be the correct one. We waited anxiously on a ward whilst arrangements were made to take us over to Birmingham by ambulance. This wait was to be for about an hour but every minute seemed like an hour in itself.

Finally they were ready to move us and we followed as Kaine was wheeled to the elevators to transfer us to the bay where an ambulance stood ready to take us on the journey to Birmingham. Kaine, although stable, was still a deathly colour and this was extremely distressing to Karen and myself. When we arrived at the all too-familiar

Children's Hospital we were taken straight up to our ward and a room away from the other patients was where we found ourselves; whereupon Kaine was examined by one of Mr Hamilton's team.

Kaine's records and past history facilitated a rapid confirmation of what we already knew and the operating theatre was made ready as her condition was deemed to be an emergency.

We watched yet again as our daughter was taken away and we prayed that everything would be fine. For myself this was the first time that I'd experienced seeing Kaine when her shunt had failed as the last time Karen was alone with her at the flat while I was at work. I appreciated now what Karen had gone through alone that morning as the fear that I felt when I first laid eyes on her in the pushchair gripped me.

Waiting was something we endured but could not get used to; what seemed like an eternity had passed since Kaine went for the operation but finally she was returned to us. Had I known that morning what the evening was to bring, I would never have gone into work, but that knowledge was unattainable. It was just fortunate that I had been there when Karen had got back from the town, as while I was at work there was little chance of her being able to get in touch with me as those days were the ones in which mobile phones had not reached the proliferation that they have in the present day. Kaine was transferred from the hospital gurney onto her bed and again our parental instincts were to hold her tight and comfort her. But we couldn't. We were grateful that she would be okay but this spectre of repeated emergency operations was one that we would have to live with from now on. Of course as I couldn't predict that morning that Kaine would be in hospital by the evening, neither could I predict that the series of emergency operations I had envisaged Kaine going through would be short.

A few hours later Kaine came to and was in great distress; in her little mind she must have wondered why this kept happening to her. If I could have made it all go away I would have, but she was still so young that we couldn't even explain to her why she found herself in hospital yet again. In the early hours of the next day after Kaine had calmed down and was sleeping, I made my way home. I wouldn't be going into work that day as I would inform Roy first thing that morning before he set out to pick us all up as was his routine. I would head back over to the hospital in our car, by now we had sold the Vauxhall cavalier and bought the yellow Volkswagen polo mentioned at the outset of the book,

When I arrived at the ward Karen was holding Kaine and giving her some breakfast as the poor little thing was starving. I always viewed that as a good sign as her appetite signified how she was feeling and if hungry, then she must be feeling better I reasoned, and this cheered me somewhat. Karen, though, looked tired and drained; there was a look in her eyes that I had not seen before. Maybe it was the same in my eyes, for I certainly felt it. This was a look of resignation to something inevitable that was to happen; maybe it was premonition who knows? Shortly afterwards when Kaine was home from hospital, we were at home just the three of us, and I took a photo of Karen and Kaine together. That look was present in her eyes then, immortalised by that photograph, and proved to be eerily prophetic to the subsequent events that were to take place not long afterwards......

CHAPTER 19.

Intensive care.

A few days later and we were picking up where we left off. I returned to work and resigned myself to the next time Kaine was taken into hospital. I had no idea how soon it would be. Inside I felt something was going wrong yet couldn't put my finger on it. A few nights beforehand, it was shortly after Kaine had come out of hospital, I had a dream that upset me very much, but I kept it to myself and this is the first time now that I have ever related it. I dreamt of Kaine dressed in white, walking with another figure dressed in white also; they were walking away from me and Kaine turned around and smiled at me, whilst smiling, saying one word; it was the word I used everyday to her before I left for work; 'bye-bye'.

I couldn't shake off my depression that day, I eventually dismissed the dream as the workings of my sub-conscious mind playing on my worries and pushed it to the back of my mind and forgot about it in the weeks that followed.

November 1989 was approaching and the Christmas of that year would have been Kaine's second; already Karen

241

was planning what to get for her. Fate was to wield its cruel influence on us though. I was working in Worcester at the time, the whole crew was split up between jobs, Roy on one, Wilf on another, and I was with Dickey and 'Basha' aka Barry Sherma or 'Shirley Temple' as he was referred to in the pub where we all drank on a Friday after work, as he had blonde curly hair. This was the Vic in Lyng lane West Bromwich more commonly referred to as the 'Scaffolder's Arms' due to the predominant numbers of building site workers who drank the place almost dry every Friday. It was a typical honest working class pub, you could leave your wallet on the counter while you went to the toilet and it wouldn't be touched.

Dickey drove an old Fiesta held together by rust with red flecks where the paint used to be, we used to rib him that an antique vintage motor such as that shouldn't be used for work. His answer was typical of Dick's wisecracks 'second class transport is better than first class walkin'.' He was correct of course, it started every day and got us to Worcester and back every night.

Dickey hadn't a driving license, and for those wondering why he had a car but no driving license, they would be told he needed it to get to the pub; he was about as legal as the Kray twins, and so consequently I did all the driving; we would drop Basha at home and then I would drop Dick at his house in Walsall and carry on to my own.

One night Kaine took bad again; we phoned the ambulance and found ourselves repeating the journey we had made last time to Manor Hospital and then on to the Children's Hospital. I followed in Dick's car as there was little petrol in our own. The same procedure followed as

Kaine was operated on and the shunt replaced. A young student doctor was present that evening and was able to observe the operation as part of his training. I was getting Karen and myself a coffee from the machine whilst we waited when I encountered him on his way back from the operating theatre. He had been present when Kaine was admitted and so knew me as her father. When he saw me a smile spread across his face.

"Mr. Lawlor, I have good news for you. The operation has been completed and your daughter is fine; it all went very well," he said.

"Oh thank God, that's great, thanks for coming to tell me," I said in return.

"That's my pleasure, I'm very glad it's worked out okay for you." From his smile I could tell how pleased he was for me and Kaine's mom. I felt the relief I had always felt after the operations had taken place in the past, but I was saddened now by the successive failure of these shunts. I asked one of the doctors there why this kept happening and he produced a spare so that he could explain in detail how they operated and what could cause failure to occur.

As I said in the book earlier in my description of the shunt- it looked like a small tube with a series of tiny holes at the top end through which the fluid drains to empty the chamber in the brain. These holes can clog up with natural debris from within the body, and they are particularly vulnerable to clogging after the procedure has been done, as the likely-hood of debris is increased from the operation itself. So it was explained that on a child totally shunt dependant as Kaine was, that this was a sad fact of life and we could expect more of the same.

I didn't know whether to tell Karen this or not; I decided not to that night as I didn't want her to become any more upset than she already was. It was three o' clock now in the morning when Kaine was brought back from theatre. She was as usual heavily sedated. I had to get back home in time to get Dickey and Basha to work. I'd phoned Darren, one of the other guys working on another job, earlier to meet me at my house after this,

he could go to Worcester in Dick's car after I'd dropped it off to him and this would enable him to pick the lads up that evening, then the three of them could carry on to Worcester for the rest of the week, Darren taking my place as the only one with a driving licence. Dick wouldn't risk long journeys in the car so these arrangements had to be made.

While Kaine was still unconscious from the anaesthetic, Karen decided to come back with me to get some clothes for her stay and after I dropped Dick and Basha we could both go over together in our own car. The night staff at the hospital assured us that Kaine would be fine while we did this. We waited at Kaine's bed side until the early hours of the morning then I drove us back home where I dropped Karen off and went straight to Dick's and then onto Bash's place explaining on the way what had happened. After dropping them both at Worcester, I drove the return journey as quick as the morning traffic would allow me to get back to meet Darren at my house as he had to come off the other job.

When I got there Darren was waiting for me and Karen was talking to him at the door. From her appearance I could tell that something was wrong, I pulled up, jumped out of the car and asked her what was wrong.

"Kaine's in intensive care," she sobbed. "The hospital's been on the phone, we have to get there straight away."

"What's happened to her? She was okay when we left." I said, shocked now at her words.

"I don't know, come on we gotta go!" Her voice was getting frantic now as she had been waiting for my return for us to leave. I threw the keys to Darren and barely had time to give him directions to get to the job, but that was the very least of my concerns.

We jumped in the car and headed for the hospital. I had to stop for petrol as we were nearly empty and this took precious minutes from us. I was growing more and more desperate to get to the hospital to find out what had happened in the few hours from when we had left Kaine in the hospital's care to now when we didn't know why? or how? our daughter had ended up in the Intensive Care Unit. The very name sent shivers through me as I drove as fast as I could to get there. Upon our arrival, we were met by one of the female doctors who had monitored Kaine from when she was admitted. She ushered us to a room where the three of us entered, and asked us to take a seat. The look on her face was grave. I had searched the faces of many a doctor over the times we had been coming to the hospitals, both Sandwell and the Children's Hospital whenever they were to inform us of how Kaine was progressing; the look on this woman's face told me that the news was bad; I didn't know what to expect; we had brought Kaine for a shunt replacement which had been done. had not the student doctor who had observed the operation said that everything was fine? We had not long left her, what had gone wrong?

I held Karen's hand as she had started to cry by now, obviously picking up on the doctor's dour countenance.

"I'm afraid early this morning there was an emergency with Kaine. Shortly after you left, Kaine displayed signs that the newly inserted shunt had mal-functioned, and was taken back to theatre to have the problem corrected."

"Why is she in the intensive care unit?" I asked, my mind struggling to keep track.

"I'm afraid following this further procedure your daughter developed neurological dysfunction and bradycardia; in plain terms her brain couldn't regulate her heart properly and she went into cardiac arrest and has had to be put on a ventilator in the intensive care unit."

"A ventilator?" Karen asked.

"Life support," the doctor said quietly

"What's her condition now?" I asked desperately hoping that her response would be a positive one. She continued in the same level-pitched tone that she had used throughout this brief conversation so far.

"We won't know for some time how Kaine is until she recovers consciousness." By now my wife was inconsolable; my mind was reeling, this wasn't happening, it couldn't be happening. But it was; we only wanted to be with her now.

"When can we see her?" Karen asked through the tears now flowing from her reddened eyes.

the doctor had graciously passed her a handkerchief to wipe away her tears. If only the meningitis could have been wiped away without trace as easily as tears could be, then this sad scene unfolding before us might have been avoided in its entirety.

"Due to the nature of intensive care, we will have to make arrangements which will take a little while; I'll get someone to make you both a cup of tea while I attend to this."

She then left us alone; bewildered and with a million questions racing though our minds; the foremost being, what would be the outcome of all this? would recovery be possible? Probable? And probably the biggest one of all going through my mind and heart; Why us? Why Kaine? We hadn't done any wrong to anyone; all we had tried to do was to work hard and put a home around our little girl. This was so unfair. I tried to pull myself together for Karen's sake more than my own, I couldn't go to pieces, someone had to remain strong in our blackest of hours. I latched on to a piece of the conversation that we had with the doctor. She had mentioned Kaine recovering consciousness; this was hope, a beacon of light in the dark. Maybe in a few hours when the medicine they have given Kaine takes affect, she'll wake up and be as right as rain again; yes that's what's going to happen, I naively thought, I was sure of it. But something in the doctor's eyes when she had said that had told me otherwise, maybe it was because that when she had mentioned this she had automatically looked at the floor, and when telling us something she was more certain of, she had looked me in the eyes. I was no psychiatrist, but I could tell when being told the truth and when maybe I wasn't....

Looking back now I can't blame her, we didn't know it yet but Kaine would never open her eyes again. And in the next few days this reality became more obvious as we desperately clung to every ounce of hope that the human body can muster. The saddest part was that we convinced ourselves that Kaine would recover; it was painfully obvious to those fully aware of the trauma that Kaine's brain had suffered that this was a forlorn hope. This we chased for five days and sleepless nights, where the extent of the boundaries of our world became the Intensive Care Unit ward where the focus of our entire lives lay in a coma, breathing with the aid of the ventilator now sustaining Kaine's existence for us. Some time later we were told that we could see Kaine and were now led to a part of the hospital previously unseen by us. As we approached the door to the ward a sign on the door read clearly, in large capital letters,

'INTENSIVE CARE UNIT PLEASE REFRAIN FROM MAKING

EXCESSIVE NOISE.' It was the quietest room full of children I have ever been in. I can't recall now how many beds were in there, even if there were only one, it was still too many. I was shocked at the sight of so many desperately sick kids. Each had their own dedicated nurse on hand keeping a close eye on their little charge. Most were babies, some premature, others a little older. I noticed one young lad of about six or seven though; totally incapacitated, unconscious and hooked up to life support, and obviously in a very serious condition. I thought of his poor parents. I should have saved my sorrow for myself for when I saw my own daughter Kaine I nearly passed out from shock; Karen gripped me tight with fearful expectancy and physically shook when she saw her.

Kaine was on her back dressed only in her nappy, a needle was inserted into her foot which was hooked up to a drip of some sort; a bandage was wrapped around this secured by surgical tape. To her arm a second drip was attached. The ventilator tube was inserted into her mouth and held by surgical tape to keep it in place. On her chest were two little pads connected to what I think was a heart rate monitor; this had a series of red digital readout numbers and I noticed that they fluctuated but I couldn't know whether this was normal or not. A plastic clip which resembled a clothes peg, light green in colour was attached to one of her fore fingers and this in turn had a wire attached which led to another monitor. Kaine's chest rose and fell as the machine did its unerring duty; her eyes were closed to us and to the world. Would she hear us? Tenderly I touched her face as my own tears welled at this terrible sight; Karen held her hand and whispered 'my little darling we love you.' What could we do? there was nothing in the world we could do to stop this.

Kaine's dedicated intensive care nurse was a young woman, she looked a little younger than us; she introduced herself as Kaine's nurse, and she told me that she was keeping a close watch on Kaine's condition. Whatever else she may have said I have no recollection of as my brain was incapable of absorbing anything more than what lay before me.

At that time of the morning we were the only parents there apart from another woman who sat holding a little boy's hand, he was also unconscious. She turned and looked at me and as our eyes met, no emotion came from either her or me, I saw only an empty despair recognisable only by those who share this feeling. She turned her attention back to the young lad. Kaine's immediate neighbour was a small baby of about four months.

Compared to the baby in the next bed Kaine looked big by comparison. The whole scene was totally wrong, these kids shouldn't have been like this but they were.

The eerie silence continued as not a sound came from a single child in there. The constant beeping of the monitors and the sounds of the other medical equipment were unremitting and even when the nurses spoke with each other, it was in hushed tones.

We knew that we were in serious trouble, but we couldn't quite comprehend how this was likely to turn out for us. With the benefit of hindsight now it couldn't have ended any other way than it did. We were prepared to accept that Kaine might well be permanently brain damaged, but personally, my mind was made up. If it was to be that both myself and Karen were to become her full-time carers then that was what it had to be; we were her parents and that love was unconditional. I'm glad that day that I made my decision, as my conscience remains clear as to how I would have reacted if that were how Kaine's life had turned out. But it was not to be. We, however, were not to know that at this time, and hope, as always, springs eternal even in such grave circumstances as these indeed were.

CHAPTER 20.

The eleventh hour before midnight.

On the first day of November Kaine was responding to some stimuli and her limbs moved, although only in reaction to pain. Her pupils were unevenly dilated and her breathing controlled by the life-support equipment; she wasn't responding to her name or wouldn't or rather couldn't open her eyes.

Looking back over Kaine's medical reports for the five days leading to the early hours of the sixth of November, it was obvious that my little girl had sustained severe brain trauma due to the failure of the shunt to drain properly; this is known in medical terms as cerebral oedema and was the primary cause of her death due to brain-stem failure.

We stayed by Kaine's side all through this period hoping against all hope for the elusive miracle for which we had prayed. But over the next two days as the time went by her condition deteriorated; we weren't told any of this by the nurses as they went about their work checking

Kaine's progress or lack of. Her eyes gradually became dilated and unresponsive to light and that was followed by a gradual cooling down of the skin as her brain decided that one by one, her bodily functions would be turned off.

On the third of November, Mr. Hamilton came to check on her. He was a curious man; he seemed completely immune to our feelings as Kaine's parents. As he checked the reports from the monitors and the nursing charts, he just turned to me and said,

"That's it; I'm afraid there's nothing more we can do." And walked off. It would be easy to dismiss him as unfeeling and callous; for a long time I thought he was. We had a further meeting with him some weeks after Kaine had died to ascertain the full reasons for her death, and came from his office none the wiser and more upset than when we went in. I didn't find out until years later when I obtained all of Kaine's medical records and found his personal correspondence between himself and Mr. Hockley, his partner (who had performed the very first operation on Kaine due to his being on leave,) what his true thoughts had been. Although not dripping with sentiment, his professionalism was apparent, and for that alone I am grateful that he had done all he could to save Kaine. A room had been found in which both myself and Karen could stay at the hospital, due to the more serious condition that Kaine was now in; we could stay on the ward as long as we liked as long as we didn't interfere with the care the nurses were administering to the children. That is when I became an eyewitness to the dedication of those women and the outright professional attitude in caring they displayed, and I can't praise them high enough for that. Most of our time was spent with Kaine, we got very little sleep. On the fourth day we were by her bedside; all our relatives had been informed that there was very little hope now and had come to the hospital to support us in the final hours of Kaine's life. Late in the evening of that day, I looked at Karen and she was exhausted due to the strain of this terrible ordeal. Kaine's bodily functions, such as passing urine, were no longer controlled by her brain. As we were to find out later, her death had already occurred; it was the ventilator breathing for her. Her heart continued to beat due to this but the part of the brain controlling temperature was no longer operative and so her body was cooling down in response. Her bladder was emptied by a nurse pressing down on the area where this was and so this was when I realised that she was no longer capable of any of the bodily functions which happen automatically.

I told Karen that I would stay a little while longer with Kaine and that she should go back to our room now and try to get some sleep; this she reluctantly agreed to. I said that I would wake her in a few hours and that she could take over from me so I could do the same. But I already decided that Karen would need all the rest she could in order to be able to face what was gradually becoming clearer to me; and so I let her sleep. The time I had left with Kaine was limited and so I was going nowhere that night. I wanted to be with her to the bitter end, and that was how it was going to be.

There were other parents coming and going throughout the day but most found staying there unbearable. It was, but each has to make a choice and mine was to stay. Throughout the night and into the early morning of the fifth day, the nurses checked on Kaine. Nothing was said and I knew that this was bad, as I saw the reaction of the other nurses to the improvement in the condition of the little baby next to Kaine; it was slight but they were all overjoyed. I'm sorry to say I didn't share that joy as it only emphasised to me that Kaine was showing no improvement and in this I gave way to tears. One of the nurses tried comforting me but it was no good. I was happy of course that the little child was improving and would survive if this continued; but human nature can be selfish and I wanted Kaine to have that improvement in her condition as it felt that improvement was in short supply on that ward, only the very fortunate could partake in it with precious little left over for the rest. The fifth dawn that cold month came; for the world outside it was Guy Fawkes Day. No doubt preparations for the lighting of the bonfires and the setting off of the fireworks that evening were eagerly anticipated by young and old alike. For myself and for Karen it was one more day where hope was fading. Karen came back onto the ward and asked me why I hadn't woken her when I had said I would. I simply told her that I had wanted to be with Kaine. She had brought me some tea and a sandwich; I didn't feel like eating though. The night shift handed over to the day shift; at least they could leave now and forget all this until they were required to take up their duty again; but for us it went on.

The nightmare we were in had an expiry time however; it would culminate in a decision no parent should have to make but is necessary as I was to find. During the day the medical team we were to meet again later on came to the bedside to perform responsive tests on Kaine. All the data that had been collected by the ITU nurses was logged and viewed by the senior member. It made harrowing reading. I have read it all since.

From the early morning of the emergency with Kaine, her brain had swelled and infarcted causing massive brain damage; in turn the brain gradually shut down all vital functions until the main stem itself expired. The tests gave this indication. However conclusive testing would still have to be done for to ascertain for certain that brain-stem death had occurred. The hour for this was set at midnight….

Kaine was to be moved to a more private area for these tests to be conducted. This was so that any other parents in our position would not witness what was an extremely private time, but it also meant that they wouldn't hear the reaction of other parents to the news that their child had died.

We were asked if we required any religious help; a miracle would have done nicely but they were in very short supply in Birmingham's Children's Hospital Intensive Care Ward that day, as I well knew. I did ask however if a Catholic priest would be available to administer the last rites to Kaine. This I was told would be arranged for us later in the day. Karen was inconsolable by now and I took her off the ward to the waiting room where our relatives were. And where Karen's mom could try to ease her daughter's pain.

While we were off the ward, the staff moved Kaine's bed and all the equipment into a side room where we would have the privacy needed in the hours left to us. It was a step closer to the inevitable. When Karen was up to it we went back in a couple of hours later and found

Kaine on her bed in the room. The plastic and metal framed chairs that we had on the ward were replaced by two more comfortable looking armchairs. All the room had been arranged so that we could sit in the chairs and hold Kaine as well making us as comfortable as possible during our wait. As the time went by one of the nurses came to us and quietly told us that a Father Gregory had arrived and was waiting for us to let him know when we were ready for him. Darkness was now falling outside and I could hear the first explosions of the fireworks being set off in premature expectation to the main event.

Karen and I looked at each other; this was going to be the first step to letting go of our baby. I asked if she was ready, she asked for ten minutes, the nurse nodded, and left the room leaving the three of us alone. We had taken it in turns holding Kaine every couple of hours, but for this we put her on her bed ready for the arrival of Father Gregory. In due time a slight knock came on the door and he entered. He was an old man with grey hair and he was wearing spectacles. After he introduced himself he asked if there were any special prayers he could say for Kaine. Neither I nor Karen knew any as we were not religious at all, And so we left that to his judgment. He said the Lord's Prayer and asked for forgiveness of our sins. And then he gave Kaine the last rites in Latin.

We had a brief conversation in which he offered us some comfort but we just wanted to be left alone now with Kaine and so he politely left. The noise of the fireworks was getting louder and louder and we dimmed the lights and waited for the clock on the wall to signal the time for the final tests on our child to be completed.

I sat with Kaine in my arms and Karen sat opposite me; the room was darkened and warm. I held her close to me and kissed the top of her head. Sleep was creeping into my exhausted mind as I struggled to stay awake. I found myself dozing fitfully, I leaned closer to Kaine after looking at the time once more and whispered, 'not long now sweetheart'…..

CHAPTER 21.
Angels' tears.

The rain was beginning to beat heavily against the window of the funeral car where we had sat waiting for the rest of the mourners to get to their vehicles and take their positions behind us for the journey back to our house. Karen gently squeezed my hand bringing me back to the present.

"I think we're ready to go," she said to me.

"Erm, yeah okay," I said. "I was just thinking." I added.

"What of?" she asked.

"That beach in Wales with that couple with the dog." I said, in response.

"Why them?"

Karen looked at me slightly puzzled by this.

"No reason." I said, "I just was, that's all." The driver started the engine and slowly pulled away from the church-yard closely followed by everyone who had come that morning; we were minus one person though on the return journey home, the most important one; Kaine....... I had thought of the beach in Wales with that older couple walking hand in hand along it, with the dog barking at the waves; it was such a tranquil scene, peaceful and carefree. I had imagined Karen and I with Kaine a little older with our dog doing much the same thing had we moved to Wales that time. Those sweet thoughts would never be, and Karen never did get to put those ribbons in pigtails on her little girl. Our world had ended that day. Would it ever begin again? It was too soon even to think, I felt suffocated and crushed by the weight of my own sorrow for us. Time would tell if time was to be the great healer it was said to be.....

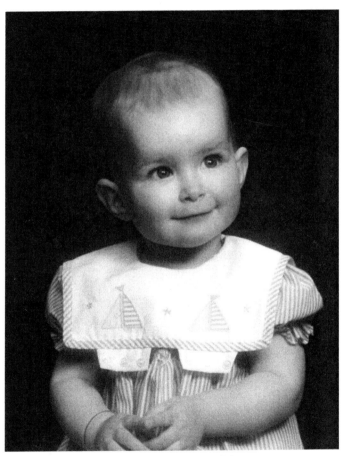

Hauntingly beautiful

First born.

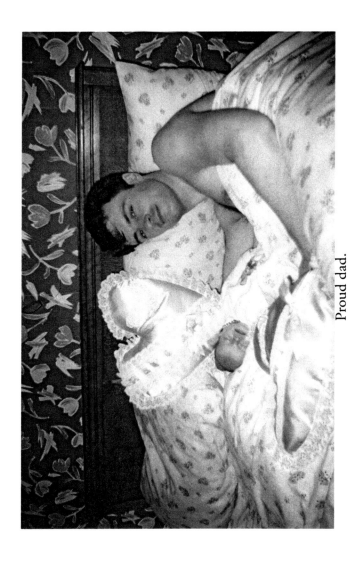

Proud dad.

Mother and child.

Fresh faced and raring to go.

Happy birthday Kaine.

How's this work?

Happy family.

Sitting pretty.

Father and daughter.

Soap and bubble.

Home sweet home.

I'm outta here.

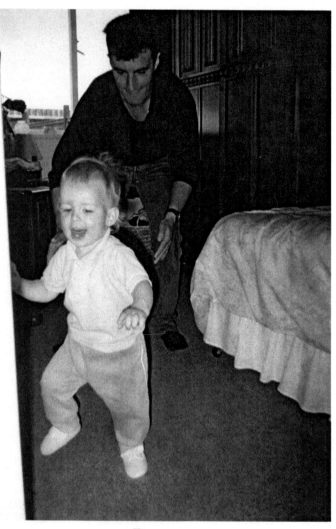

First steps.

Two quid and a mad bank manager.

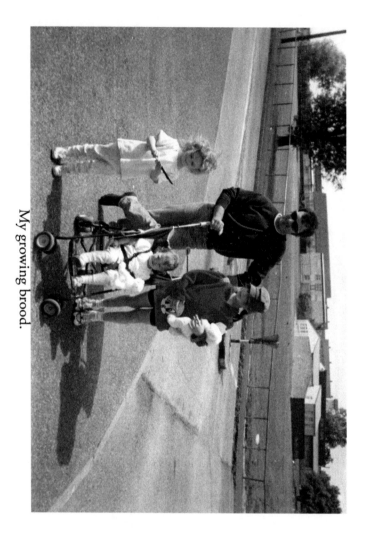

My growing brood.

AUTHOR: Joseph JP Lawlor.
COPYRIGHT NO: 0146318409.

PART TWO.

CHAPTER 22.
Angels' tears. (Part two)

The main car retraced its course now back to Willenhall, to number 41 Villiers Street, to the house that was now a shell for me. All the food and drink had been laid on for our guests. When this was consumed they would return to their homes leaving us to pick up the pieces of our shattered lives.

I have often thought about the death of loved ones as in the world we now inhabit it is a daily occurrence; sometimes through natural causes, a lot by illness, and much of it now down to violence. It is hard to take, one can never get used to it. But there is something more terrible in losing a child, all those unfulfilled dreams and plans; not seeing them grow and have children of their own. One wonders what kind of person they would have been. All these things I had hoped and wondered about my own daughter, and in an instant it had all stopped. I felt powerless to express my feelings. People say things like, "I know how you feel." But unless they have experienced your trial then they can't possibly know, and I wouldn't want them to.

However we had guests to attend to and the next few hours would be taken up with looking after this event at our house.

It had been decided that it was still too soon to return home properly as Kaine's toys and clothing were all still where we had left them. How were we going to put them away? Those thoughts were beyond me at that present moment in time. That was a task I would have to steel myself for; in particular taking down her cot which still resided in our bedroom. Karen had decorated the other bedroom in readiness for when Kaine was old enough to sleep in there; sadly this now was not to be.

The car had gathered pace as we drove through the streets lashed by the rain that fell from the sky that terrible day. The weather suited the occasion, for if it had been sunny I think if it were possible I would have felt worse. I wanted the world to mourn with me and in my mind the rain from the skies that day were the tears of the angels that wept for our loss. That is what I wanted to believe and in a small way I drew a crumb of comfort from my reasoning. The question remained in me though, as to why Kaine had died. I could accept an older persons passing, having first experienced the life this planet had to offer, but one so young? Kaine had just begun to learn to walk, her mom had been out a few short weeks earlier and bought her first pair of shoes measured for the purpose, and now she lay buried in them. The injustice of this was monstrous. The thoughts too big for my comprehension, the uncertainty of God's purpose, burned in my mind, unreachable questions unanswered by the invisible realm so silent to me in my need for knowledge of my little girl's welfare. The experience we had had just after leaving the hospital that day only served to confuse me all the more. I would search for the answers that the philosophy of the invisible realm kept so well hidden from view, …..but for now the sausage rolls and vol-au-vents were waiting to be uncovered and passed around as people made idle chit-chat with each other as they stood in our living room saying 'so sad'. I wondered if there was a bigger picture to all this and I implored the Almighty to let me in on the big secret because at that moment I can tell you I was a very angry and confused young man.

I kept my thoughts and feelings to myself. I had always been a deep thinker, but this baffled me completely. Yes, I had heard of children dying, a class mate of mine named Larry died at eleven years of age back in Ireland years earlier; we weren't especially close, but we used to play cowboys and Indians together with the other kids from our road; we were the same age. He though, suffered from epilepsy; sadly, one grey morning, he died in his mothers arms at home. I remember his death affected me deeply at the time, and periodically throughout my life, I had often thought about poor Larry and how he never got to play cowboys and Indians again with us. I had wondered how his mother had felt, as we were a noisy bunch of kids running about the place back then. She must have heard the squeals of the other children of the road playing outside and this would have been a reminder to her that come the prescribed time that all the other mothers had to shout for their kids to come in; she would have to remain silent. I had often seen her coming back from the shops with Larry by her side chatting away in his youthful excitement to his mother, but now every time when I saw her after Larry's passing, an aura of sadness was her only companion. If I had any feeling of inquisitiveness about how she had felt, then I'm sad to say at twenty six years of age in nineteen eighty-nine this feeling was completely satisfied within me…. The days that followed on from Kaine's funeral grew progressively darker; I remembered it rained almost constantly for three days after that. We were staying at Karen's mom's house for the foreseeable future as a Christmas in the house we had striven so hard to acquire, without the one person we had worked so hard for being there, was quite unbearable. The nights were the worst for Karen. She woke up sobbing for the little girl we had had to leave in the lonely church graveyard; wind and rain lashed and eerie in the darkness. No words of mine could comfort her in her loss, and she didn't want to get up in the days that followed. I went into the bedroom one cold morning and found her staring blankly out through the bedroom window from where she was lying.

"Would you like a cup of tea?" I asked.

"No thanks," she said not breaking from her gaze into space.

"I was thinking of going to the old church later to sort out the flowers." I said. "Do you want to come with me?"

I was unsure what was for the best but I feared for her mental state just lying there alone with her thoughts.

"Yeah okay," she answered, after a pause. It would be hard to go there but it had to be done. This would be the first time that we had been back to the grave alone and we could be together again the three of us I thought, if only for a short while.

Time had little impact as my focus on everything had taken a skewed angle. It was late in the afternoon when we finally got to the graveyard, already it was beginning to darken, hurried by the gloomy clouds that hung low in the sky still rain laden and threatening to burst at any time. The flowers that had been brought to the churchyard with the funeral were all laid on the top of the freshly turned earth. The constant rain had beaten them down and they were bedraggled and limp. The cards of sympathy with them, inside the plastic covers were barely legible now. This was where people had poured out their sincere sympathies for our loss. All were destined for the bin as decay took them. I could see that the earth over Kaine had sunk due to the torrential downpour of the past few days. I couldn't leave it like this and so we resolved to come back early the next day to clear everything away and think of some appropriate surround while we waited for the ground to settle and lay a memorial stone.

The threatening sky fulfilled its promise and the rain came once more. Karen and I embraced each other, totally alone by our daughter's graveside, and our tears flowed together for the love we had for our lost child. We walked back to where we had left our car, glancing back occasionally as we went, involuntary reactions to something, someone we were leaving behind us as we went. The seat for Kaine was still in the car and I thought to my self that I had better remove this as it was a constant reminder, as if we could forget; nonetheless we couldn't help but look at it as we got in the car.

"We can go to B&Q," I said to Karen as we drove from the car park. I had to switch the headlights on full and the screen wipers were at maximum to cope with the downpour of rain.

"What for?"

"Well we can go to the garden section and get some top soil to fill the ground, and I can put kerb stones around the perimeter for now."

"Okay we'll do that," answered Karen, slightly lost still as if some invisible coat of numbness was wrapped around her.

We headed for the nearest warehouse which was in West Bromwich town. The plan was that we could pick these items up along with some fresh flowers, and bin bags for the ones ruined by the rain. The following morning, weather permitting, we could go up there bright and early and do our work for Kaine. This was all we could do now, as even in her passing, we were acutely aware that we still wanted to do the best we could for her as we had striven to do in life.

We got what we set out for in B&Q and made our way back to Karen's mom's house. Pat did all that she could for us in those days following Kaine's death and I can't thank her enough for that.

We all sat down to our evening meal and the conversation remained pretty much as normal; the weather was discussed, even the approaching nemesis of Christmas being broached. The thoughts were that we'd cross that ravine when we had to.

That evening I had some 'phone calls from my old work colleagues at the Market Hall. The first was from Carol who was heart-broken for me, she and I had become good mates working together all that time, and I had shared my innermost fears with her when Kaine had first contracted meningitis. Anne called later and was upset for me also; understandably so as she knew Karen as well from when she came to the market to pick me up after work. Alan rang me later in the evening and uncharacteristically was stuck for words. But it didn't matter; sometimes more can be said without the use of mere sentiment, and I appreciated the words he couldn't say to me. The following morning the sky had cleared briefly, enough for us to make our planned journey to All Saints' Church. The ironic thing was that we would literally be only hundreds of yards away from where Kaine's life had begun, that being Sandwell Hospital. The irony was not lost to me as I had followed the same route to the church as to the hospital except, that this time there was to be no joy at Kaine's birth; just a hollow emptiness that would never be filled.

When we arrived there, I was surprised to see an old gentleman near where Kaine was buried and he appeared to be doing something. It was early in the morning; I'd deliberately chosen the hour so as not to be disturbed in what I wanted to do. It turned out we both had much the same idea. The grave next to Kaine had recently been dug and filled; it, too, was covered in flowers that had been destroyed by the rain. The man was tending to his own daughter's grave; she had been forty when she died, he was in his sixties, I was in my twenties. Side by side two fathers of different ages attended to the same task; looking after their little girls. We spoke very little as we went about what we were doing, he finished before I did as he had started earlier. Before he left he laid a wooden plaque by his daughter's flowers…. Margaret E. Field passed away 1989. He said 'goodbye' and I never saw him again after that. Some ten years later her stone was taken up, and when it was re-laid, his name had joined hers.

We had taken up all the flowers that were ruined and managed to salvage those that weren't. We had bought some vases for the purpose of renewing the flowers periodically and Karen busied herself with doing that whilst I filled in the depressed soil and laid the kerbstones in place. When I'd formed the perimeter around the grave with these, I then filled it with gravel to prevent any weeds from taking hold. A small wooden cross I'd made, with Kaine's name across the centre piece, finished it off.

We stood now observing what we had achieved for her; it was the best we could do for now. It would be twelve months before we could lay a proper memorial stone to honour her short life; in the meantime this sufficed.

Economic necessities meant that within a few weeks I would return to work, but Karen made the almost daily pilgrimage to the grave for weeks after that to tend to the flowers. I would go there with her on the weekends and sometimes find flowers left by persons unknown. This happened a lot as we had left a small teddy bear by the cross thus identifying the site as a child's grave; and even strangers were moved to show their sorrow. The weeks passed and I found that being at work helped as my mind was kept busy in other areas; I found out later that not having a proper period to grieve for Kaine was more damaging to me, but for now I felt better in myself. I was young and thought I could bounce back, even from the enormity of this tragedy that had occurred. But the mind is a complex thing and it can hold many facets that are not always apparent until time has gone by, and an event can reveal the damage done in earlier times. A trigger would be required for this and little did I know it then, or even suspect, that when we went to Kaine's final resting place, the secret deeds perpetrated by men lay undiscovered as yet beneath the soil. Covered by the flowers that were lovingly laid with our caring hands and with unsuspecting minds, the trigger that would ruin our lives lay dormant…..

Karen had taken a job in a chemists shop in Wednesbury, I was pleased as I thought this would focus her mind elsewhere and find the same relief as I had in my work. During her brief lunch though, she would make the journey to the church daily, for her lost child.

Christmas was soon upon us that year and it seemed that this was the worst year of gloomy weather we had ever endured; interest rates were beginning to bite hard as the brakes were applied with more vigour by the government to slow-down the economy as we all slid towards the recession of the early nineties. Things were looking dire. Work was slowing down as the pulse of the country slackened and the building industry suffered. It looked as though not only were we to have lost the most precious thing in our lives but that the very roof over our heads was also at risk as the mortgage rates soared so did the repossessions and the evictions. We were two months in arrears with our mortgage due to the time I had been at the hospital and the subsequent weeks off I'd had after the funeral. We had letters from the Building Society regarding this and I had to make an appointment to see a someone from the Alliance and Leicester during the week, thus missing another days pay. When we got to the branch where our mortgage had been arranged, we found ourselves at the counter in front of a stone-faced woman who had no sympathy whatsoever for anyone 'criminal' enough to have been caught in arrears with their mortgage. People stood behind us in the queue and were quite clearly in earshot of the whole conversation.

"We've come about this," I said, passing the letter detailing our arrears to the hatchet face in front of me. She looked at the letter in much the same way as an executioner would have looked upon a death warrant.

"Is there any chance we could see someone in private about this matter, as the circumstances are quite delicate to discuss here," I said, hoping that some favour might be granted.

"I'm afraid that's not possible as all our interview rooms are being decorated. Whatever you have to say you'll have to say it here," she said unflinchingly.

"I would really prefer to discuss this in private." I protested. But to no avail.

"As I have already explained," she now said with the air of the most strictest, frigid school headmistress you could ever imagine,

"We haven't any rooms for you to see anybody in. You can always come back another day when there are, but even then we can't guarantee that one would be free. So whatever you have to say, you will have to decide whether to say it here now, or book another appointment," she added more forcefully this time.

I was stuck between a rock and a hard place. I didn't want to let a whole room full of perfect strangers know we were in straits with our mortgage in the circumstances we had been through, but on the other hand, I had taken the day off work specifically for this and could not afford it, and to take another day would sink me even further into the mire.

So we had little choice, we stayed. We both cringed with embarrassment as she read the contents aloud for all to hear.

"So, you said there were 'delicate' circumstances as to why you owe us money," she began, looking at me over the top of her glasses. There was little I could do; 'hatchet' face deserved it.

"Our daughter has just died and I've been off work through that; that's why we are behind with the payments. Do you want the keys now? Or would you rather accompany us back to the house to supervise our eviction personally?"

You could have sliced the air there with a knife, and then like spectators at Wimbledon, all eyes were now on hatchet face. She seemed momentarily stunned. Her lips formed a perfect imitation of a hen's arse and she began again.

"Well, quite obviously, the building society doesn't want to seem harsh in the face of such sad circumstances; would you be able to catch up if we increased your payments slightly?"

well what else could she say? By now she was hated by everyone present; I could nearly smell a lynching.

"Yes, I think we could manage that." I said in return.

I was also thinking, as maybe 'hatchet face' was, that the bad press that this, potentially, could generate might have had a bearing on the matter.

"Very well. I'll have a letter sent out to you for you to read and, if you agree, sign and send it back to us."

I was waiting for the smack of a gavel accompanied by the words 'case adjourned.' But she held herself in check; ah well! she could get to wear her black cap another day.

We left the place in a hurry, the atmosphere that prevailed in there made me feel ill. But at least we had some time now. We had evaded eviction that day, now I had to concentrate on work and try to keep what was left of the home we had around us.

We couldn't bear to throw any of Kaine's clothing or toys out and so the painful task of bagging and boxing everything up had to be done. This was tackled by both Karen and myself. We did this with a resigned air of sadness but it was necessary to do. I took the cot apart and with the boxes and bags put it in the loft for safe-keeping. Soon nothing physical of Kaine remained, only her photographs that we had taken and framed; some were professional, others just snapshots that were particularly good and so were framed as well.

And so with everything put away in the loft out of sight, we waited for the dust to settle and got on with what was left of our lives; the future was altered somewhat now by the absence of Kaine. What would we do? It was too soon to ask the question or plan anything; in truth we hadn't got the answers. The future to me seemed like a beast one prodded gently with a stick aware that it could either devour you or lick your face tenderly. Who could know? But I can look back now and say for certain that something changed in me the day Kaine died. I wasn't aware of it then but the desire to express my feelings as I'm doing now has always been there since then, I just didn't know how to do it.….

CHAPTER 23.

The second Christmas.

"It's not flowers, but presents she should be getting."

Christmas that year had a bitter sweet flavour to it. We bought a special wreath for Kaine to lay on her grave. Others laid flowers. I remarked to my grandmother how nice they looked, and she summed it up in the no nonsense Cork accent I had known all my life, with the words; 'it's not flowers, but presents she should be getting on this day.' She always had a way with words; maybe it was because we didn't live all that far from Blarney Castle with its legendary Blarney Stone, who knows; but she was right. Kaine should have been getting the presents we had planned to buy for her.

Over the holidays, I invited an old mate of mine for a drink, none other than Nobby; we had a good old knees up, and reminisced over our crazy days at the market of which he of course, was still a part of. For myself, however, I was happy as I was, and where I was, and I had no intentions of stepping back behind a butcher's counter again. Still it was good to see him, and hear about all the goings on at my former place of work, and I was glad that Alan was still doing well and also Paul with the two shops they now had.

Things were up and down in the construction industry for a while and occasionally the thought entered my head where I was beginning to regret not taking the managers job that Alan had offered me; at least it would have been stable and the money consistent, but I loved the out door life of construction. There was a benefit, if it could be called that; having the worry of finding decent consistent work meant that I didn't have a lot of time left over to dwell on our loss of Kaine. We went to the church without fail every single week and changed the flowers in the vases every Sunday. Other plots were being opened and filled as the time went by, and I noticed one weekend that a young woman was tending to a freshly-laid grave not too far from where Kaine was. It transpired that she had lost two children of differing ages for different reasons, unknown to anybody but her. To lose one was bad enough, but two was, well, beyond comprehension to me. And I thought back to the questions I had for God on the day I would meet him. And so life continued for us. The child we had had was no longer with us, and we were too frightened to try again in case anything went wrong. We continued, instead, to work and to pay the bills until the acute pain of bereavement lessened somewhat, and time did its best to heal the wounds inflicted by the cruelty of chance. After Kaine had died we had attended the church services for weeks afterwards trying in some way to unravel the mystery of why God had decided that Kaine was better off with him than with us. That made no sense, and it didn't matter how many prayers were said and how many hymns were sung in there, no-one it seemed had got the answer to this most puzzling of enigmas, why would God give us the power to reproduce, and then take our child from us? Francesca said that it was a mystery and that we weren't supposed to know, which, really meant that it was she that didn't know. (applying logic to the situation,) If I had been going to a doctor with something wrong with me and he had told me, after years of looking, that he had no idea what was wrong or what the solution was, then my faith in him would be shaken. And so I stopped going to the church. But it didn't mean the end of my search for the truth though.

CHAPTER 24.
Memorial.

Just over a year had now passed since Kaine had died. It was around this time that we had to think about a more permanent memorial stone for Kaine. The work I had with was fairly consistent and Karen had left the chemists and returned to her old job at Coral bookmakers. Our combined wages enabled us to keep our heads above water, just. All our money was taken up with keeping the roof over our heads and we had very little spare to save for a decent memorial stone for Kaine. Help, though, for this, came in a surprising way. My being employed in the construction business as a self-employed contractor meant that a yearly set of accounts had to be submitted to the tax office for approval. My accountant sent me a letter telling me that I had a two thousand pounds tax rebate that year, and this was what we used to get the memorial stone for our daughter. We had a meeting at our house with the rep for the memorial company to decide on the design and the inscription to go on it. I had disliked the white marble stones as after time they tended to stain quite badly as this gave an appearance of neglect, and this we did not like. We settled on a black polished granite with kerbstones filled with white gravel and a central vase for flowers. It cost a little more than the money we had had from the tax rebate but this didn't matter it was the best we could do for Kaine and it was a beautiful memorial for our beautiful girl. The inscription we wanted to keep simple and to the point and so after discussion between Karen and myself, we decided on a teddy bear motif with the inscription;

Kaine Lawlor.
*26th April 1988 + 6th November 1989
Beloved daughter of Karen and Joe.
To all the world a baby,
To us the world.

There was nothing more to add to that. It said it all. A few weeks later the stone was laid. Karen and I stood looking at it in its entire splendour. It was perfect. But of course we knew it wasn't, how could it ever be? That was the last earthly thing we could do for Kaine. All that could be said had been said, and all that could be done had been done. Her memorial stone stood as a final silent reminder of the love lost and Kaine's brief life. As we walked away from the church that day our only thoughts were that we would return every week in order to clean the polished granite, and replace the flowers as they wilted.

As for us personally we resolved to live out the rest of our lives and never forget Kaine; my writing this book twenty-one years on from her birth is testimony to that. She never leaves my thoughts.

CHAPTER 25.
Good news and bad news.

Life regained its normality in the sense that work continued as did the daily problems life throws at you. These however were small fry to what we had been through but needed attention nonetheless. We resumed our social life with our friends and adjusted to being a married couple without children and a measure of happiness with each others love returned for Karen and I. We were given a little kitten who we named Brandy because of his colour, bless him; he was a lovely thing to look at, but alas completely stupid, as he was always getting into situations he couldn't get out of. No matter how many times I climbed the tree at the bottom of the garden to rescue him, a few days later he'd be back up there on the same branch, terrified of going higher and too scared to climb back down again. But it was no matter, we loved him anyway. The scrapes he constantly got himself into only served to endear him to me all the more. And besides, his presence was therapeutic, and he was company for Karen when I was away working.

It was early in nineteen-ninety one when Roy came to me on site one day and said. "How do you and Basha fancy a trip to Grimsby?"

"Don't sound too good Roy. Name of a town starting with 'grim' doesn't exactly inspire confidence that it's gonna be a nice place."

"Nah, Grimsby's all right, it only for a couple of weeks anyway."

"What doin'?"

"They've just built a big power station up there, your mate Darren's brother Chris has done the sheeting and there's some snagging to be done there."

"Oh right, just me and Basha?"

"No I'll be comin' too, you don't think I'd let you two idiots loose up there without supervision do ya?"

"S'pose not."

We were used to splitting up to cover different jobs by now, so I thought a couple of weeks in a different place would do for a break. We had been working at home for a few months now, and periodically getting away was a good thing; but not for too long though. Karen was well used to the routine of my work, as from when she was young she had known Roy to be away for periods of time working, and accepted that this was part of the life of a construction worker, as it was not always possible in our trade to work at home constantly.

Upon my arrival home that evening I broke the news. Kaine had been gone from us for some time now but I didn't think that Karen would relish the idea of being alone even for a short period of time.

"It's only for two weeks and I'll be back each Friday," I said to her.

"And besides, you got Brandy for company and you can always go to your mom's if you need to; the dog is there too." I added by way of reassurance.

"Well the cat's not much company; he spends most of his time stuck up that tree!" she said, smiling.

"Ha ha! I know maybe we should have called him Red instead of Brandy he is a ginger cat after all." I said referring to my old mate Red in the market.

"Well two weeks ain't so bad though is it?"

"No, then we got a spate of work around here according to Roy."

"Oh that's good, so you'll be home for a bit, I ain't felt myself lately; I think I'm coming down with something," Karen added.

"Well, just take things easy then," I said to her, not thinking too much of it. And so the following Monday morning I had a bag packed ready for my early pick up from Roy, we headed over to Basha's house in West Bromwich and from there headed east to pick up the M1 motorway to Grimsby. I myself was feeling better as time was the soothing balm it was said to be, and I had thrown myself into my new job with enthusiasm to try and forget the bad times I'd had. Karen also seemed happier now as she was working back with her old friends and this gave her support when I wasn't there.

We had two weeks there and the weather was improving steadily thereby lifting my mood even further, I felt I could start to enjoy my life once more now albeit saddened by Kaine's loss; but this was out of my control and comprehension, I was a small part in a big world and an even bigger cosmos. Who was I to question the order of things and how they went? It was just one of those things

I told myself, even though I didn't believe it deep down. And so I adopted a new philosophy, one ancient in origin but valid throughout the ages nonetheless. 'Let us eat and drink, for tomorrow we may die.'

We found ourselves frequenting the town's pubs and having a good laugh with the other contractors who were working on site with us, the money problems started to ease as the interest rates were forced back down again. We had work for now, but, there were no guarantees that it would last, so we took what came. I soon found that there was a lot more to be done at this job than we had previously thought, new drawings came in as alterations needed to be done to accommodate new machinery being fitted and moved. And so the original two week stay turned out to be twenty-two weeks. Not that I minded. The extended work gave added security and so I felt settled. We were away four nights and back every Friday to depart again early on the Monday.

One day we had finished work and we were having our dinner in the dining room when the landlady came in and called to me.

"Joe, you've got a telephone call from your wife."

"Okay, thanks, I'll come and take it now." I went into the hallway and shut the door so as to be out of earshot from the other guests there.

"Hello" I said.

"Hello, it's me."

"I know that silly, what's up? Is everything okay?" I asked. I wondered why it was that Karen was ringing me because I usually rang her around eight o' clock in the evening.

"Well yes, and no." she said and sounded a bit worried.

"What's the matter?" I was beginning to get worried now.

"Can Roy hear you?" she asked.

"No, he's in the dining room eating," I said, worried that something had happened to Pat.

"I don't know how you're goin' to tell him this, but they've been burgled."

"Oh no!" I said, "How's your mom?"

"She's a bit shook up; they've had all her jewellery and Nan's as well and it's really upset her; plus they've had his new portable telly, that's why she's asked me to call you to tell him in case he shouts at her."

"Well it's hardly her fault unless she left the front door open; she didn't did she?" I asked, fearing she actually had and was anticipating Roy's resulting wrath on the matter.

"No, 'course not; they got in through the back window by stripping the wood beading out and then removed the glass!"

"Okay, I'll tell him gently then so as not to upset him too much."

"Hold on, there's something else," she now said to me.

"What else?" I asked, thinking that we had been done over as well.

"You know I said I had been feeling a bit off."

"Yeah." I thought this was because I'd been working away a lot.

"Well I've been to the doctor's and......"

"And what?" I enquired, eager to know why she'd paused.

"I'm pregnant."

"Oh!" was all I could say.

"Oh? Is that it?"

"I'm a bit stunned."

Everything that had happened flashed through my mind once more.

"How do you feel?" Karen asked me.

"How do I feel? How do you feel more like?" I said, wondering how indeed we both felt about this news. We had exercised caution but not always, and this was the result.

"I feel okay, I'm happy."

"Well if you're happy then so am I."

"Are you sure Joe? We've been through a lot ain't we?"

"Yeah, I know, but so what? Kaine's gonna have a brother or sister by the sounds of it so what's wrong with that?" I said, adopting a positive manner now. And that's how I felt. I wanted children, so did Karen; it was only a matter of time before we tried again. It just so happened that nature told us that this was the 'again' that we had been unconsciously planning, and that was that.

"Good! I'm glad you feel like that." Karen said to me.

"Right I'd better give Roy the bad news about the break in and our good news as well."

"Okay, will you call me later?"

"Yes of course I will, I am pleased and I love you."

"Love you too, speak later," she said, and rang off.

I returned to the dining room. My mind was pre-occupied more with my own news and expectant fatherhood again than telling Roy that somebody had made off with his telly in the conservatory and the family jewels.

My mind turned to Kaine, and a slight wave of sadness went through me; it was April, the month of her birth, and she would have been three years old by now. I wondered how she would've responded to a sibling, but for now I put my thoughts away for another time.

"Everything okay?" asked Roy, as I sat back down.

"Well, yes and no," I said wondering which bit of news to deliver first. I thought I'd use the age-old method of letting him choose.

"There's good news and bad news, which do you want first?" I asked him.

"I suppose I'd best have the bad news first."

"You've been burgled mate." I said, thinking just get it over with.

"What?!" he exclaimed, in obvious shock at this unpleasant happening.

"'Fraid so mate, they got in through the back window and took all Pat's jewellery and her mom's as well. She's a bit upset, that's why she asked Karen to ring me to let you know." I left the departure of the telly for Pat to tell him.

"What's the good news?" asked Basha.

"Karen's pregnant again."

"Fantastic! we got to go out and get drunk tonight at that sort of news, ha! ha!"

"We go out and get drunk anyway." I said, as was indeed the case most nights. So I was to be a dad again, my mind was in a whirlwind of thought. Karen was early in her pregnancy so we had months yet to plan and prepare for the event. But fear lurked in my mind; if anything were to happen again I wouldn't be able to cope, and neither would Karen, we would be devastated beyond repair. However I had to try and dispel those thoughts and let nature take its course now as new life once again grew inside her. I was excited that I was to be a dad for the second time in my life. I called Karen later on as I had promised. Also a little time had given me the chance to digest this bit of news. Obviously we were overly concerned now with her health arrangements, but apart from the usual checks and scans as the baby developed, there was little else to do but wait for the nine months to tick off and await our new arrival.

That April was to be the beginning of a tour around the country for me, we went on two more jobs and as luck would have it all three jobs that year were coastal locations. the spate of work we had at home was done by Wilf and the other lads, while Roy, Basha, and I did the away work. The remaining weeks we were to spend in Cleethorpes came to an end; the next job would take us even further from home, we were to head north of the border to Kirkcudbright in Scotland. The weather, though, was glorious, and on my return home Karen was suspicious that we had gone to Spain and not Scotland at all! Judging from my colour she could have been forgiven for thinking this. She was well along now with her pregnancy and when we went to the churchyard on the Sunday, as was now our habit, I wondered if Kaine could see what was happening and if she longed to be back with her mom and dad to share in the excitement of a brother or sister. That was a mystery I couldn't know though, but the mystery we could know was what we were to expect to have to buy colour-wise, for our unborn child. The miracle of the ultra-sound scan furnished the news; pink it was to be. Another little girl for us, not to replace Kaine though, for that could never be.

It was half-way through one week that Roy had a phone call asking him to go on another job on the south-west coast, near Bridgwater in Somerset. Roy chose me to go with him, and so I found myself, with him, saying farewell to the boys, and doing the marathon journey from Scotland to the West Country of England. The bonus was that we were to be given a holiday caravan on Brean Sands as our accommodation for the duration of the job. This was an unexpected bonus too for Karen the following week as she came to be with me along with her brother Lee, as the sea air would be good for her. While Roy and I were at work Karen took the car and with young Lee toured around the countryside or went to the beach. This was an advantage also for myself and Roy, when we got back after work Karen would have a meal ready for us.

We walked along the sands in the evenings in the coolness of the summer twilight discussing our new child growing steadily inside her and we spoke openly of Kaine, and about how we missed her and still grieved for her loss. This was tempered, though, by the excitement of our new child. We had settled on a name for her, she was to be Jordan; Kaine's first sister.....

CHAPTER 26.
Two quid and a mad bank manager.

At last the job ended there and as the autumn turned into the beginning of winter I found myself back in the West Midlands once more. November was nearly on us and Karen was heavy with her pregnancy now; she was due some time in late December or early January, and so it was getting close.

Work, however, resumed its roller coaster pattern as we entered a period of slackness once more. I always found this frustrating as one minute we were on our feet and the next knocked back to square one again struggling to pay the bills with a baby well on the way, and Christmas to cope with also.

My frustrations began to mount at my enforced idleness. I loved the building trade but it wasn't giving me the security I needed to make proper future plans, as you just never knew when a job might end of be put back or cancelled. I'd never had those fears in the market as we were always busy and food would never go out of

305

fashion, buildings could be put off, eating couldn't. I faced a dilemma. I considered going back to shop work as exactly that, going back that is; forward was my motto but I needed more security in my employment; how was I to achieve this? In construction I was a small cog in a big wheel where I had no control over events, decisions made by others in board rooms would result in either my employment or the opposite, as I was now experiencing first hand.

To return to work behind a counter was not for me as I was now conditioned to being self employed and felt I couldn't go back to any other way of life other than that. But I had to provide for my wife and expectant child.

One Saturday, when we were out shopping, I spotted a fishmongers trailer stall at Wednesbury market; it was then that it hit me, why not do the same with a butchers trailer stall? I would be my own boss and dictating my own future with my own business.

My mom was selling an old caravan which I bought from her for a hundred quid, that was where I would start. I sat up late one night and drew the plans for my tiny little empire, I knew enough about the building trade now to know my way around technical drawings and put together an impressive building schematic drawing of my trailer stall complete with refrigerated meat counter and work block and storage counters. So the business plan was thus. To build a mobile butchers stall up to environmental health standards put it on a market, buy my stock and sell, sell, sell! I knew I was good at that as I'd proved time and again working in the market. So I'd got the plan, got the caravan, I'd got the idea and the drive, only problem was I'd got no money!

The next morning I showed Karen what I'd been doing for half the night.

"That looks good," she said, yawning, as she put the kettle on.

"Good? Good? It's, bloody brilliant! I exclaimed full of the excitement a mad scientist might have at discovering anti-gravity boots or something.

"Okay, calm down, okay, it's really good then, have you decided how you're gonna pay for it?" she said, now bringing me to earth again with a thump.

"Ah well, I was gonna ask the bank for a loan to do it with."

"Joe, you've got two quid in your pocket, what bank manager in his right mind is gonna lend a bloke with two quid to his name thousands of pounds to build that?" she asked.

"Looks like I'm goin' to have to find one that's as mad as me then eh?" I replied, undeterred by Karen's negative feelings towards my brainchild. I was on fire now, this would work no doubt about it.

My first port of call was to the catering manufacturer's office where I spoke with the manager there. I explained my intentions and told him I needed a close estimate to build the counter and the storage tables and block for cutting I had also added in the requirement of a water heater and sink plus the stainless steel panels to cover the walls which were required for hygiene purposes. The man was sufficiently impressed with my drawings and took copies so as he could work out the cost of this. My next call was to the timber merchants. The whole structure was easiest made from wood, and covered with ply panelling painted white as this was the most cost effective way of

307

building it; the fixing materials I required for the rest would be acquired at work when I eventually returned, and this would complete my ensemble. A few days later I had a call from Middleton's with the costing of the counter and the rest of the equipment I needed. The counter was the most expense; that was two thousand pounds and the rest could be done do for six hundred quid. A total of just over two and a half grand. I'd estimated two thousand pounds for the building of the shell of the stall, so I had it. Four thousand six hundred pounds to build. Five grand with initial stock. I'd got two quid; I needed a mad bank manager!

I called my bank to make an appointment to see my manager there. I had no savings and no money in my current account. At least though, I wasn't overdrawn. My unbridled optimism was my only weapon along with my rolled up drawings as I went for my appointment on the following Saturday morning, dressed in my best suit and tie. Trying to look as business-like as possible and confident, I waited outside the office of the man who held my future in his hands. They were the bank that liked to say 'yes'; I was about to test that advertising boast to the limit.

Would you lend a guy with no money five grand because he's got a great idea? Even saying it to myself it sounded ridiculous. Ah well! I was here now anyway.

The door opened and I was asked to come inside by an older gentleman with greying hair. Not surprisingly he had a printout of the current status of my account in front of him. He looked at it, looked at me, and smiled.

"Well Mr. Lawlor, what is it that I can do for you this fine morning?" he asked.

"I've got a business idea I want to discuss with you." I said, feeling nervous, and convincing myself that he would burst out laughing at my bare-faced cheek for asking him for money with not a dime in my account. He remained serious but pleasantly so; he looked at my rolled up drawings and asked.

"Is that what you have in mind?"

"Yes sir it is, allow me to show you." I said.

"Certainly." he responded. I then spread my efforts before him. I figured that I'd gauge his reaction by the look on his face when he saw what I had in mind.

"Hmm, that's very impressive, have you drawn them yourself or had them done professionally?"

"I've done them myself." I said. He pondered my drawings and read the attached business plan I had written out explaining what my intentions were, and how this creation of my mind would come to fruition and make a profit.

"Well I'm a bit confused, perhaps you could enlighten me?" he now asked. I was wondering what was coming next.

"This is clearly a set of detailed schematics, as you've indicated, for a mobile butchers stall; according to your business plan you are the butcher and this will be your business, is that correct?" he asked whilst holding the drawings with my written plan and looking intently at them.

"Yes sir that's correct. Why may I ask?"

"Well, if you're a butcher, how on earth did you happen to get the know-how to draw technical drawings to this standard? And I see here in your plan you've said that, to keep costs to the minimum, you would undertake the construction of the project yourself. Forgive me Mr. Lawlor, but we deal with many butchers and many builders and ne'er the twain ever meet. So are you a butcher or a builder?"

It was a fair question, I hadn't really thought that it would be an issue, but I was able to furnish him with the answer. He seemed quite impressed with the fact that I was able to do both the trade of a butcher and have the necessary skills to build the stall. But there remained the small detail that I had not a groat to my name so to speak.

"Hmm, your account does not reflect your abilities by the looks of things, but I see here in the past you were a steady saver."

"The building trade has been up and down, as you can see from my account; that's why I put my plan together to fix what seems to be a recurring problem." I said.

"Yes, I see what you mean," he said to me without looking up from my drawings.

"Right, I'll take this under consideration and write to you and let you know." We shook hands and asked me to wait while he too copied my drawings for what I assumed was further perusal.

I felt totally drained on leaving his office. I had no idea how my idea would end up in his considerations. The optimist in me kept telling me he'd be mad not to lend me the money, and the pessimist couldn't speak for laughing at the thought!

When I arrived home Karen was eager to find out how I'd got on. I told her that he was considering my plan and that he would write and let me know. At this news she was surprised as she had honestly thought that

I was going to be flatly refused there and then; it was still possible however that could well turn out to be the case. But I would have to wait and see.

I put all those thoughts from my mind and got on with the rest of the weekend as there was little else I could do now but wait for the letter from the bank.

Monday morning saw me off to work with Wilf and the boys in the van.

The week went by at the normal pace until Thursday morning when I got a message from the site office to phone home; my initial thoughts were that Karen had gone into labour early and I was panicking a bit, but that wasn't the case.

"It's me, is everything alright? What's the matter?" I asked her on ringing home.

"Nothing, you've had a letter off the bank."

"What's it say?" I asked, excitement now mounting.

"I'll open it then shall I?"

"Yeah yeah, hurry up!" I was desperate to hear my fate.

"Dear Mr. Lawlor," she began,

"With regards to your recent appointment with me to discuss your business loan, there are a few items we need to clarify with you before a final decision can be made. An appointment has been made for you on Friday morning this week at ten am. If this is inconvenient could you please ring me to arrange another time. If I do not hear from you I will assume that the original date and time is acceptable and look forward to meeting you again very soon."

"Wha hoo, YES!" I shouted, nearly deafening Karen in the process.

"What you getting excited for? It doesn't say you got it"

"It don't say I ain't neither does it?" This was one step closer to realising my plan for my own little business; dare I think that I would indeed clinch the deal? I would find out early the next day.

The next day I was at the bank early again for my appointment. I was suited and booted and hardly able to believe that my scheme warranted a second look by the bank. Nonetheless I was prepared for what the out come might be.

"Hello Mr. Lawlor, nice to see you again, please sit down," the manager said to me.

"Now then, we hear many, many ideas for businesses here at the bank, and only the ones that make good sense make it to a second interview."

I could feel my stomach tightening in anticipation now.

"I appreciate that sir." I said, trying to keep calm.

"If we lent you the money, how long do you anticipate before you can build it and get it running?"

"No later than February next year."

"Hmm, and what sort of turnover are you expecting to make and what percentage would you hope to make in profit?" he enquired further of me.

"Well, I would hope to do three grand a week with a clear profit of twenty nine per cent which is the average but this can fluctuate upwards or down according to the market I'm on and time of year." I said, relying on my previous experiences with my own counter in the Market Hall in Birmingham.

He thought for a while now, looking again at the drawings I had furnished for his appraisal. I hardly dared to breathe, wondering what his decision might be. After what had seemed like an eternity to me, he said,

"Very well, we'll lend you the money Mr. Lawlor, terms to be agreed with you and us…..blah blah blah."

I didn't hear anything after that; as I was stunned to have done it. It took all my self control to stop me from jumping on his desk, kissing him on both cheeks, and punching the air in triumph! I waited while the paperwork for my loan was being drafted, thinking of a future where I was going to be my own boss with a business that could keep us secure at last, I felt so proud of this achievement and couldn't wait to tell Karen. By the time I'd got out of the bank I was on cloud nine, my mind was racing ahead at a thousand miles an hour. All the plans that had kept me awake for the past few weeks would now have to be implemented. But first I was going for a pint to celebrate!

By the time I got home I was fit to burst with my news.

"Well, what happened?" asked Karen.

"I got it!" I said, unable to keep my excitement under control any longer.

"You're kiddin' me!" she said in disbelief.

"Nope. I aint kidding, better watch out cos there aint no stoppin' me now." I said to her, overjoyed that I was going to be the designer of my own future from now on.

Karen was pleased that I'd achieved my goal but for her, her priority was the growing bump once again making an impact on her body and on our lives once more. As for me, I was also eagerly anticipating Jordan's arrival as well, but now I also anticipated bring my child up with a comfortable life fashioned by the business I intended to build up from this little acorn. The date we had been given for Jordan's arrival was hovering very close to the Christmas festivities and we wondered whether we might have a joint Christmas present in the shape of a baby girl on the twenty-fifth of December.

This was as yet though a future not realised and I for my part wasted no time when the funds were in my account from the bank in putting my plan together. I soon got to work building the trailer with the help of one of the lads who drank in the 'Scaffolders Arms' (the Vic), his name was Anton Phipps, he was a carpenter by trade and a good one at that; we worked every weekend on the project and I enjoyed every minute of it.

As I was busy doing that, Karen was busy being very pregnant. We entered the month of December in 1991 and knew that very soon now the child we had lost was to have a little sister. I had little time to worry. As to the actual birth and the health issues surrounding that; as it was very early after Kaine was born that she had contracted meningitis, most likely at the hospital, I had my suspicions that she had contracted the disease at the moment she was born, when the mid-wife had cut her head in the process of delivering her. It didn't mean to say that I hadn't thought of these things, it might be fairer to say that I was frightened to contemplate them very much as I hoped that Jordan's arrival in the world would have none of the fraught difficulties and the fatal consequences that Kaine's birth had had.

The month went by very quickly as December tends to do with the preparations for Christmas taking precedence over everything else. We went to Karen's mom's house for our dinner as we always had done, and this year we were expecting at any moment to rush off to the hospital with Karen being in the condition that she was. However that didn't happen; as we enjoyed our Christmas dinner, our little bundle decided to stay put.

The next day Karen and I were at home, preparing Boxing Day lunch not thinking that anything out of the ordinary would happen, as we had felt sure that if anything was going to occur then it would be on the twenty-fifth. We sat down to dinner when Karen suddenly looked at me and said,

"Oh, I think it's time to go to the hospital," thereby spoiling what looked like a very nice dinner.

Three hours or so later and Jordan Emily Catherine Lawlor entered the world on the afternoon of the twenty-sixth of December 1991. I've often teased her since about her ruining my Boxing Day lunch and how I never got to eat it because she, selfishly, decided to be born. It didn't matter, and all that concerned both her mom and I was that she was healthy; and she was. We couldn't help but keep a close eye on her though over the coming weeks as we were terrified that something might happen to her the same as had occurred with her sister. Thankfully nothing of the sort happened, and Jordan remained a healthy baby, nursing at her mother's breast and feeling content with her new life.

So Jordan was with us now, I continued to work and pay the loan to the bank on a monthly basis; on the weekends myself and Anton worked on the trailer. We had a relatively busy period of work early in 1992, apart from a short spell, during which I had work I did with my brother Michael laying the ducting for cable T.V. all over Birmingham. I was in the Longbridge car plant for a while in the late January and February, and then we had two jobs in succession very close to home. One was on Strawberry Lane industrial estate, this was to be a significant development in my future and my business but

I didn't know it yet, and I will get to it later; the other job was an ambitious project to erect a brand new factory over the existing factory near Cannock.

By now though, the trailer was complete, and stood resplendent as the newly named 'Butchers Joint' ready for my business adventure into the unknown. I was still waiting for the refrigerated counter to be completed, as this was a rather intricate piece of equipment to build, and so I had to wait for the phone call from Middleton's to let me know when to bring the trailer in to be fitted with all the new equipment I'd ordered for it.

I busied myself with buying the other bits and pieces of equipment I would need in preparation for the grand opening. As to the actual market I had in mind well, Willenhall was the nearest to my house. It wasn't a hugely busy town and had a number of butchers already trading in the town centre, but I was confident that my experience would see me through when it came to market work. In the meantime little Jordan was coming along and growing steadily, she was a little 'cranky' at night but in the event she turned out to be a 'cranky' teenager so I figured you can't do much about your personality! I was as pleased as her mom was that she remained healthy though. I got Kaine's cot back down from the loft and re-erected it in our bedroom for her; we also went through Kaine's clothes that we had put away for Jordan but as we decided that she looked too much like her sister in these so we chose instead to buy new for her.

We now felt it was time that we could let go of just that little bit of Kaine and took her clothes to one of the charity shops in the area; we kept some of the items that we particularly liked, though, for sentimental reasons.

The time also had arrived for the fitting out of my trailer; I felt excitement at the prospect of starting my very own business at last, but not without a certain nervousness accompanying it as well, as this was the first time I'd ever set out on my own. Plus I'd got a wife, a new child and a house to keep.

When the trailer was returned to me, the pride I felt in seeing the representation of my mind's eye in its physical form was abundant. I felt a huge satisfaction for what I had accomplished so far. But that, as it turned out, was, so far, the easy bit of the game.

Everything was in readiness now to start. I was two months behind with my own schedule for a start date which I'd indicated to the bank. This was mainly down to the building of the counter and my work commitments still with Roy, but the beauty was, that as long as I made the loan payments, which were easy to manage due to the increased work we had had, then that at least was no problem. My real problems started when I had to tackle the world of beaurocracy in the council. I applied for a trader's licence and a health and hygiene certificate which was granted without a problem as the trailer stood head and shoulders above anything else of the time, as even the fishmonger's stalls on the open-air market relied on a table with ice to keep the stock fresh. The real problems were the ridged rules to which the council officials swore an undying oath.

"I'm afraid we can't let you put your stall on the market in Willenhall or Walsall as it doesn't fit the description of a traditional market stall," I was told by the official inspecting my brainchild.

"That's the whole point, if it were a traditional stall I couldn't trade in meat as I'd need a constant temperature to keep the produce cool and fresh and washable non-porous surfaces and storage. That's what the health people of the council have written in their guidelines for the selling of fresh meat on the open air markets," I said in disbelief and protest at this unbending attitude of the council official.

"That's as it may be Mr. Lawlor, but I'm afraid if your stall doesn't look like a traditional market stall, then I'm afraid I can't let you stand it on one of our markets, even if the interior meets the stringent needs of the council's requirements to sell fresh meat." So here it was, beaurocracy at its tail-chasing best; one office saying one thing and the other office saying something entirely different; and here I was right in the middle of it with a five grand state of the art fully refrigerated fresh meat stall and nowhere to stand it.

It was no wonder we were in recession I thought. I was not going to be beaten by petty politics though. I used to drink in The Royal George pub in Willenhall on occasion; the pub itself is situated right by the main bus stop at the very start of the market and so in the ideal position to catch the shoppers as they entered the market thoroughfare. The car park of the pub was right on the doorstep of the market itself so I had the idea that if I parked on there, then for all intents and purposes I was on the market but the council officials couldn't touch me. I had a street trader's licence and a health and hygiene certificate from the very council that were now preventing me from trading on their market, so I was untouchable to officialdom. The pub was privately owned and I struck a deal with John the landlady's son who ran it, and that was that. On the following Wednesday morning, which was market day, the 'Butcher's Joint' opened for business for the first time.

I attracted a lot of attention, and, as I anticipated, the crowds exiting at the bus stop to go shopping were easy to attract and sell to as the years of practice I had in Alan's shop had honed in me. I'd lost none of my edge as I sold tray after tray of meat in the opening hours of my first day.

Karen had phoned the local paper the Express and Star, and a photographer turned up and took my picture; the result of that was a piece in the paper that evening, telling the story of how a local man had turned a caravan into a mobile butchers shop and was beating the recession. All good publicity. The council fumed but could do nothing about it for now. Karen came down to see how I was getting on and with Jordan sleeping peacefully in her pushchair it reminded me of the reason I was doing what I was now doing. The first day ended in success, I had Friday and Saturday to prepare for and was now buzzing with excitement. The other butchers in the town were understandably none too happy at this latest hotshot turning up and diluting even further now the limited trade that was available in the town. I was, however, a skilled market salesman and I regarded that as my advantage; people bought for two reasons quality, and price. I had low overheads and could deliver on both counts, and I had the experience to sell like no-one else was doing in the town.

It wasn't long before a barrage of complaints arrived from the other butchers in the town to stop me trading as in the following weeks I was cleaning up on the market days and was looking to find another market to try and get onto on Monday, Tuesday and Thursday. Officialdom complained to John who had allowed me on his car park but as he had said, it was his car park and he could allow who he liked on there; we were breaking no council bye laws and they knew it. The pressure was on however and it amazed me how the inflexible council was bendy enough to look back in time and discover that they had, some years before, given the George a grant to re-surface the very car park I now stood on. They threatened John that they would ask for the money back if he didn't stop me from trading off his property immediately. And that was that, I couldn't blame John, he faced a hefty bill from the council and so I was out of business. For now....

CHAPTER 27.

"Daddy, why is the sky all scratched?"

I felt very put out by this unexpected turn of events; I couldn't believe the lengths the council had gone to in order to placate the other meat traders in the town centre. It was futile to complain though, faceless beaurocracy hides itself well and it seemed it had conspired to remove the wheels from my wagon or trailer to be more accurate, and achieved what they'd set out to do. I searched in vain to put my trailer onto other markets but they were either already occupied by another meat trader or were asking for extortionate rents for the stand. I was in a bit of a dilemma; I had the business loan to maintain now, and no means to do it.

Thankfully Roy was still busy and I had work to return to and so I could still keep myself afloat; but paying for a business that wasn't operational was no good and so I felt a little down and out at the failure to make a success of my dreams. At least I had the cold comfort of knowing that it was not my own doing that had put me in this position, only that of the narrow minds in the council offices, and so it was my turn to fume.… But only for a while. I was fortunate enough to have a large parking facility where we lived and so I put the trailer away and wondered what to do with it. I could have advertised it and sold it and more than covered the money I actually owed on it; I even thought of building more of them to sell at a profit but that was something I kept in store now as a back-up plan for if I found myself out of work again.

Six months went by and little Jordan Lawlor was getting bigger, our lives remained as normal as anyone else's with a young child and in Jordan, the pain we once had when Kaine died was eased. As the time passed, the fears we had of her contracting any disease such as the feared meningitis faded from our minds but we were always on our guard in case anything went wrong with her health; fortunately the only things to come her way were the usual childhood ailments such as chicken pox and a few sniffles; and that was all.

One Saturday again I went for a drive by myself and went past the site on Strawberry Lane where we had previously done one of the construction jobs in the year before. That one was the closest job we'd had to my front door as it was only three miles from my house. One morning I had actually walked to work, this was indeed a contrast to the other jobs I had been doing all over the country. That industrial estate had been a big one with quite a few businesses on there, however the recession had taken its toll since then and quite a few had shut down. But now they were opening back up again as the fortunes of the economy were once again revived. While I was actually working on Strawberry Lane, there was a corner of the estate where a guy had set up a little caravan and had sold sandwiches to us and the factory workers in the area. We used to watch as he hitched up his caravan every day at two o' clock, and with a cheery wave to us working on the roof in the hot sun, he'd be off. I remember one of the lads saying to me one day.

"Now that's the kind of job I'd like; finished every day for two, in the pub for half past!" It didn't take much to put two and two together; that guy no longer traded there anymore, probably due to all the factory closures, but that trend was reversing itself now as things improved.

I drove back home and opened up the trailer that had been sitting there doing nothing from the time the council had shut me down six months earlier. My mind was ticking over and the plastic nylon cutting block was removable, the space left was just the right size to fit a gas hob connected up to a cylinder for fuel. A flue fitted in the roof would take the heat of the cooker safely away, and that was all I needed to do to put my trailer back in business. Instead of selling meat as a market trader, the 'Butchers Joint' was to be converted into the 'Pit Stop Café' I already had my street trader's licence the refrigerated counter was ideal for cans of cold drinks and cold sandwiches, and everything else fitted the bill perfectly. I spoke to my mate Nigel Lowe, who used to be a chef, and had, in the years previous, ran his own snack bar on the same estate and had done very well out of it until he had the notion to sell up and go around the world 'searching for himself'. We used to joke that all he had to do was look in the mirror and there he'd be, but that was Nigel for you.

"What d'ya think?" I asked him on explaining my plans for the trailer.

"Great, go for it; I've still got me chef whites, you can 'ave em if you like."

"Thanks mate, they'll look good from the hygiene point of view." I always knew that people were fussy about certain things and that food was top of the list when it came down to hygiene and preparation. I also had the added advantage of being in the building trade and knowing what to look for in the perfect sandwich. If you got that formulae correct you were onto a sure-fire winner. And we were. I quickly got to work and converted the former butcher shop into a state- of- the- art mobile kitchen; the gas hob replaced the block and I fitted the flue to the roof of the trailer and we were ready for business, and so in the closing months of 1992 the 'Pit Stop Café' was born. Karen and her mom Pat ran it to begin with while I continued to work with Roy; they took thirty-two quid on the first day, small beginnings of a business that would soon grow to take almost two thousand pounds a week four years later.

We went from strength to strength as the added convenience of a mobile phone for orders swelled our takings and put us under severe pressure to cope with the amount of people falling for the 'formula one' gut-busting sandwich; which was basically a full English breakfast between two thick slices of crusty bread. The hungry factory workers couldn't get enough though and I was eager to satisfy their demands.

Jordan was growing now and while we were at work with the café, she went to a private nursery in the town called 'The Wonder Years'. The lady who owned the business had also had the same tragic experience as we had, of losing her only daughter but due to cancer; it was she, (before she died) who had suggested to her mom the name for the nursery because, as she put it, the early years of a child's life are full of wonder and so this was what she had called it when she opened; sadly, after her daughter had passed away.

I liked that she had called it 'The Wonder Years' and it was particularly poignant that it had been her daughter's suggestion to call it by that name. We shared a common event, tragic for us both, and wished each other well at getting through it. Jordan attended there until she was eligible to go to school and it was evident that she enjoyed the company of the other children there at the time.

Business was booming and our daughter was growing into a healthy young child. I used to sit her on the counter of the trailer with a Wagon Wheel chocolate biscuit to munch on while I cleaned up after a busy day and she would ask me loads of questions as young children are prone to do. I cottoned on very quickly that the best thing to do when faced with the never-ending barrage of questions ranging on anything that caught young eyes, was to answer as honestly as I could as the standard 'it just is' answer didn't satisfy Jordan's insatiable curiosity. However one question she levelled at me defied all reasoning until I realised what she meant.

"Daddy, why is the sky all scratched?" she asked one day, whilst looking up at the clear blue sky.

"But the sky isn't scratched," I answered, wondering what she meant.

"It is though," she insisted. And I looked again at what she meant. It was then that I noticed what had caught her attention; she was looking at the vapour trails left from the jet engines of the passenger aircraft that flew at high altitudes.

"Oh, I see what you mean; those are left over from when an airplane flies very high in the air." I said, pleased that I could offer an explanation for her question.

"So it's the airplanes that scratch the sky then," she reasoned.

"Yes darling, it's the airplanes that scratch the sky." I loved her dearly and she was so special to me after the pain of losing her sister.

The 'Pit Stop Café' continued to be a flourishing little business for the next four years which meant that Jordan remained an only child for the time being. Karen, however, wanted to have more children, and was finding the strain of running a very busy business and looking after another child very tiring. In spite of that, we knew that the only way to have any more kids was for her to give up full time work and become a 'stay at home' mom. I had ambitions for the 'Pit Stop' as I eventually wanted to go from street trading to owning our own café in bricks and mortar. Further into the future, I had my sights set on a restaurant; my brother Michael had, in his other life, been a chef at the Grand Hotel in Birmingham city centre and my sister Marie had been a waitress and the idea of a nice family business was forming in my mind; if they were willing to work with their big brother in his projects of the future. My good mate Nigel, as I have said, had also been a chef and had helped me out many times at the café to cover at different times but had no interest at all in going back to catering full time, and so that was him out of the picture as a replacement for Karen.

"You could always sell it," Nigel said to me one night we were out having a pint together.

"And do what?" I asked. "I earn good money from my business and I ain't keen on working for anybody else but me."

"Yeah, but if you get rid of it you wouldn't 'ave the problem of trying to juggle a life and a business all together."

"I know that but I'm still gonna have to earn a living."

"You know Jon Legge, don't you?"

"Not well, but yeah, what about him?" I asked, curious as to why he had mentioned him.

"Well, his mother told me he's looking for a good salesman as he's just been promoted at work and needs to build a team."

"He works for BUPA don't he?" I asked.

"Yeah; she reckons the money is fantastic. He heard about you flogging meat in the town and worrying all the butchers so much that they got together and had you closed that time, and he was asking what you were up to."

"There's a big difference flogging meat and sellin' medical insurance though mate."

"You can sell anything though, you know what you're like," Nigel now said to me.

"I dunno, I'll 'ave a think about it. I know Karen's getting really fed up though and is pushing me to do something about the situation 'cos she really wants another kid." I didn't think much more of it until a few days later when my mobile phone rang. It was Jon Legge on the other end of the line.

"It's Jon Legge mate, how you doin' Joe? Nige' gave me mom your number, I hope you don't mind me ringing you?" he asked.

"No, not at all Jon, what can I do for you mate?" The conversation I'd had with Nigel the previous few nights before came back to me.

"Well I don't know if you are aware but I've just been promoted at work and I'm looking to build a sales team around me, and Nige' reckons you're a man that I should have a word with about that."

"Well I'm very flattered mate that you thought of me, but I don't know anything about healthcare insurance."

"Joe, you'd be trained to do all that, and listen, the money is phenomenal, I kid you not. Can I pop around and see you one of the nights and I can explain more to you face-to-face? That would be better, eh?" he asked, and we arranged for him to come and see me one of the nights later on that week. I would have to talk to Karen about this, there was a lot to consider, I had my own business and a successful one at that, I was my own boss and that meant a lot to me, but the least I could do now was to give Jon a hearing as to what he had on offer. He drove a very nice car and was obviously doing well, he was always suited and booted and seemed happy and content; but Jon was first and foremost a salesman. I'd have done well to have kept that fact in mind.

It was a few nights later when Jon came to see me. I'd discussed the whole thing with Karen by then and she was keen for me to find out more about the offer that he had in mind. I'd told her that the only way I would give up the business was if the alternative occupation gave me more money or better prospects; preferably both would be the ideal scenario. I still knew next to nothing about BUPA but I admit that the thought of a nice clean job in a suit instead of catering whites and smelling of cooked bacon and sausage at the end of the day was starting to appeal to me. Jon arrived at eight on the dot suited and booted as ever and as cheerful as a day in May.

"How are you Joe?" he asked as he thrust out his hand to shake mine.

"I'm fine thanks Jon, come in and sit yourself down."

"So Nige' was saying you weren't happy with your business any more?" he asked of me whilst getting comfortable on the settee.

"No that's not strictly true Jon. I'm happy enough with the business, it's the circumstances it's causing for me and Karen that I'm looking to change." I said.

"Oh right, in what way?" he asked me.

"Well we're really busy and it's really taking over our lives. We want to expand the family but we've got no chance as we are right now, so if there's a better offer out there that can allow Karen to stay home and we can do as we planned, then I'm listening."

"Well, I'll tell you now Joe, you'll have a lot more time on your hands if you come and work for me."

"Jon that could be a problem, because I'm very much used to working for myself now and I don't think I'd be happy in a situation where I was being told what to do again."

"The position I'm offering you Joe is self-employed, you'd be running your own show. I'm just there to collate figures and offer assistance when needed, if needed that is. I got guys on my team that I don't see from the beginning of the month to the end; they just fax their figures over to me."

"Sounds interesting mate, what's the salary like?"

I was more intrigued by the self-employed aspect and that I wouldn't be tied to a desk in an office somewhere.

"Fifty to sixty grand a year is no problem Joe for a good advisor, and from what I've heard about you that ain't a problem. Nige' told me you frightened all the butchers in Willenhall to death a few years ago when you first set up."

"Well, they weren't pleased to see me; they were happier to see the back of me that's for sure."

"Ha! ha! I'd love to have been there when you showed up."

"That money you just mentioned, is that straight up?" I asked, not daring to believe it.

"Absolutely Joe, listen I can take you over to the offices in Birmingham one of the days and you can have a chat with the guys and see what kind of set up we have running there. If that impresses you then we can talk more, I'd give you a job tomorrow, I'd love to have you on board mate." The evening ended with my arranging with Jon to go to his offices in Birmingham a few days later. The only problem I could foresee, if everything worked out, was what would we do with the business? I would cross that bridge when I came to it, but for now I had to concentrate on the next few days in front of me and what my future, and this unexpected offer, might bring.

I went to Jon's offices in Birmingham; ironically enough these were only a mile or so from Birmingham's Children's Hospital where Kaine had been. I tried not to think about this as I drove past but it was impossible not to do so. Following Jon's directions I made my way into the impressive building that housed BUPA's offices. Jon met me in the foyer of the building. I had taken the precaution of going suited and booted myself so as not to look too much out of place. Jon behaved impeccably as always, and put me at my ease with these very unfamiliar surroundings.

"How you feeling?" he asked.

"I must confess I feel a little nervous Jon." I said.

"Don't be, you're among friends."

"I only know you though mate."

"That's all you need to know though Joe, ha! ha!"

"Okay then, I'm here, so what's the deal with this BUPA thing then Jon?" I asked, being keen to find out why I should give up a busy, highly profitable business and don a suit every day for ever more.

"Well, going off our conversation the other night and what you were saying it appears to me that you want a job that has stability and is obviously profitable, but also you need time to be with your family," he said.

"Yes that's pretty much it, but there remains the problem that I know absolutely didly squat about the health business." I said.

"Joe it's a product just like anything else, if you can sell then you can sell anything, it doesn't matter what it is. You can be trained to do the job, our training is excellent and BUPA will look after you in that respect."

"Okay, I can see what you mean about it being a product and to be fair to myself I do know how to sell, but only if a product is viable, and private healthcare costs money, where-as the NHS is free; that's some serious competition you got going on there, Jon."

"All our market indications are that we can compete with the NHS with the business private sector Joe. We got directors on waiting lists to be seen who can't afford to be off work with anything for too long; think about your own case, if something were to happen to you and you were off work for any length of time waiting for a hospital appointment, how would your business do without you at the helm?"

"Hmm, that makes more sense to me to be honest Jon, yeah you've got a point." And he had, my own experiences with my business led me to the conclusion that if I needed a product like that, then I would be just the man to sell it to me. Jon sold me the job, but ultimately it was my decision. I must admit, though, that the surroundings swayed me as well; a nice fluffy office and a suit with a PhD in style was an attractive proposition after all the years of manual work. If the salary was equal to the rest of the deal then I was thinking that I would make more money, be free of a business that, although I loved, was tying me down somewhat, and give Karen and I the freedom also of expanding our family. I'd always wanted kids plural; having been raised as an only child by my Nan in Ireland due to family circumstances, fostered in me a desire to have a family of my own around me.

"Lets go meet some of my team and have a chat with them and see how they're doing, it might give you a bit more food for thought." Jon introduced me to a few of his lads on his team. They were friendly enough men but not the kind I was used to dealing with in my everyday business of selling sandwiches to the starving; as the factory, construction workers, and, not forgetting to mention, lorry drivers who were my customers all invariably introduced themselves as being on arriving at my counter. They seemed happy enough though and appeared to be doing well for themselves, so maybe it was time yet again for another change; one of progression I hoped. I had never seen myself as a suit and the prospect was quite daunting to me, but what's the difference? A suit contains a human being and it's the human being that makes the difference not what he's wearing. It also struck me that if Karen and I had had healthcare cover when Kaine had become ill in those crucial early days when all the difference could have been made by an early diagnosis of meningitis, then Kaine might have survived and our tragic past could have been averted. Maybe there was an opportunity in this offer to do some good, I certainly had the experience of the bad. I told Jon that if it was okay, that I'd need to discuss this some more with Karen and ring him and let him know what I would decide to do. This was not a problem and Jon shook hands with me as I departed the building, promising to ring him in a few days.

I certainly had a lot to think about. The conversation we had had about the salary revealed that it was commission based, with the potential to earn a hell of a lot of money. It also had its pitfalls and I was to find out later about those. It was a chance but I wasn't afraid to take chances. If it worked then I'd be better off than ever. If it failed though, well then I would have to start again…..

CHAPTER 28.

"Hello BUPA, good-bye Strawberry Lane."

Karen and I talked it over. We were concerned that Jordan was in need of attention as she was getting older and that was a factor but not the only reason that I decided to take Jon up on this opportunity. I had a gut feeling that I was doing the wrong thing, and if I've learned anything over the years it's this; your brain may work it all out and it may seem very logical, and the right thing to do; but never, ever, ignore your gut. With that in mind I made what was possibly the worst decision of my life; it was my decision though, and I'll take responsibility for it. We decided to sell the Pit Stop Café and I was to embark on being a suit for the first time in my life. Also, for the first time in my life, I learned that appearances can be deceptive as I witnessed, first-hand. The genial pleasant façade I had met with my new colleagues at BUPA'S offices was simply that, a façade.

I did my training with BUPA and 'hit the road running' as the saying goes. I made sales for the four months I spent there but in that time I also saw how the men in suits were stressed out beyond belief as the burden of their extravagant life-styles took its toll. It soon transpired that the commission- based pay deal was a house built on sand that could shift at any given time and make you penniless at a stroke. I witnessed more than one physical fight in the office involving men who obviously were feeling the strain of sales work. It struck me that in all the shops and building sites I'd worked in and on, I had never witnessed anything as vicious as the day when one of the guys snapped and literally tore his colleague's shirt off him. This was unsettling. But I didn't blame my mate Jon for this, he genuinely thought he could help when he offered me a job there. but as I know from my past, decisions made in boardrooms can have far reaching consequences for the people whose lives they affect. And some genius came up with the idea that we were only to sell the most expensive BUPA policy and nothing else, and that made a life as a BUPA suit untenable for me.

As ever plan B had to be implemented. I could see the writing on the wall. After my first month at BUPA, I knew I'd made a terrible mistake. This was a rat race and no doubt. I wanted no part and so set out an exit strategy for myself.

I still had my building experience to draw on and with that in mind I approached one of the guys, who coincidentally, had been in the same trade as me, which of course was roofing and cladding. I suggested that we form a partnership together as he was in a bad position also with the shifting policies of the office and was looking for a way out of it as well. We rang a roofing company based in Birmingham and got our first contract with them. From there, things progressed rapidly as we made an impact; due to the fact we were both penniless after our BUPA experience and took any and all work that was offered to us. From the ashes of the disastrous decision which I had made four months previously came our own company. I was back on track. However a partnership was not for me and after quite a few profitable jobs we decided to split and I went on to form my own company.

The year was now 1997; we were approaching the tenth anniversary of Kaine's birth. Being on my own business-wise suited me, I no longer wished to work away from home as I had been doing. Jordan missed me as I was away a lot. It was in this year also that myself and Karen fulfilled the desire we had to increase our family, I was earning good money and was happy to be back amongst the kind of men I was used to, but this time I was the boss. I was very fortunate to acquire work contracting to a company called Ascon Roofing, the owner was a guy called Keith Carter. He remains one of the men I respect to this day, a tough- talking no-nonsense Black Country bloke who knew the score and gave my company more work than I could handle. The beauty of it was that Keith didn't work out of town and all his contracts to me were either in the area of the West Midlands or just on the peripherals and this suited me fine.

I was happy to be working back in my trade, sad I had lost the 'Pit Stop Café' but financially I was better off for doing so. Also in the tenth month, on the fifteenth day of nineteen-ninety seven, Karen presented me with daughter number three. Little Keira came into our lives, Jordan had a sister to play with at last. Jordan knew of her sister Kaine of course, but was too young yet to understand what had happened to her.

Keira was a sweet little thing with bright blue eyes that shone from a little doll-like face, she was perfect in every way as was Jordan. I couldn't help but feel the same old fears creeping back though as the early weeks of her life went by, understandable I know but terrifying none the less. But we were fortunate as well with Keira that the only ailments she had were the usual childhood common-o'-garden variety and she soon progressed to be a fine healthy adorable child. The intense grief I had felt at losing Kaine was lessened by the passage of time and the arrival of her sisters was a balm to soothe our pain; but Kaine would never be forgotten by her mom or me. As we watched Keira and Jordan grow I wondered what she would have looked like as she changed physically. In her photos she remained a perpetual baby and toddler who never grew beyond her short eighteen months, but it was not good to dwell on the past. We had two healthy girls to raise and we were thankful for that.

The year wound it's course from 1997 into 1998, Kaine's tenth year from her birth. In my minds eye, as I have always done at every year passing, I tried to imagine what she would have looked like now aged ten. But it was to be a significant year though in other ways.

I was at work one morning when I had a call on my mobile. It was Karen as I could see from my caller ID screen. I didn't think too much of it, probably Jordan playing up not wanting to go to school or so I thought.

"Hello, what's up?" I asked her.

"You might well ask."

"Have I done something wrong?"

"Depends how you look at it."

"What are you going on about?" I asked, becoming more puzzled by Karen's strange tone of voice.

"I'm pregnant," she said, and paused.

"Okay, you're pregnant." It was a surprise but a nice one, and I decided to play it cool.

"Is that all you have to say?"

"What do you expect me to say? No you ain't or something?"

"Joe, what about the house?"

"What about it?"

"It's too small for five people!" she now exclaimed.

"Relax, we can solve that problem. How are you feeling?" I asked her now.

"I'm ok, I'm pleased; are you?" she said.

"Me? I'm fine, I'm happy. Don't you worry about the house you just leave that to me."

"Joe this is the last one. Your gonna have to get yourself fixed!" I thought that asking the doctor to 'fix me' when apparently there was little wrong with me was a bit funny but I knew what she meant, in both respects. My family was complete now apart from losing Kaine; we were expecting our fourth child and enough was enough. I knew Karen was struggling with the room we had at the bungalow it was a two bedroom dwelling which I had extended by building a porch and conservatory. Jordan occupied the second bedroom and Keira was in the cot in ours; I had to do something quick and I didn't just mean get fixed!

When I arrived home that evening I was greeted by Jordan, as ever pleased to see her old man unless she had done something wrong, and knew that an unfavourable report of her day's activities might grace my ears. She had taken a dislike to school and, on occasion, put up a vigorous protest at being dressed and taken to an institution that little Jordan found totally unnecessary and a massive hindrance to her own vision of utopia. That didn't go down well with me as my grandmother's words that education was the key to success shaped my outlook. Try explaining that to a seven year old who thought teachers were her personal jailors! Anyway she wasn't always in the bad books and that evening Karen and I had a lot to talk about regarding our newest arrival and a bigger nest for the chicks.

"We're gonna have to move," she said to me after dinner when Keira and Jordan had settled down for the night.

"Yep, I know that; you'd better start looking at properties then."

"Ok I'll start straightaway, we haven't got much time to lose."

Clearly now Karen was worried at the sudden prospect of another child because we were experiencing a little overcrowding right now, and this would be made worse when child number four arrived. Keira was still but a baby and Jordan's resistance to and dislike of school was an added stress; but I took all this as part of life's path that we had to follow and assured my wife that, although I was busy at work, I would take as much responsibility as I could with the kids in order for her to get through her last pregnancy. And this led in turn to that other little matter that I had to take care of; so subsequently I made an appointment to see my doctor and all was arranged to have the operation to get 'fixed'. It wasn't too terrifying and I was back at work the day after, risking the 'John Wayne walk' if the expected swelling was to occur. Thankfully, in my case, I managed to avoid all mishaps and carried on as normal.

Karen meanwhile was busy looking for a new home and was becoming more comfortable with the idea that she was to become a mother of yet another child after my assurances that I would help out as much as I possibly could. One of the lads who worked for me at the time told me that his wife was looking for a part time-job, cleaning and such-like, and so I was lucky enough to be able to hire her for a couple of days a week just to take the burden off Karen that little bit. She had developed a condition called pre-eclampsia, and needed to rest, as this would endanger our baby if she didn't. It worked well; we looked forward to buying a bigger home and were trying to decide on a name for our new child after finding out first of all what Mother Nature had in store for us. In the event Mother Nature decided that we were to have another little girl. I cared little about the question of the gender; only that when she was born that she'd be healthy. The same fear that haunted me regarding Kaine's birth had lost none of it's cold sting as I worried constantly for my children's health on their arrival into the world. But for now all we could do was plan for her arrival; the pram, the cot and clothing were not a problem as Keira would be scarcely out of them by the time our newest chick was ready to fill them.

And so with less than nine months to go we had to find a suitable house for our expanding brood. I came back from work one day and found Karen had been to the estate agents and had spotted a house for sale not far from where we lived that seemed to fit the bill. It was a four bedroom property with a spacious garden. We went to view the house and found it was owned by a pleasant man who found himself now divorced and childless. The house was ideal for us and we set our hearts on it immediately. In conversation with the owner, we agreed the asking price and discovered that due to his status he himself was on the lookout for a smaller property. The former salesman in me took over.

"Would a two bedroom bungalow with a nice little garden be in the range of what you see yourself in?" I asked.

"That sounds ideal," he replied. So I invited him to take a look at our house; if he liked it then we could sell him ours thereby completing the sale of both properties between the two interested parties and eliminating chains and gazumping which still existed, although to a lesser degree. The next evening he came to our house, and he liked what he saw, particularly the conservatory I had built, and so and it was a done deal. We informed the estate agents that our intention was to complete the sale between ourselves and that was that. It transpired however, some six weeks later, that the chap couldn't raise a mortgage. It meant putting ours on the open market. It also meant he couldn't sell us his house as he had no means to buy another property. Karen was gutted, I was bitterly disappointed.

So the question became how could I get larger living space without the nightmare of entering the property sales world? The answer was simple and required no moving on our part and no increase in debt. As we lived in a bungalow the loft floor space was massive, equal to the entire square metre-age of the building; and so we converted the loft into a massive bedroom more than capable of accommodating our children to begin with. Afterwards it became the main bedroom in the house as the kids grew older. With permission granted for the extension to our property we went ahead and completed a beautiful bedroom ready for when baby Jenna arrived to take her place in our family. We settled on the name Jenna in the usual way, arguing over different names and settling on one that we both liked. So Jenna it was and with the house ready after some months of preparation with the construction of the new loft conversion, it seemed that we were ready to receive at last the fourth and final member of the family.

This was to happen as I was at work one fine day in late August of 1999. A call came through as we were in the middle of a construction job on the Pennsnet Industrial Estate in Dudley, West Midlands. This was not far from home, and, having jumped in my van, I made my way over to the main hospital in Wolverhampton where Karen was already on the maternity ward. It was around six o' clock in the evening of the 26th when I walked in to the Birthing Suite and found her in an uncomfortable state. It wouldn't be long now, I thought, before we would have our baby with us and it would be all over. Karen felt the same way and yet when it was time to push, she felt instinctively that all was not right. Hours later we were still in the same position and, as had happened in the past, our concerns went unheeded by the midwives at the hospital. The memories of ten years prior had not left me; but now I was older and the youthful politeness that had prevailed within me then in the face of the older, more mature medical people, was pushed aside by the anxiety I felt for my wife and my as yet, unborn child. Karen was asking for an emergency Caesarean to deliver Jenna as all attempts to give birth naturally were fruitless; and she was nearing the point of complete exhaustion.

"You can do it, just push harder!" the midwife kept on saying over and over, and ignoring her pleas. This was our fourth pregnancy so we knew what to expect. After Kaine's birth Karen had never been in labour more than five hours with any of our other children, with Keira being the quickest to arrive.

"Can I have a word?" I asked the belligerent midwife who was attending to Karen. We left the room and entered the corridor.

"I'm not telling you how to do your job, but by now that child should have been born and now both the baby and her mom are in distress. I've lost a child in the past and I've no intentions of losing either her or her mother because you won't listen. I KNOW something is wrong in there NOW are YOU going to get a doctor to attend to my wife? Because if YOU don't, and something happens to either of them, I'm going to hold YOU personally responsible! Am I making any sense to you?" I was deadly serious and she knew it. She stared hard at me in defiance at her perception of been told what to do.

"I would greatly appreciate that if you would." I added further, without breaking my stare back at her, this broke the tension and she simply nodded her acquiescence.

Twenty minutes later a young female doctor in her late twenties was in the room. An examination confirmed that Jenna was in the wrong position to come into the world. She wasn't breached, she was in the right position,

being head first but she was facing the wrong way and had to be turned around. I breathed a sigh of relief; at last we could get some proper help with the delivery of our child.

And so at six o' clock the following morning Jenna Lawlor, Kaine Lawlor's youngest sister arrived at New

Cross Hospital, Wolverhampton; ten years after losing Kaine. I felt relief now that this was the final time both Karen and I would face the heart-stopping moments immediately after the birth of our children. Jenna was here safe and sound, her journey had been a little bumpy but she had made it nonetheless. I was a happy dad and Karen was a happy mom. We now had three fine healthy girls, a nice house to bring them up in, financial security, due to our business, and the memory of losing our first daughter (healed somewhat by the flowing river of time) fading from our memories and our children giving us new hope in their youthful splendour. Nothing could go wrong now could it? Unknown to us and to other parents who were unfortunate enough to share our common past, a dark secret was about to be revealed that would horrify and chill us as parents, and those who weren't, to the very core.....

CHAPTER 29.

The Bristol Royal Infirmary, Trigger to the past.

However that August the only thing on our minds was securing our family. Three girls, what a handful! I felt content in myself now that I was a father for the last time, and all that was left for me was to bring my girls up well and healthy. It was a few days later that the kids could all be united with each other, and so it felt that we were all set; we were happy and content with what we'd achieved despite the very early events surrounding Kaine, whose memory would never be erased from our lives. I pondered the past and wondered how the girls might react when told that their oldest sister had died before they were even born. However my life had automatically become filled with other things to contemplate and any lingering thoughts I had regarding that sad time were gradually being forced further and further to the back of my mind as running my business and taking care of our family presented themselves as the first priorities for me.

It was in that very year though that the trigger to the past first came to my notice one day as I sat in my van having breakfast. We used to have the radio on as we sat and had our break, a routine that was the norm on nearly every building site in the land, I didn't take much notice of it, it became just background noise as we were either chatting away or reading the daily newspapers. This particular morning however a news item pricked my ears. The newscaster announced that an inquiry into the Bristol Royal Infirmary had revealed that the hospital had kept hearts from children who had died there; the amount being significant. The item relayed that the hospital had retained these hearts after post-mortems had been held to establish the cause of death of these unfortunate children. My mind immediately flashed back to the time that Karen and I had gone to the Children's Hospital in Birmingham a few days after Kaine had had the post-mortem to establish the cause of her death. Could they have done the same with my daughter? The thought was too horrible to contemplate. And this enquiry related to an entirely different hospital anyway. Surely this was the action of someone who, quite clearly, had no compunction about desecrating those little children's bodies. It could have no relation to our own case, I told myself. It would probably turn out to be the work of some deranged mortician I thought; yes some uncaring individual working alone; this would surely be the answer.

However the seed had been planted. The news went on to the other news-worthy items of that day and I tried to dismiss the thought from my own mind when it was time to go back to work. But there had been something about Kaine's remains that day we were in the mortuary that had told me that all was not as it seemed. I knew enough about human anatomy to know that Kaine's eyes had looked very different from when we had last seen her. I could tell that her optic nerves had been severed. But that day in our immediate grief and sheer upset, all I had wanted to do was to leave the hospital and drive those images from my mind. There was also the question of Kaine having been dressed completely differently from that night we had changed her nappy and put a clean romper suit on her before we laid her in the Moses basket to take her to the Chapel of Rest. Why had she been dressed in a cotton sleeveless dress that neither Karen nor I recognised? Who had undressed her and redressed her in this item of clothing? Those questions weren't that significant at the time but nonetheless had made enough impact on my mind to now recall those very questions to which I had sought no immediate answer at the time of our grief. But now, in the light of these revelations about the Bristol Royal Infirmary, would the answer to those two questions take on a more sinister meaning? I would find out much later as the storm clouds gathering around the Bristol Royal Infirmary started to spread out over the rest of the country.

It would be a while yet before our part in this tragic play would come to pass but a bad story is a good story for the news media, and like a dog with a bone the news people pursued this particular story with enthusiasm, and it wasn't too long before this seemingly innocuous piece of news was to envelop the country and shock people into disbelief at the numbers involved with this scandal. But for now I didn't want to contemplate what might have been done; speculation was, for me, a painful pastime and so I returned to work that day to finish my shift and go home to my family.

That night when I got home, I decided not to mention to Karen what I'd heard on the news earlier in the day. Even-though ten years had passed, the thought of anything happening to Kaine would still be very upsetting for my wife. The thoughts had flitted in and out of my mind all day but I'd more or less successfully convinced myself that it was a West Country problem and it would have nothing at all to do with us. Of course I felt complete empathy with the unfortunate parents of those children that were affected by this, but my own take on it was 'there, but for the grace of God, go I, and the thought of Kaine's grave and memory remaining undisturbed was one that I sought to keep preserved within me. I didn't want Karen to hear about this news as it would have upset her and this was not what I wanted either; but if she did come to hear of it, I thought that as of yet Birmingham's Children's Hospital had not even been mentioned and so I prepared myself with that to counter any fears she might have had.

The News at Six carried the item I'd heard earlier; to the kids it made no difference, Jordan was an eight year old with Keira a toddler and Jenna a mere babe-in-arms as of yet. But to Karen the news was horrifying to hear. I didn't relate any of my earlier thoughts about Kaine's post-mortem to her and from her reaction to the news I gauged that she too thought it an isolated incident also affecting just one hospital. Sickened though we were that it happened at all, it was still incomprehensible that it could happen elsewhere. But the story gathered pace as the news media went to work, and it wasn't long before more sordid details were now emerging from the shadows of the mortuary rooms, the next round of revelations more shocking than the first, involving another hospital in another part of the country, and like a fire spreading throughout a burning house, as each room was consumed I could feel the heat of the flames of this particular story getting closer and ever closer to us.....

CHAPTER 30.

van Velzen and Alder Hey Some days later (as the saying goes amongst journalists) the story developed legs, and refused to go away, I listened intently to the news bulletins as the focus shifted from the Royal Bristol Infirmary to Liverpool's Alder Hey Children's Hospital where an even larger collection of children's organs, primarily hearts, was being reported as having being kept for study. One man who had worked there became the focus of attention as his private collection of children's organs became the fulcrum of the story so far. It was the stuff of horror movies, but this was no fictional Doctor Frankenstein; although when one contemplates the scale of the activities that went on there, the name might have been better-suited to him.

The individual involved, (and I choose the word 'individual' carefully as I want to expand on that) was Professor Dick van Velzen, a Dutch pathologist who had been working at Alder Hey Children's Hospital since his appointment in the April of the year 1988 as Chair of Foetal and Infant Pathology. He had assumed his post in the September of that same year. It was to be the beginning of an era of unbridled woe, both for the

350

hospital administrators and also for the many parents of the children who came under his remit in this new post of his. But Professor van Velzen's sudden arrival under the unwelcome glare of the media spotlight happened due to a chance remark made by a medical witness named Robert Anderson. This man was giving evidence in a totally unrelated case linked to the Bristol Royal Infirmary where an enquiry was in process relating to the death of an infant girl by the name of Samantha Rickard who had unfortunately passed away whilst undergoing open heart surgery at the Bristol Royal Infirmary. Unknown to any one at the time this poor girl's passing would spark off a chain reaction throughout the country; with potentially violent scenes, directed toward pathologists working in the sphere of foetal and infant pathology.

It was some years after her daughter's death that Samantha's mother Helen demanded her daughter's medical records from the hospital when, in 1996, she had heard of excessive mortality rates at the Bristol Royal Infirmary compared to other trusts elsewhere. Within the files she had discovered a letter from the pathologist in her case that who had retained her daughter's heart. Helen Rickard decided to leave her work and set up a support group called the Bristol Heart Children's Action Group. The group's primary function was to field enquiries from other parents whose children had died at the B.R.I. Naturally people were concerned at this alarming news that the hospital may have kept organs of children who had died. This was a totally new and disturbing concept to the public who, up until now, had never imagined anything of the like could happen in civilised society.

The group set up by Helen Rickard discovered worrying evidence relating to the quality of paediatric care at the hospital, and in February 1999 the group called a press conference to inform the public. This was the first time that the topic of organ retention had made it's way into the public domain. And this in turn led to a formal public enquiry in September 1999, chaired by Ian Kennedy.

This was the news item that had pricked my ears as I sat in my van that ordinary Thursday morning having breakfast with the lads. I had no idea at the time of the far-reaching consequences the impact of the news would have on my own life and well-being, all that was yet in the future, for now all I could do was listen as aghast as any one else at the news that the Bristol Royal Infirmary habitually kept the hearts of children who had died there.

"What the 'ell would they want to keep them for?" asked one of the lads of me whilst chewing on a sandwich.

"Beats me mate." I said in return to the question that would be repeated in the inquiries that followed by parents and lawyers acting on their behalf. Although my answer to that question had been somewhat rather flippant at the time, in my mind the cogs had slowly turned and had awakened in me the memories of Kaine's passing and her post-mortem. I assured myself once more that not only was this another hospital in another part of the country, unrelated to Birmingham's Children's Hospital, but that if any question arose as to the practice of wide-spread organ retention, I could console myself at least with the knowledge that Kaine had died of cerebral oedema, which was a swelling of the brain. This, I naively thought, had no relation to her heart. Of course, at that time, I had had no access to my daughter's medical records and up until now I had had no desire to trawl through them.

It was the next round of revelations that shone the torch on Professor's van Velzen's activities at Alder Hey that really set the cat amongst the pigeons in the hayloft; it was the proverbial 'lifting of the lid' that sent the people in white coats into a flap and diving under the tables of concealment (a place they had operated in for so long) as the wrath of an incensed collection of parenthood started asking some very hard-to-answer questions of the 'professional' class. One man's face was proffered as the root of all the evil that was to be revealed, for van Velzen the game was up. He was solely in the frame, for this, but was he the only one to blame? The almost off-the-cuff sounding remark that the heart specialist Robert Anderson made at the Bristol Royal Infirmary inquiry; that Alder Hey had an even larger collection of hearts, inferring that this was nothing out of the ordinary, must have astonished those in attendance. I'm referring to the lay society here as it has since transpired that the medical profession had, for a long time, been aware that organs left over from autopsies were routinely retained. The resulting furore from this information sent a posse of news teams and journalists galloping to Liverpool's Alder Hey Hospital, eager to be the first to break the news to the as yet unsuspecting public. But an even greater awakening of the parents directly affected by the under-cover activities was gathering pace as more and more enquires started to flood in regarding the cases of their loved ones. The numbers were high, it seemed that the undertaker's remark to me that day in his office (that children didn't die that much these days) was an inaccuracy. Once the numbers of organs retained by Alder Hey were released, one was left in no doubt that the mortality rate amongst children and infants was still much, much too high; but to arrive at the figures by counting the left-over hearts of those very children and babies must be the most horrific of accounting practices imaginable!

Professor van Velzen had been busy since his appointment at Alder Hey where he had found that he had had a free hand to do whatever he liked when it came to the remains of children. The public inquiry into the Alder Hey scandal, as it had now become widely known as, revealed that he had ordered the systematic unethical and illegal stripping of every organ of every child who had lost it's life and had had a post-mortem there. So now the public were horrified to learn that not only hearts had been retained but pretty much every other internal organ along with them. More was to come however, as this storm now touched land, so to speak, and like a tornado it tore through the lives of those directly involved. Tongues, penises, eyes, and most disturbingly, a child's head in a jar were revealed to have been found amongst his macabre collection. Hitchcock would have been hard pushed to sell that story to the general public in one of his films.

This though was no work of fiction, this was real; the child's head in the jar had once belonged to a real live child, who in turn had had real live parents. If the identity of that poor child was ever discovered I pray that its parents were never told of the revelation. It strikes me as odd that the object of fascination to these medical students was completely overlooked as once having being looked upon with love and hope when alive. I wonder if they ever thought of that fact when busy severing it and placing it in its medical goldfish bowl as an object of study. I will return to that question a little later, but for now other events in my life at the time were formulating; some expected others, not. I was a very interested observer of events relating to the Alder Hey scandal at this time. As van Velzen's activities suddenly became known, another hospital not far from there was now caught in the domino effect of the practice that was now revealed. The story being thrown to the media was that this Professor van Velzen was rogue had and operated with arbitrary indifference to the effect of his actions, and that he was solely responsible. I remember van Velzen's protests at the time that he was being made a scapegoat by the General Medical Council, and that the practice of organ retention was widespread throughout the medical profession involved in infant pathology. The revelation that another facility at Walton Hospital had in it's possession the organs of over seven hundred patients tended to lend credence to his claims that he was not the only one involved; and as van Velzen, couldn't split himself into two, then neither could he have been responsible for the retentions of organs at Bristol Royal Infirmary or Walton Hospital, as it seems he himself had been a very busy man with his activities at Alder Hey, falsifying records and post-mortem reports and also medical records, not to mention the failure to catalogue the organs that were removed; which incidentally may have helped him to avoid prosecution in the United Kingdom. All was revealed by the damning Redfern report at the end of the enquiry.

Scenes of outrage were recorded as the scale of the scandal grew. Bad enough to lose a child but then to have it's body dissected and stored; parents demanded explanations. The fallout was getting ever larger as the hospitals involved decided to come as clean, as they had to when it was realised that it was now impossible to contain this colossus that was threatening to ruin careers as well as the lives of those closest to it's appalling revelations.

CHAPTER 31.

The Redfern report.
van Velzen alone?

The Redfern report was meant to establish what exactly had being going on. The stage was set, the villain of the piece sat squarely in the centre of the ring of accusation, protesting in absentia that he was not the only one who should have been there. I tend to agree, but the public were demanding a full public enquiry into this man's practices; he certainly didn't act alone, as the sheer numbers of retained organs at Alder Hey would suggest that he would have had to work double shifts to cope with the amount of work that came his way. No, he was responsible for the specific order to strip those children of their organs both internal and, as we found out, external as well. The most disturbing aspect for me personally was the discovery of a number of complete children's bodies which had been kept and stored at the hospital. To me it was incomprehensible that that could be so. What! did no-one know who these children belonged to? Why were their bodies not claimed by the parents? And what purpose did it serve to store these children there instead of giving them their right to burial or cremation? These were questions I had, but as yet no answers were forthcoming, and in truth it was difficult for me to want to know the answers to those questions.

In December of 1999 an inquiry was started which resulted in the Redfern report, in which it was established that from van Velzen's appointment in 1988 up until the year 1995 the retention order at Alder Hey had harvested over two thousand organs involving more than eight hundred and fifty children. I listened to the news and read the reports in the newspapers incredulous at the sheer scale of his seemingly unfeeling barbarity; was he a butcher or a doctor? Even the use of the word 'doctor' is wrong I know in his field, but I thought this to myself as I pondered over the reasons for the retention of so many organs; the storage of these items alone must have presented a formidable problem for the hospital, hadn't anyone noticed what was going on there? Two thousand items sitting on shelves would hardly indicate a lack of enthusiasm by the Pathology Department in the taking of those organs. The hospital were saying that this man had operated under a cloak of secrecy and that, for the main part, they hadn't known what he was up to. The facts revealed by the subsequent Redfern report were that the hospital had known that there were concerns about him prior to his appointment there, and on point number one, had gone ahead and hired him anyway, and on point number two, once he had been hired had done absolutely nothing to supervise his activities and had failed to respond to complaints about him. That would lead me to believe that they hadn't cared what he had been up to as long as he had got the job done. It seems they hadn't reacted until the nasty stuff had hit the fan and all had been revealed by the nosy media types telling the great unwashed exactly what had happened to their dead kids. How inconvenient, now look at the mess we're in Stanley!

The whole debacle concerning the lack of supervision at the hospital to control the amount of retentions of organs this man had been taking was mind numbing to me, but as yet we remained unaffected. So far three hospitals had admitted to keeping children's organs. The thought gradually took hold in me that maybe we weren't in the clear regarding our own situation. I still didn't want to think about it. The horror stories I had been hearing so far must have been catastrophic for the families involved I thought to myself; one never ever gets over the death of a child, one only learns to live with the pain to an acceptable degree. It was beyond comprehension that anyone would be so cruel as to put another human being in the position of having the agony of a child's death increased by the thought of a desecration of that little person's body.

I hid myself from the very thought that it might have occurred to my Kaine. I didn't want to know anymore and so I stopped reading anything relating to the Alder Hey scandal. It was their problem not mine I said to myself as I kept my head down and tried to get on with my life; three other children to care for was what I should be concentrating on, not anything else. Other events in my life, however, were to come to the fore now and shake our foundations.

My Nan in the meantime was succumbing to old age, and with my mother in hospital as well it was a worrying time for the family. With that thought in mind, I visited with my uncle one night to discuss the on-going situation with my mother when he produced the Evening Mail newspaper.

"Here, have you seen this?" he asked me and proceeded to hand me the article to which he was referring. There was a photograph of a man named Matt Redmond; he was holding a photo of his daughter who had died years before. Mr. Redmond had formed a group called 'The Stolen Hearts Bereaved Parents Group.' I briefly read the article. What hit me immediately was that it involved Birmingham's Children's Hospital. I stared in disbelief at the print; here it was in black and white, the hospital's involvement in the organ retention scandal. I could no longer hide from it now. It was staring me in the face.

"Can I keep this Tommy?" I asked of him.

"I kept it especially for you Joe knowing the situation with your Kaine."

"Thanks, I'd better be going." I said and took my leave. Troubled and upset I made my way home unsure what to do about this shocking revelation about the hospital where my daughter had passed away and had undergone a post-mortem. My mind kept seeing Kaine as she had lain in the room in the hospital that day. There had been a reason we had had a closed coffin for her, I hadn't known at the time exactly why, but now that I knew, I was upset and angry. I didn't say anything to Karen about the article in the paper. I took it from the car and placed it in my van. We didn't have that paper in Wolverhampton and no mention of it had, as yet, made it to the news. It would have been unlikely that Karen would have caught the evening news anyway as Jordan and Keira were always glued to the Simpson's when I got in from work and so I'd watch the news on the television we had in the conservatory.

I was pretty sure by her manner when I arrived that it was not a thing that she'd heard as she would have mentioned it to me upon my arrival. Troubled, I wondered what to do about this now. Once the information was in there, there was no going back. I decided that the next day I would ring the hospital and make my enquiry, then conclude if there was anything to be upset about.

The following day I left for my work as usual. Later on that morning it was my intention to call the number that was in the paper to satisfy any inquiries on the subject of possible organ retention. I was still hoping that it was something that wouldn't have anything to do with us, but deep down, Kaine's eyes told me that it was something we as her parents should be very concerned about.

On the stroke of eleven I went to my van and took out the paper. My hands were shaking as I dialled the number given for the hospital; what would I say? Have you got my daughter's organs? This was a situation I hadn't wanted to find myself in. Kaine had long since been laid to rest and even though she was always a part of my life, it somehow seemed that even making this phone call to the hospital that I had vowed never to return to was renewing the pain of her loss that had faded from my mind. The number I dialled changed to the ring tone; I was expecting it to be engaged, and maybe hoping it would be.

"Hello, Birmingham Children's Hospital, how may I help?" asked the female voice on the end of the line.

"Er hello, I er, I saw in the paper an article about organ retention and it had this number to contact." I said nervously to the person on the other end of the line.

"Please hold while I put you through to the Organ Retention Department." She said...What! The Organ Retention Department! I nearly passed out with shock; the very thought that they even had a department to deal with this sent a shockwave through my entire body. I couldn't believe my ears; I hadn't known what exactly to expect, but I certainly hadn't expected that!

"Hello, Organ Retention Department, how may I help?" another female voice asked of me... How could she help? Tell me it's not true! That's how you can help love! Nonetheless I steadied my voice to complete my inquiry.

"Hello, I've seen an article in the paper about the hospital being involved in organ retention, like that Alder Hey affair." I said.

"Are you inquiring as to a relative?"

"Yes I am, my daughter died in Birmingham's Children's Hospital in 1989."

"Can you give me her details? And yours. We require her name and date of birth; the date she died." And the cause of death."

"Yes, yes of course."

This was like a bad dream. Here I was talking to a perfect stranger on the other end of the phone about my deceased little girl, and she, although being polite, was talking in a manner that for all intents and purposes would make it to appear that I could have been booking a bus ticket. But nonetheless I gave her the information she required.

"Okay, I'll send a letter out to you."

"Hold on, I'd like to know if the hospital has got her organs now!"

"I understand how you must feel Mr. Lawlor but I'm afraid all that has to be checked and there will have to be some extensive work to be done before we can say for certain whether or not we have any of your daughter's organs here at the hospital. You wouldn't want us to make a mistake now, would you? and give you any wrong information."

Two points crossed my mind immediately; the first was how the hell could she understand how I felt? And the second was that if they had my daughter's organs, they had already made a big mistake!

"I don't want a letter sent out in case my wife sees it before I can tell her." I was keeping my cool, but I could hear the emotion creeping into my voice.

"Well we have to send a letter to you as those are the inquiry rules, but we can call you a few days in advance of the letter going out to pre-warn you if that would be of any help," she said, somewhat more understandingly.

"Yes I would prefer that, I'll give you my mobile number." There was little point being angry with the woman on the phone; it wasn't she who had been responsible for the deed that I now thought was a strong possibility of having actually happened.

"How long before I know anything?"

"There are a lot of enquiries coming in. I'm afraid it may be a while, it could be a couple of months."

I gave her my mobile number and that was that, I was in the system. The conversation had lasted five minutes and thirteen years of my life had regressed just like that. What was I to say to Karen? My mom was ill and my Nan also, now getting worse with every passing week. Not good, not good at all. I felt as if my own heart was being slowly removed. The weather was worsening, dark clouds on the horizon ahead.....

CHAPTER 32.

Kaine's own eyes told me what they had done to her.

I stared at my phone in disbelief at the brief conversation I had just had. A million thoughts ran through my mind. I felt conned and deceived; the hospital should have contacted me I thought, not the other way round. But then again does a burglar who steals things contact all his victims upon discovery of his crimes? Not really. I thought about the horror stories I had been listening to, and reading in the media about the Alder Hey affair. No, this couldn't be I thought, but that was wishful thinking on my part. If the media were running a story on the Children's Hospital's activities then there must be some mileage in the content. I pushed my construction helmet back on my head and rubbed my forehead wondering now what to do, what even to think. Was every child a victim of organ retention? Kaine's eyes that day in the mortuary once again told me all I needed to know. But to what extent? I was not stupid, and I realised that a post-mortem involved intrusive invasive techniques in order to establish the cause of her death. And I thought most reasonable-minded people could accept that, as we had. This was different however. We had come to terms with the fact that Kaine had died, and that had been nobody's fault. The ultimate culprit for her death had been the meningitis disease. But that had been thirteen years ago, and the very thought that the grave we diligently visited every week contained the incomplete remains of our little one was a hammer blow for me.

I decided to keep my findings to myself that day and now returned to work, but I couldn't shake the off feeling of deceit. If it were true that Kaine's organs had been kept by the hospital way back in 1989, then we had all stood there like fools on the day that we buried her saying 'good-bye' to the shell of what was once my little girl; the same little girl who had sneezed that night I was in the bath because the bath bubbles I had placed on her nose had tickled her and had made her laugh. My memories hadn't faded, they never could. It was the other events happening in my life however that were to take precedence over the as yet speculation as to what had or had not occurred to Kaine. I kept wondering whether or not to tell Karen of the suspicions I'd had and the subsequent phone call to the hospital. It crossed my mind now that I felt privy to a secret that had been kept, it was not a good feeling. The other thing was that sooner or later with the media coverage of this particular news item that it would be only a matter of time before Karen found out anyway, and so I decided to tell her myself.

That evening after the kids had gone to bed, I decided to pick a quiet moment to tell her. I knew she'd be upset by this news and I wasn't looking forward to bearing what might be bad tidings. In truth I was upset as well; all day long the call I'd made to the hospital had been replaying in my mind. It was as if Kaine had died all over again, but this time I had to hide my feelings from everyone present.

"So, how's your day been?" she asked me, picking up on the pensive mood I was now in.

"Not too good."

"Is the job not goin' too well then?" she asked, not suspecting the bombshell I was about to drop in our lives.

"It's not the job." I said, looking down at the floor as I sat on the settee.

"What's the matter? Is something wrong Joe?" She was asking with more forceful enquiry now as to the nature of my demeanour. I felt the pressure of the day's revelations building in me and took a deep breath.

"You remember all that in the news a while back with the Alder Hey stuff and the kids' organs?"

"Yes what about it? What's that to do with us?" she said, and I could see the change in her face.

"Everything."

I was aware of the impact that word would have on her, but there was no other way to say it.

"How do you mean? Kaine was in the Children's Hospital in Birmingham! Oh my God!" She put her hand to her mouth as the realisation hit her.

"No Joe, don't tell me that, please don't!"

As the tears for Kaine once again flowed, I realised the full extent of the pain from the re-opened wound that had been healed by the thin layer of thirteen short years.

"I really didn't want to tell you this but I saw no alternative." I said to her as I held her in my arms, trying to comfort her as best as I could. I let her cry for a while until she was ready to ask me how I knew about these things. Eventually she calmed down enough for me to show her the article in the newspaper that Tommy had given me. I tried to tell her that we weren't one hundred percent sure yet as enquiries had to be made. But the fact remained that hundreds of families were now affected by the growing catchment area of the scandal of organ retention. Our case fitted the bill; a young child, unknown cause of her death, and finally a post-mortem in a hospital that implemented the same policies that Professor van Velzen had, and had been castigated about in the press and television. One didn't need to be Sherlock Holmes to put everything together. Upset wasn't the word. But all we could do now was wait for the coming phone call and the letter from the hospital before we could say with any certainty what had happened that day Kaine had had the post-mortem.

Other considerations in our life made self-indulgent thoughts superfluous as the kids were young and needed constant attention; this helped but didn't make it go away. The worsening situation with the other members of my family was also making a large impact on my life at the time.

The weeks passed and I visited my Nan and mom in turn watching as both old age and illness reduced them both to all but shadows of the women they once were. Finally on March 26TH 2001, my mother succumbed to cancer. Less than one week later, on my birthday, my dear old Nan lost her fight for life also. We reckoned they'd planned it, as they loved a good old fight but always loved each other dearly and so couldn't bear to be apart for very long. We buried them both together to the music of bagpipes playing Irish laments in New Oscott cemetery, Birmingham, where my old granddad had been waiting patiently since his death in 1966 at the Longbridge car plant where he had been working. It seemed as if he had been waiting for his dear wife to join him and finally in 2001 he had got his wish, and his only daughter, who was my mother, had joined him also. The knees-up we had for them both in celebration of their lives surpassed anything the Hamstead pub had seen in all the years my uncle Tommy had drank in there. I was as drunk as a lord and happy to be with my family in this time, but I knew that in a few days the reality of what had happened would kick in; sadness gradually replacing the happy feelings of the huge send-off we gave the indomitable two Irish women to whom I owed my life. I knew I was in for it; I just didn't know how deeply these two combined events, and the future was yet to affect me......

CHAPTER 33.

Instead I should've left flowers at the storage room door.

We owned a nice caravan in Mid-Wales and decided to get away for awhile to get over the double funeral of Mom and Nan. They do say that all bad news travels in threes; I wasn't to be disappointed. Karen took the kids in the Shogun jeep we had at the time down to the van, I would join her a few days later. I decided that I would ride my Honda motor cycle down there as I could have a ride through the countryside if I felt things getting on top of me. I was all set, I called Karen on my mobile and told her I would see her in a couple of hours. I then clipped my mobile phone onto the hands-free set attached to the fairing and connected the ear phones to my helmet in case I was needed. As I rode along the winding country roads the sun shone brightly. I glanced at the mobile and could see it was flashing an unknown number. I slowed to reduce the wind noise and hit the answer button with my fore-finger.

"Hello? Is that Mr. Lawlor?" asked a woman's voice.

"Yes it is, who's this?"

"It's a bad line Mr. Lawlor, I can hardly hear you," she said.

"Hold on love, I'll just pull over and turn the engine off. I'm on my motor bike."

"Is that any better?" I asked when the noise of the wind and machine had gone.

"Yes, that's much better, It's Birmingham Children's Hospital here Mr. Lawlor. You made an enquiry some time ago regarding possible retention of your daughter's organs."

I felt my heart sink.

"Yes I did," I said, dully.

"I'm sorry to tell you that the outcome of our enquiries here has led to the discovery of a number of your daughter's organs stored here at the hospital." Silence was all I could manage.

"Are you okay Mr. Lawlor?" she asked.

"No." I answered.

How could I possibly be? Silly question really. Every time I had gone to pay my respects at my daughter's grave for the last thirteen years, I should have gone and left flowers at the hospital store room as well.

"I'm sorry to have to give you this news Mr. Lawlor," she added, rather hesitantly.

"Why should you be sorry my love? You didn't do it did you?"

I was calm like I was when I first accepted Kaine's death.

"Well, I'm sorry all the same. A letter formally telling you of the results of our searches and enquiries will be sent to your home address; is that still Villiers Street?" she asked.

"Yes." I said. I hung up not wishing to prolong the call. I sat there in the middle of the most beautiful surroundings of the countryside on a glorious day in mid-April, removed my helmet and cried for my daughter once more. Thirteen years from when we lost her, it felt like it had happened all over again.

After a while sitting there on my motorcycle in that lay-by in Wales, I gradually tried to pull myself together. I'd been expecting the call, and had long suspected that the content would be in the negative as regards to myself and my wife Karen. So now I knew; soon Karen would know. What was to happen now? What were we to do? For now I couldn't even think straight. My life as it had been was now beginning to unravel. I pulled my helmet on and disconnected the mobile phone from it. I pulled out onto the main road and gunned the powerful engine until I was doing over a hundred miles per hour. I felt an anger rising within for which I sought an outlet; the adrenaline produced by the high speed I was now travelling at provided the perfect conduit for it's escape. I overtook cars as though they were stopped as I raced through the bends of the meandering roads. I could feel sheer frustration at being fooled and cheated of my young daughter's life. How dare they keep any single part of her! She was ours, mine and Karen's; they had no right! The sense of outrage building within me was palpable. The parental instinct that all creation has for the protection of their young was boiling within me. And then the other three young lives I was responsible for flashed up before me. I'd better slow down! I'd be no good to them, dead also, or even seriously injured, and why should I hurt myself? I'd been hurt enough. It was time to make those responsible stand up and account for what they had done. I needed an explanation. Why were we not told? What exactly had the hospital got? No, it was time for rational thinking, not blind reaction.

I slowed to a more acceptable speed and continued my journey to the caravan site. It was situated in the beautiful peaceful Welsh countryside, a trout river ran through it and for me it was a paradise to lose myself in whilst the rest of the rotten world got on with business as usual. I pulled into the car-parking space next to our car and dismounted.

"Daddy!" came the cry of anticipation from Jordan and Keira as they ran excitedly towards me. "Hello, you two." I said as I knelt down with my arms out to receive my warm welcome from my two girls. They had been down by the river with their mom, and had heard the noise of my engine as I crossed over the bridge.

"That's your dad here," Karen had said to them and off they had run to greet me. Karen came over from the river as well carrying Jenna in her arms. I looked at her and wondered how on earth I was going to tell her about the conversation I had had not long before.

"How was the ride down?"

"Eventful."

She looked at me and knew straight away all was not well.

"What's happened?"

"Not now, I'll tell you later."

I was aware of the little ones eagerly pulling at my hands willing for me to come down to the river to see what they had been up to.

"You've had that call, haven't you?" she said to me, reading correctly the look that was in my eyes.

"Yes." I answered, and she just nodded.

We both had known that it was going to be bad news. It had been a feeling of expectancy, hard to explain but there all the same, the question was; now that we knew, how on earth were we going to deal with news like this?

The trouble with life is that it's a learning process from beginning to end. It's your first time, you've never been here before, and you'll always be the new kid on the block as the world changes rapidly around you. But this was totally unique for us. We'd experienced the death of a child, a parent's worst nightmare, and come through relatively unharmed, or so I had thought. But now; how were we to react? What were we to do? Who could guide us? The answer for me was no-one, I felt totally alone…. And I was.

For me and Karen the nightmare of Kaine's death was brought back to us, but this time we both reacted differently; I was cut to the quick. Later on that evening I sat down at the outside table set we had and pondered life and it's twists and turns; it seemed not to do one any favours. Alan, my former boss, had always said of it, "you're goin' along the road and all seems well, and suddenly a hole opens up and down you go." I could hear his voice and see his fore-finger pointing skywards as he uttered his pearls of wisdom to us as young men, who at the time laughed at his sardonic winsomeness; how right he was. I hadn't known it then, but now I did. The hole had opened up. I was about to fall in…..

The first indications I had that all was not going well for me was when my sleep was interrupted by bad dreams that also disturbed me through the following days. I also had a rapid decline in my personal interests;

this also included work. I can look back now and see as clear as daylight what was beginning to happen to me, but then I was non-plussed as the changes in my thinking patterns and the functions and stability I had always had so solidly in my life began to leave me feeling bewildered and alone.

In the following weeks at work I lost my temper more and more with the lads who came to me with any and all trivial problems that were now of no importance and to me mattered less than an ant; ironically enough, that's just how I felt, like an ant separated and lost from the rest desperately struggling to find his way home. Nobody understood, not even Karen. I sought solace more and more down in the pub where I would sit alone at the bar trying desperately to find the answer to this most perplexing of problems, what the hell was wrong with me!?

"You're depressed," said my doctor, "take some time off and you'll gradually start to feel better." He was a genius! Take some time off and I would gradually start to feel better! I had never thought of that; and while I was off work the fairy life coaches would erase all memory of Kaine's death and hide those nasty organs in the jars so that I'd never have to see them in my mind's eye ever again! But alas it didn't work like that. I did take his advice though. I'd had enough. I told the lads I was shutting up shop, and I was sorry but they would have to find other employment; they could've carried on without me if they had so chosen; in all honesty, at the time, I didn't care. And that was another indication how far from home my mental compass had taken me. Never in my life had I not been bothered about other human beings feelings. It used to make me happy to provide work for my lads and to see them prosper through our mutual efforts but now all I could think of was, what the hell am I struggling for? I'd always done my best and worked hard and for what reward? I felt as though life had delivered the mother of all body blows to me. I needed change in my life, but what change? I felt as though it was me who had been put in the sealed glass jar. Inside, I was screaming in frustration; they could see me, but no one could hear me and I couldn't get out.

They say never make big decisions that effect your life when your feeling down or depressed, very true. The problem with that piece of philosophy is, if you were capable of making a correct call in times of stress, then most likely you are not depressed, that's why depressed people make bad calls, and I was about to make one.

Karen was also feeling the strain of what had transpired but to me she seemed to be handling it much better than I now was. When Kaine had died in 1989 it had been the other way round. It has become obvious to me since then that what I was suffering from was regressed grieving or post-traumatic reaction to Kaine's death, triggered by the deaths of my mother and grandmother in the same week followed by the final blow of the confirmation of organ retention on our child's body. Enough for any one to handle I would say. And in my floundering state I wasn't handling things at all well. I drank more now that I was off work and obviously that caused problems between myself and Karen. It was also upsetting for the kids to see their parents arguing, something that was relatively new; of course we'd had rows in the past but these were now different. I could feel us growing apart, Karen dealing with life and me not dealing with anything. I felt she couldn't understand what I wanted to do. How could she? I didn't know what to do.

One day she came to me and asked if I minded if she took the kids down to her sister's place in Somerset, where she had moved to some years before.

"It'll do us good to have a break from each other" she said. I had become uncharacteristically moody and more and more sullen over the weeks. I didn't blame her. In fact at the time I thought it was a good idea. I could go out and get drunk without having the arguments when I staggered back home. We were sinking into an abyss and there was nothing I could do about it. The bad dreams continued. Jordan's hamster died and we buried it in the back garden and it caused me such upset with the dream of death that followed that I didn't feel right for weeks afterwards. What was happening to me and my family? We were coming apart at the seams.

Karen took the kids down to Somerset; ironically her sister Diane and Carl didn't live all that far from the water plant we had worked on together in the nineties. Carl and Diane had settled there after experiencing their own problems and seemed happy. Maybe Karen thought that that would apply to her if she followed the same path.

She 'phoned me a couple of days later to let me know the kids were well.

"I think we should move down here Joe," she suddenly said to me.

"Karen, where to?" I wasn't keen. I liked my house as I'd worked hard and it was home to me.

"I've been looking at some houses to rent and there's a nice village called Nether Stowey where there's a house up for rent. Why don't we just have a look?"

"Okay, I'll come down on the bike and we can take a look at it." I really didn't want to but felt that maybe Karen had a point; getting away from the overly familiar surroundings of the area we were in might just be the change I thought I was desperately seeking. But the gut instinct I trusted implicitly after the ill-fated BUPA job I had taken years before was tugging away at me; should I once again ignore it to my detriment?

A few days later I travelled down to Somerset. Carl and Diane lived a few miles from the centre of the town of Bridgwater; it was a decent enough place I thought, yet nice as it was, it was an area of Britain though that I had never really felt that much excitement about. I was pleased to see the kids and they were equally pleased to see me but I still had that underlying feeling that everything had changed and could never be put right again. I couldn't put my finger on exactly how I felt but I knew that the feeling of happiness was no longer present within me as it had previously been and it felt as though a great weight had been added to my heart.

We went and had a look at the house in the charming and pleasant village of Nether Stowey, a three-bed room property with an open-plan living room, hallway and stairs, a large garden and parking facilities for our car and my bike. 'Nice enough' I thought to myself, 'but it's not for me.'

Karen, on the other hand, was overjoyed with the place, and it was obvious that she wanted to up sticks and move lock stock and barrel to the coast. I was in a bad position. Division was evident, I really didn't want to move to Somerset, yet I wanted to make Karen happy and also the kids as well, which was a major factor. We still had a lot going on with the hospital enquiries as we were receiving letters every few weeks keeping us appraised of the coming public enquiries that were generated by the Alder Hey and other hospitals' complicity in organ retention, in which the Birmingham Children's Hospital had now too become deeply implicated.

"What do you think?" Karen asked me.

"It's nice," I said, "but I don't know."

"Well I do!" Karen said, quite emphatically,

"I think it's just what we need, and if you don't want to move here I do! I'm going to put in for it." She told me exactly what she wanted with no ambiguity.

"Well okay then, put in for it and see what happens, but there's no way I'm selling our house until we're positive that this is the right move for us and the kids." I was in fact thinking that we had no chance of getting the place. It was in a nice area surrounded by fields, the village had three charming pubs and a school nearby.

"There must be hundreds of locals after this place, the owners were unlikely to let it to out of towners who had just shown up." I said to myself. I'd leave it to the law that rules, the law of Sod; because the more you want something the more unlikely it is that you'll get it. I should have looked at that law in reverse because two weeks later Karen walked into our conservatory at home and announced that the house was ours if we wanted it. This was something I hadn't wanted yet now I'd got it! The choice before me was simple. I could live in Somerset with my wife and kids in a charming little village where the most exciting thing likely to happen would be an over zealous cow mooing noisily in the fields surrounding us, or I could stay and wallow in misery.

"Carl can get you work there with the company he works for. It might be good for you Joe to get back into the saddle again and take your mind off things. All you've been doing is trying to drown your sorrows."

"Karen, if only they would drown then I'd be happy."

"Well, that's no good to you or anyone else. You've got the choice Joe, either come with me and the kids. Or stay!"

I hadn't got much choice. My world had disintegrated around me to the point where I was losing my identity. I had always been a worker. But, for the past few months, I'd just worked on the house and done little else. Personally I was suffering as my mind struggled to keep pace with the overwhelming negativity that was replacing the irrepressible enthusiasm that had been my trademark and had pushed me to achieve success where others had seen only failure. I was tapped out for a solution to my problems, and this in turn sank me even further as I had always been able to rely on my brain to think my way through difficulties. Karen wanted us to move to an area where we knew virtually nobody and take work with a firm unknown to me. However a number of factors were now closing in on me. I wanted to get back to work and I wanted my wife and kids around me. If a move to Somerset might achieve the happiness that had eluded me since the bad news we'd had earlier in the year, then I was willing to give it a go.

CHAPTER 34.

Somerset blues

Some weeks later we moved to Nether Stowey. I had secured a contract with Carl's company to fit a roof and wall clad a building to house turbines for the generation of power in the South Wales town of Aberdare. We moved without incident and as I had said that there was no way we were selling our house until I was certain that this was the right move for us, we hadn't. There wasn't much I was certain of back in those days and the feeling I had in my stomach told me I was making a big mistake, but I was aware that I couldn't trust my own judgment and so I decided to soldier on with what we'd got.

Karen had secured a place for Jordan at the local school but little Keira had to wait for a place to be found for her. She had already started school in the West Midlands and now found herself missing her schoolmates from home in this new area. Jenna at this time was still too young to go to school and so Karen was at home with the two kids as I took to the unfamiliar roads of the West Country working with a local lad with whom Carl had teamed me up with. I found it all hugely unsettling and the move to an aesthetically nicer area did absolutely nothing to improve how I was feeling inside. In fact, I felt worse. I missed the hustle and bustle of the West Midlands and I needed the familiarity of home. My hands were also tied by the knowledge that the company I was working for had a monopoly in the area as to choice of labour and could dictate prices for the jobs and send you where-ever they felt like sending you, and they did. The only choice you had was either to like it or lump it. It also turned out that the contracts manager I had to deal with was a complete and utter ass and we couldn't see eye to eye. I hated the quietness of the place and the change in our lives that was happening to us all. The point I'm making is that I perceived a change happening at a time when it wasn't change that I felt I needed. I was yearning for nostalgia. I wanted to travel back to a time before all this had happened; in short I could no longer cope. I was a fish out of water and I wanted to get back to my roots.

A huge row with the company I was with over money settled things for me. I told Karen I was no longer happy there and wanted to go home to work with the firms in the Midlands who I knew were honest and fair. We came up with the half-baked plan that I would work in the Midlands area and travel back down to Somerset on the weekends; in effect treating our home as digs, working away all week and then travelling back. We rationalised this completely inadequate plan by saying that we were not uprooting the kids again. Who were we kidding? It was a sodding mess and that was no exaggeration. I was more unhappy now than when we had first moved down there.

It was a good job that I'd stuck to my guns over the house. A week later I was back in the Midlands. One phone call to Yorkshire Sheeting had got me a contract working for a number of weeks on the Toyota car manufacturing plant in Derby cladding a new building. I was at least working again now and earning decent money as I had always done.

But work and money were not the answer to my state of mind. I was struggling with the bombshell that had torn our lives asunder and still had found no way to deal with it. All I knew was that it was pointless trying to run away from something that was carried around in the mind. I could have gone to the ends of the earth to escape my problems and when I got there the same problems would be there too. I wanted my wife and my kids back with me. That I knew with certainty. All else I was still struggling to piece together.

We were now in 2001. Karen drove up with the kids one of the weekends to visit me and I told her that I was never going to be happy living in Somerset and that what I needed to do had to be done where we had started out from.

"What DO you want Joe?" she asked me.

"I want for us to be happy Karen, to return to the life we had before all this crap about the organ retention stuff came out."

"So, what are we going to do?" she asked.

"I've got a job coming up where I can earn very good money from it. We can redecorate the whole house. I'll buy new furniture and refit the kitchen. We can move upstairs to the loft and the kids can have the downstairs bedrooms." I said. I was desperately trying to come up with a solution to make us happy once more. I was in fact though like a wounded soldier who had been a good marksman but now, through the blurred vision of his emotional pain, kept missing the target. But I was getting closer to the solution of the problem that had gripped my mind and repulsed all efforts to release me from the constant sadness that I now felt. Except that is when I got drunk.

And so four months after making the trip down the M5 motorway we found ourselves doing precisely the opposite trip back up. Karen carried everything she could in the car and then I hired the biggest van available at the time which was a Mercedes sprinter. Two trips in that exhausted me completely, but I did it nonetheless. I made good my promise to re-decorate, buying new furniture and beds.

The conservatory was attached to Jordan's bedroom and so as she was getting older we designated it as part of her private area. The compensation for that was that I built a shed workshop equipped with wood work tools which was a former hobby of mine, and a summer house for us to relax in during the summer evenings that would follow. I tried my best to settle down to work and normality now we were back home. Although I still felt the sadness that was in me I managed to conceal the worst of it and looked pretty much the same good-humoured bloke everyone knew, but for me inside that guy was now a distant relative. We knew that we had to face the inquiries of the hospitals. The Alder Hey Redfern inquiry had been the first to come to the public's attention, and with it had come the media interest generated by a story which at first had shocked everyone who heard it. For me it had been a nightmare to listen to, but I was forced to face it by my own desire to understand the motives behind the practice of organ retention.

Now we faced our own Alder Hey; this time it was the Birmingham Children's Hospital that came under the scrutiny of the media. I decided to contact the man who had been the subject of the news report in the paper that my uncle had given to me. I was about to enter a tunnel of confusion and personal distress; how would I come out the other end? I'd have to enter to find out, but all I knew was that I had to do it....

CHAPTER 35.
Stolen Hearts, Stolen Minds.

I dug out the copy of the newspaper article first given to me by my uncle alerting me to the issue of the Children's Hospital being involved in the practice of organ retention. In the article I read that Mr. Redmond had set up his support group for parents affected by this; it gave the name of the firm of solicitors who had launched legal action against the NHS for the unlawful removal, retention, and disposal of parts of children's bodies, and also for the resulting distress caused to parents as a result of handling the issue. The name of the firm handling this was Irwin Mitchell. I obtained the telephone number for the Birmingham office and was put in touch with the man handling the inquiries related to the case, a chap called Mark Danesi. I spoke with him and explained how I had recently become aware that our daughter's organs had been retained by the hospital and I was at a loss as to how to proceed. He took all my details and explained how the whole issue was taking shape; as it was an on-going investigation into the amount and extent of the practice by the NHS and it's affects on parents in the locality of the Midlands and beyond. He explained that if we wished for the firm to take on our case that paperwork had to be sent out for us to read and sign. I was unsure about entering into the world of legal action against the NHS at this point. I felt in my heart that a compensation claim was somehow an insult to my daughter's memory; as if an opportunity had presented itself to make money from an horrific episode of life. In the preceding few years the 'compensation' mentality had been steadily growing in Britain as a plethora of lawyers appeared on the television urging people to get in touch with them with complaints about anything relating to accidental injury, ranging from a broken fingernail to a broken neck, and promising thousands of pounds to the injured party. I viewed this as ambulance-chasing Americanism that had now reached our shores threatening to paralyse the good old British attitude of 'getting the job done no matter what'. Now people were suing their bosses for the most trivial and ridiculous of things including psychological damage for being asked to work overtime! One case in particular I had read involved a guy who had sued his former employers and had won his case; he was awarded fifteen hundred pounds in compensation. He was then presented with a bill from the lawyers who acted on his behalf amounting to…. you guessed it, fifteen hundred pounds. As far as I was concerned this was a matter of honour for my little girl; her body had been desecrated and in my eyes, no amount of money could compensate me for that, and in saying that I'm sure I speak for all the other parents who were affected in the same way. I had never made money my god. As long as I had enough to live on and raise my kids in relative comfort I was happy. Of course I always believed in prospering by honest ability and to this day I feel the same way and I'm not ashamed of that.

Kaine's death had been the result of meningitis. No-one could go into the dock for that. The fact that she had contracted the disease in the hospital in which she had been born was for me a point of contention which I could never view as an act of God or a deliberate act by a human-being. It had been unfortunate in the extreme. I'd accepted that, and had managed to get on with the rest of my life. My personal search for the answer to the question I alluded to in the early pages of this book had been answered; personally I had felt at peace. Now like a wound re-opened the pain had flooded back and was threatening my mind. I was now on anti-depressants and sleeping tablets, and drinking way too much. Bad dreams relating to Kaine's death ruined my following waking hours and my previously good relationship with my wife was now strained. This was no broken fingernail, it was a broken heart. What price tag does that come with? Is it cheaper if you buy in bulk? Apparently for the lawyers acting for the NHS it was; an offer of a thousand pounds for each case was on the table. That was five hundred quid each if you came as a couple, single parents were better off!

I was flabbergasted at this act of contemptuous arrogance. I would have had more respect for a letter stating admittance of guilt and offering an apology and would have it left at that. That at least would have been honourable.

They were of the impression that it was about money I thought. How silly and stupid do you have to be, to be an intellectual not to recognise the plain facts of the matter? It could never be about money! I never wanted to see the NHS in ruins, paying out the millions of pounds in compensation now being talked about by the media thereby damaging an institution that belonged to us all and which we would more than likely need again in the future. That was not what it was all about.

The same arrogant ignorance of the ordinary person's thinking ability that had led them to believe that they could arbitrarily take our children's organs without bothering to ask if we even minded now fuelled the thinking of the opposition lawyers acting for the intelligentsia.......

'Ah, they're too stupid to understand, let's just offer 'em a grand, so they can buy cheap smokes and booze, because we know they'll always lose.'......

.....Well, not this time. Mark Danesi sent to me the legal documents required, to be filled in and returned to his firm should we choose to become part of the collective group of parents now lining up to take legal action. Included with them was the address and phone number of the 'Stolen Hearts Bereaved Parents Group', I decided to contact Mr. Redmond before proceeding any further. Both myself and Karen discussed the options open to us as regards the organs that the hospital had admitted to keeping; they had sent us letters of apology for the distress caused and offers of counselling. I viewed all with suspicion. They had kept secret for decades a practice unacceptable to the general public; the explanations offered that they didn't think they had been doing any wrong, didn't wash. Why had it not been out in the open then? Very rarely does honest business have to be conducted under the cloak of secrecy. And so I wrote to Mr. Redmond outlining our recent inclusion in the expanding scandal as it was referred to in the press. A few days later I received a letter in return inviting us to join the Stolen Hearts Group and benefit from the up-to-date news that came with the enquiries that the group were forging ahead with. I decided to call Mr. Redmond to speak with him further on the whole issue before agreeing to anything.

Mr. Redmond was a former City Councillor and an M.B.E. He was the chairman of the Stolen Hearts Bereaved Parents Group, his daughter Karen had died in 1966 from a failed heart operation and it had been subsequently revealed that forty-two body parts had been removed from her and retained by the hospital. As for my Karen and I we, as yet, had no idea how many organs, or of what type, had been retained from Kaine by the hospital. I was relying on Mr. Redmond's experience now in dealing with these matters as to the best way for us to proceed.

I gathered from Mr. Redmond's accent he was of Irish descent; he certainly knew his way around officialdom as his conversation with me was indicating, probably due to his post as a former City Councillor.

He reminded me of a fierce little terrier, fearless and indignant in the face of huge bureaucracy and with a willingness to right this heinous wrongful act that had been perpetrated on our children. He urged me to write to the hospital to ask for a number of things that in all honesty I had not even thought of. Amongst the list was a request for any photographs of our daughter taken by the hospital for identification purposes. I was going deeper into this ever sinking quicksand that was now becoming the main focus of my attention. I didn't want to be a bereaved parent in a bereaved parents group asking for my child's organs back, please. The idea of disturbing Kaine's resting place was abhorrent to me. But here we were, there was no going back to not knowing. I cursed the day I had had the radio on in the van and had heard that first news item about Bristol Royal Infirmary, but like a forest fire it had spread and spread and here we were in the middle of it all. There was only one way out, and that was through; I couldn't go back, neither could Karen. More revelations were to come, all not good; the drip feeding of information to the press only made recovery (if that were possible) all the harder as enquiries revealed more sordid practices that were to come to light; like the lifting of a rock and being repulsed by what was revealed. I decided to become a member of the Stolen Hearts Bereaved Parents Group and with that to commence legal action against the NHS. Being part of the group gave us access to current developments happening behind the scenes; also the solicitors acting on our behalf issued periodical newsletters bringing us up to date on the legal process and the progression of the group action taking it's place in opposition to the legal department of the NHS. It was rather overwhelming for me personally. I was focused solely on our own case against the Trust, but now I was like a voice in the wilderness, just a small part in a big play....

It had been decided by all involved in the legal process that test cases would be put forward against the Trust instead of many cases going into the legal system and jamming up the whole process. If the test cases were successful in their challenge to the NHS then all the subsequent cases involved would be treated en masse as though they had won, or lost if unsuccessful. I could understand the logic behind the idea, but to me it hardly represented a fair hearing for everyone. The law states that not all cases are the same. Would the same be true after ten years of random murder; to take three or four test cases and judge them all on those? I hardly think so. The counter argument was that, in our situation, there were simply too many instances of organ retention to hear all the different cases separately; in case of duplicity was the expression used.

Organ retention is not the same as murder I know that, but not all cases were the same, as the media coverage highlighted. In the case of Professor van Velzen's practice of simply stripping a child's body of all its organs irrespective of the cause of death, it could be argued in that instance that the crime was the same with little difference. That may have been true in respect of the physical body of the victim. My humble argument went beyond that fact. The impact on the thousands of individual parents of the victims must have been one that corresponded to the law of human nature; that being that not all people react the same way to the same things. In the case of the hearings referring to the test cases and the reaction and well-being of the parents involved, it was my opinion that in this sense it was impossible to come to a just and fair conclusion. But like flotsam in a stormy sea we were borne along by the power and the enormity of the waves of the entire proceedings.

At least things were happening to stop it all being done again. We were campaigning for a change in the law, for fines and prison sentences against paediatricians who had acted recklessly and without thought for families.

Meetings were now organised between the parents and a body being set up to oversee the investigations into the Children's Hospital's involvement and the case was to go ahead against the NHS.

But for Karen and myself, the immediate issues confronting us regarding the retention of Kaine's organs, now had to be met. If we were to be included in the block action against the NHS, our case for hearing would have to be prepared in case it was one chosen as one of the test cases.

I had the name of the person I was to contact whose job it was to field the enquiries and requests from parents coming into the hospital at a gathering rate. The lady in question was called Sue Trimmer. On the first of September 2001 (ten days before the Twin Towers terrorist atrocity in New York), I wrote the following letter.

Dear Miss Trimmer, I would like to make a claim for all of my daughter Kaine Lawlor's remains at the hospital. This would include all organ tissue block samples and slides. I have been in contact with Matt Redmond of the Stolen Hearts Bereaved Parents Group who obviously has more experience in dealing with these issues, and he has spoken to myself and my wife at length on the telephone. He has informed me of some of the procedures used by the hospital staff, which may have included taking photographs of Kaine when she was still alive for identification purposes. If these photographs are still with her records I would like to make a claim for those as well.

In the matter of Kaine's mortal remains, could you please outline the hospital's policy for the return of these items and their subsequent Christian burial .Also it is my understanding that when we come to the hospital for our meeting to discuss the post-mortem records, you can provide a parking space for our convenience.

There is one last request I have to make. On the night of Kaine's operation to fit the shunt, we had to leave the hospital for a few hours to return my friend's car which we had borrowed. On leaving the hospital Kaine was comfortable, on our return we found that she was in intensive care. I have never been given an explanation as to what went wrong in those few hours, so I would also like any ward records of that particular night/morning. The date would range between the 1st to the 5th of November 1989.

I need not explain the emotional pain that this tragedy is now having on our lives, and I would appreciate all the help and honesty of the hospital staff including your good self. I would like to thank you in advance for your co-operation.

Yours most sincerely,

Joseph JP Lawlor. 01/09/2001.

That was the beginning of my correspondence with the hospital regarding the return of Kaine's organs and her hospital records. We had asked for her records at the time we had found out about the organ retention on Kaine, but the standard reply, that searches were being conducted and files sent for, were the only responses we were getting back from them. I'd also telephoned Sandwell General Hospital and asked for Kaine's medical records from when she was born there and when she had been treated for meningitis after it was finally diagnosed, along with those of the umpteen midwife visits and the doctors' examinations. But a 'fire' had consumed the lot I was told.

Suspicious? You could say so, the whole thing was starting to stink to high heaven. This prompted my second letter to Sue Trimmer, one which was not so polite.

Dear Miss Trimmer, I am writing to you with some concern, as I have so far received no reply to my letter which I sent to you more than two weeks ago. In my letter I specifically asked for information regarding the return of Kaine's remains amongst other issues that were in my letter and are very important to my wife and I. Normally I would concede the fact that hospitals are busy places, and I have no doubt that your office is no exception. But my patience is being sorely tested as we have waited a long time for information to come from the hospital.

I'm sure you would understand if you were in the same position the feelings of anger and frustration that we feel. So it is of no practical benefit for us if we are left feeling ignored. My telephone number is at the top of the page, please feel free to use it. But I would prefer written correspondence when dealing with those issues that I have raised in my previous letter to you.

As a last point I would like to know when we are likely to receive the post-mortem documents we asked for at the start of our enquiry. Perhaps you could let us know as this information is now long overdue as I requested those documents at the start of this year.

Joseph JP Lawlor. 14/09/2001.

I sent all copies of our correspondence to our solicitors, as I was gradually becoming more concerned at the lack of response from the hospital. The Alder Hey fiasco and van Velzen had done no favours for the medical people we were dealing with and in our eyes they were not to be trusted. The further more disturbing media revelations a few weeks later in the Evening Mail only served to reinforce the feelings of siege mentality, of 'Us and Them';

the story had now crossed over from organ retention for study and education to guinea pig type tests for Oppenheimer's deadliest of toys.

NUCLEAR TESTS CARRIED OUT ON CHILD BONES! HOSPITAL DID NOT TELL GRIEVING PARENTS OF EXPERIMENTS!

Screamed the headline on page nine on Saturday October 6th 2001. 'Birmingham Children's Hospital has admitted that bones from dead children were used in nuclear warfare experiments without the knowledge of grieving parents'.

Ran the opening lines in the report.

In a desperate attempt to justify the retention of children's body parts, the hospitals were countering with the argument that what they had done they were doing for the benefit of mankind. This I could agree with. It was reasonable. I did not agree with the way they had gone about it but I wouldn't jump up and down in protest if some Professor managed to cure meningitis or heart disease or cot death as a result of the illegal taking of organs. But hang on, nuclear testing? How were we to benefit? Nuclear war was not a disease, unless you argue that some deranged lunatic will eventually push the button and do for us all. This took the whole story beyond the pale for me. I needed to know more.

The story was taking a more sinister turn to it as it emerged, quite accidentally, that between the years 1954 and 1970 the hospital had sent over 4,000 thigh bones from deceased children to the Atomic Research Establishment in Harwell Oxfordshire. Richard Folis, a partner at Irwin Mitchell, the solicitors acting on behalf of the parents, had spotted the word 'Harwell' written on a child's post-mortem records and had written to the hospital asking for an explanation as to why the name 'Harwell' was there and what it meant. He said, and I quote,

"we wrote to them several months ago, but there has been a wall of silence."

Evidently the hospital found that to admit to such a thing would inflame further a somewhat hot situation for them. Due to the time-line involved it obviously didn't affect our situation with Kaine. But what it did reveal was that organ retention went back decades, even to a time before I was born. The hospital's silence on this issue was broken by the admission of the U.K. Atomic Energy Authority (UKAEA) that thigh bones had been taken from 4000 deceased children in order to measure the long term effects of atomic explosions on the body.

This now forced the hospital to admit what had taken place, and a spokesman for the Children's Hospital stated after months of silence on the issue,

"through our audit of post-mortems, we have identified a number of cases (4,000) from the 1960's where there is evidence that a small piece of bone was retained after post-mortem and sent to laboratories at Harwell." He went on to say,

"but there is no evidence of this practice in the recent enquiries we have had and we have not tried to hide anything; we are very sorry that this took place without proper consent. We welcome the review chaired by John Alder and will do all we can to co-operate with the enquiry."

He was of course referring to the Birmingham Children's Hospital review team chaired by Mr. Alder that had been set up and had met for the first time only the day before.

His words rang slightly hollow though for the solicitor Richard Folis acting for the parents who commented,

"I always suspected that there was a link to Harwell-it seemed a peculiar reference on the medical notes. This will only further undermine confidence in the hospital. We had been assured that there would be no more revelations to come. Once again, we only have the answers because we asked the right question. It will probably only affect a small number of people, which is just as well because many people will not be able to cope with any more revelations." Strong words but quite correct, the only option open for the hospital now was complete openness and transparency. This trust that they were now seeking would have to be hard earned by them because the collective parents had been told lie after lie concerning the bodies of their children. Was it really any mystery why they were now regarded in the same contemptuous way that had seemed to be the only way they knew how to treat others? Things were indeed happening, and as I said, the commission that was set up as an external review to the practice of organ retention had only sat for the first time the day before. This was reported by the 'Evening Mail' on the 5th of October 2001. The headline for the story ran.-

'ORGAN SCANDAL INQUIRY OPENED'

'An independent commission appointed to investigate the handling of the organ retention scandal was meeting for the first time today. Parents of children whose organs were taken without their consent will help with the inquiry chaired by John Alder chief executive of Sheffield Children's Hospital.

The Rt Reverend Mark Santer, Bishop of Birmingham, will also sit on the review team along with NHS representatives and watchdogs from Nottingham, Manchester, Southampton and Worcester.

Many parents remain sceptical about the review after being given false information by the hospital on numerous occasions.'

The piece written by Paula Marsh the Health Editor went on to relate the story of a woman and her partner who had lost their baby and had been told that their baby's heart had been taken to establish the cause of death, but nothing else. Some time later it had emerged that multiple organs had been removed for research purposes without consent. The mother commented to the paper,

"I've got no trust in the hospital now at all, it's been a devastating experience and I can't help but be sceptical." This was now typical of the attitude of the parents involved; myself and Karen included. We didn't give any credence whatsoever to what we were being told. And the lack of correspondence from the hospital in our own case was hastening my judgment of the situation. However, Matthew Redmond, the chairman of our parents group was of a different opinion as he was quoted in the same piece as saying, "he was optimistic that the group (external review team) would conduct a balanced inquiry." He went on to say,

"the process has been badly handled by the hospital and continues to be mishandled. We're going to make sure there's no stone left unturned." No stone left unturned. In that statement Matt was correct. Yet more was to be revealed; it was to propel Karen and myself onto the front page of the papers as regarding our own case.

In the meantime however, our own enquiries into Kaine's medical records and as to which and how many organs had been taken and retained by the hospital were now bearing fruit. The second letter I'd sent to Sue Trimmer had prompted a letter of apology for the delay in the response, as they were dealing with a lot of cases. We were invited to a meeting in the hospital to meet with a resident pathologist and with Sue herself to discuss the whole issue of why organs were retained and the purpose behind the practice. Fair enough I thought to myself. I wanted some clarification and where better to find it than the very place where it had all began.

I wasn't looking forward to returning to the Children's Hospital after all those years ago when I had vowed never to return that day when we had seen Kaine in the mortuary room. As regards that fact though at least, we would be spared the return to the original building that was situated in Five Ways Birmingham. That building had been closed and a brand new Children's Hospital now stood in Steelhouse Lane in the City Centre. The name had also been altered to the Diana Princess of Wales Children's Hospital in honour of Lady Diana Spencer who was killed in 1997. It was here that myself and Karen met with Sue Trimmer and a paediatrician currently working there. We all sat down together in a small room. The atmosphere was tense but not due myself or Karen. I could sense that our hosts were feeling rather uptight with coming face-to-face with the parents of a child whose body parts may still have remained within the walls of the building.

I decided to put them both at ease.

"Look, before we start, I want you both to know that neither I nor my wife hold you responsible for what has happened regarding our daughter's body."

You could almost feel the tension ease as the realisation came to them both that we were not adversarial toward them.

"Thank you Mr. Lawlor, that's very gracious of you." Sue Trimmer said in response to this absolution for the sins of her employer.

"That's okay, now all I want is total honesty on your part. Like I said, we bear no malice to you concerning these issues, you both weren't even there when Kaine died so it would be wholly unfair of me to take anything out on you."

I didn't want to give them the impression that we passively accepted what had happened, I only wished for them to know that they were dealing with a fair-minded man who was capable of listening and making rational decisions based on the answers to the questions we had for them.

The discussion we had ranged in the main, from why Kaine's brain was removed and examined and the chemical used to 'set' the tissue for it to be analysed in order to establish the ultimate cause of her death. This, though hard to hear, I could accept. Kaine had died due to the swelling of her brain and so it was completely logical that this organ would be removed and kept. That I understood. However the bums started shifting uneasily on seats when I broached the subject of multiple removal; why her organs, including her reproductive organs were taken and kept by the hospital. Even as a layman I could work out that my daughter's fallopian tubes and ovaries had nothing to do with the cause of her death, and yet here they were now listed along with her heart, liver, kidneys, pancreas, spleen and other internal organs which, to my mind bore no relation at all to cerebral oedema of the cranium.

"Let's just be honest with each other" I said. I knew they understood how I felt. I could tell from their faces that the explanations for the hard questions now posed were getting too much for them to handle.

"Look, I understand that medical students need to learn somewhere and in order to do that and hopefully become good doctors or surgeons they must have something to study. Correct?" A nod was the answer.

"I have every respect for those in the medical field trying to save lives and cure people, we witnessed with our own eyes how they tried to save Kaine and for that we are grateful. But the fact remains that Kaine's organs were taken without our permission and the practice was widespread; that's the issue here and nothing else. We're here to collect Kaine's medical records and to arrange the return of her organs to us for burial. That's all. The issues of right and wrong will be fought out in court by the appropriate people, not us not here and not now."

"Of course you are right Mr. Lawlor and can you accept our sincere apologies for what has happened; we really are very sorry." Sue said to me.

"I accept your apologies but you really are not the ones who have to say sorry though, are you? I don't expect I'll ever find out who was responsible for this, probably a good thing."

The meeting was at an end. The blue medical record box containing all the information I had requested about the last few hours of Kaine's life on the hospital ward had sat not unnoticed by me just a few feet away on top of a small table. Sue walked toward it and picked it up; she then rather self consciously handed it to me, and her face bore traces of shame. I felt no dislike toward her or the paediatrician who had done his best to explain things to us. We shook hands and parted company. As we walked to the car park Karen and I remained silent. I carried the box of records with me as Karen drove us home. What secrets were contained inside? If any? Karen didn't want to look but for me, not looking meant hiding, and I wanted to find out what had happened in those few short hours we were away from Kaine's side. When we had left she had been recovering from a routine shunt revision; on our return she had been fighting for her all too short life, I needed to know what had happened.....

CHAPTER 36.
How much is sweet revenge?

The next day I sat in our conservatory, looked at the box and braced myself to open it and read what was inside. The whole episode now was growing ever larger and consuming my life; it shouldn't have been happening but it was. Every few days post was arriving either from the hospital or the solicitors and now from the retained organs commission; I couldn't avoid it now even if I wanted to. The press also kept digging away and it wasn't long before another good story for them came to light; good for them, heartache for us.

I read the contents of Kaine's records. The bulk of it was just the treatments she had received whilst in hospital on the numerous occasions she had been admitted. Finally I got to the last hours which was what I was searching for. I was extremely upset again, when I read that in Kaine's last hours that she had suffered cardiac arrest due to the infarction of her brain, and that was how she had ended up on life-support and that we had had to switch it off six days later. At least now I knew what had happened, and now we knew what had happened behind the door of the mortuary room where her post-mortem had been conducted. The whole report was in there, every detail was discussed and charted; I knew exactly what had been examined by the pathologist. I couldn't feel hate, I couldn't feel anything. I just wanted it all to go away, but it wouldn't. I closed the medical records and put them away safely for future reference.

It was then that I decided to write this book, and tell the world Kaine's story, it was the least my little girl deserved. Out of the thousands of children affected by this her name would not be forgotten, not if I had anything to do with it....

The juicy story the press were seeking duly presented itself. As the year progressed during 2001 and was approaching 2002, the third of the meetings that had been organised by the external review team became open to us following an invitation to attend at the Birmingham and Midlands Institute, in the city. It was at the first of these meetings held on the 13th of November 2001 that I had met Matt Redmond, chairman of the Stolen Hearts Group of which we were now members, face-to-face. We shook hands and had a brief chat, and it was here also that I had met our solicitor Catherine Godfrey; she was a young woman in her twenties who specialised in clinical negligence. The purpose of these meetings was to keep the many parents there informed by way of a progress report. Progress was slowly being made with the handling of enquiries and the sifting of the data of the organs held. Obviously due to the sensitivity of the whole issue, the meetings sometimes became heated as outraged parents sought to vent their frustrations on those they thought were responsible. Karen hated the meetings and had decided not to attend anymore and so I went by myself. The overall impression they left on me was one of frustration, people wanted answers and none were forth coming as yet, as the final report was working toward it's completion. It was an extremely stressful time for all involved. The early meetings I felt were the worst. They were question and answer format with the emotion of the proceedings fuelling the tension. The external review team consisted of seven people and these were.- John Alder- chairman Christine Bosewell-Munday- project manager (relative's liaison group) Isabella Moore-consultant pathologist Professor John McClure-consultant pathologist Martyn Forrest-information specialist The Right Reverend Mark Santer-the Bishop of Birmingham (relative's

liaison group) Glen Green-chair community health council (relative's liaison group). These were the people in the firing line listening to the concerns of parents who had lost children; in some cases decades before, and were now forced to re-live the whole thing all over again. I sat and listened quietly and observed the emotions of those present; some were totally dignified, and others were completely outraged and wanted dire retribution. Others still sat in what appeared to be a state of numbness. As the meetings were approximately two hours in duration the atmosphere was tense to say the very least.

One particular couple stood out to me at one of the meetings; they said 'hello' in passing and had a brief chat with me. They had lost their only child some twenty-five years before and now had just each other, they were in their mid-fifties I'd guess. It was their manner that struck me; ordinary folk, nice, sweet even. The husband held his wife's hand throughout and whilst they sat he tenderly put his arm around her for support. The collection of monstrous circumstances that had brought such people to this room was an affront to their dignity I thought. Even-though I was there myself under much the same circumstances, and I too felt the outrage at those responsible, I kept my anger hidden. Some didn't, it was their choice. I managed to get my own sweet little piece of revenge at one meeting that was held for the release of the report put together by the people listed above. Oddly enough it was the sweet older couple's treatment at the hands of a glib spokesman representing the NHS that triggered the whole short episode but had 'Mr. Personality' stuttering like a nervous schoolboy at my hands in response to the question I put his way. But first I must tell how I was able to put the question that completely threw the whole array of suits before us into a mini-panic.

I mentioned that the press as ever kept digging away for a juicy story to hit the headlines. During the Alder Hey inquiry it had emerged that the hospital had been passing thymus glands and other organs to a French pharmaceutical company called Aventis Pasteur. The object and desire for which these organs and glands were primarily used was to develop anti rejection drugs for transplants. My own mother had some years before had a kidney transplant operation, and subsequently had had to take anti-rejection drugs for the replacement organ to function properly, so I was aware how vital those type of drugs were for us as humans. Birmingham Children's Hospital had also contributed thymus glands from operations on live children. From what I was able to understand the thymus is removed to gain better access to the heart during surgery, and as the thymus now became superfluous it was sent to the pharmaceutical company for research and development along with other organs and human tissue. The outrage at this practice was centred on the revelation that, by way of remuneration to the hospitals involved, cash donations had been made by Aventis Pasteur. The dates given for these were between 1991 and 1993; however the company involved dated the practice from 1985 to 1989. As Kaine had died in the children's hospital in the latter part of 1989 the conclusion that parts of our own daughter might have ended up being sent there became a possibility.

To be fair to those involved in this trade, some staff had thought that it was unethical to sell children's body parts (do you think?) and this had been stopped; the selling of children's organs that was, not the trading of the actual body parts. It had struck me as strange when I had read this, that whoever it was that had felt that it was the wrong thing to do and had thought it was unethical to receive cash for body parts had felt that it was perfectly okay to carry on giving, in effect, stolen items to the company involved. But the costs involved with the shipping of these items would still have had to be met.

Aventis Pasteur had issued a statement when all this had come to light saying, 'an annual donation of less than ten pounds per waste fragment was made to the hospital's cardiac department, to contribute towards expenses such as nurses training and the fitting out of accommodation for parents.'

The latter part of that statement brought home to me the irony of the fact that when Karen and I had slept at the hospital, the very bed we had slept in had been paid for by the parents of the children who had died there and we may have unknowingly contributed to further parental accommodation for others who would, in turn unwittingly join the paying-in club. It's a cynical old world eh?

James Underwood the Vice President of The Royal College of Pathologists went on record to defend the practice of organ donation with what I thought in my opinion was a lame argument to counter the growing outrage, when he said,

"a wide range of human tissue was increasingly sought after by drug companies for the use in the manufacturing of medicines and for testing new drugs; if unwanted human tissue, the detritus of operations, were not used then there would still be more recourse to animal experimentation." Now I'm not suggesting for one moment that Mr. Underwood is not correct in saying that left over waste material from a live operation instead of being disposed of could be put to better use; but consent for the use of the said tissue is the vital aspect in the argument. And he assumed that all that tissue, as he said in his statement, was unwanted. In the case of a live operation that would be entirely reasonable to assume; it would be a strange thing indeed for a person to require a superfluous to requirements piece of themselves to be handed back to them after an operation had been completed.

In the case of a deceased child however the whole attitude of the parents is altered by the intense loss of the loved one. It has to be said that parental instinct operates the same way after death has occurred as it does in life; the saying

'don't touch a hair of that child's head,' is indeed a powerful one. The psychological evidence of how parents feel towards their children is well documented as in the case of a frail looking Chinese woman whose child lay trapped under a piece of concrete after an earthquake who somehow found the almost superhuman strength to lift it off her child.

Even in the animal kingdom the protective instinct is there. A report in a New York newspaper that I found particularly moving involved a fireman who, in the process of extinguishing a fire in a derelict building found a badly-burned cat lying in the alleyway at the back of the building. Next to the cat was a kitten burned as well but still alive. Further investigation by the man found five more kittens, all with varying degrees of burns from bad to minor; the conclusion? It was obvious that the mother of these kittens had returned to the burning building time and again to carry each one of her offspring to safety facing each time the instinctive fear of fire prevalent in all animals. But the parental instinct of an ordinary wild cat overcame its greatest fear. If a cat could display such love towards its young then how on earth could it be assumed that human parents somehow care less what becomes of their children even after death? Granted some cases of humans abusing their kids are reported, but these are the exceptions to society and not the rule.

Clearly a change had to come about in the attitudes of those who, on a daily basis, dealt with what, for us, was a once-in-a-lifetime tragic event; the loss of a child.

The long-awaited report by the Retained Organs Commission had been finalised; a press conference had been arranged to coincide with the release of the report that incidentally had been sent to our home a couple of weeks beforehand with a note that the report itself was embargoed until 02.30pm Friday 29th of November 2002. In the evenings I sat in the summer house that I had built for us with the gas fire on so as I wouldn't be disturbed and read every detail of the report. I was still distrustful of any and all of the people I regarded as being complicit in the whole affair, and as the Retained Organ Commission personnel were largely employed by the NHS, (they worked for the same 'boss' so to speak); this did nothing to allay my fears that the whole report might have leant itself toward the practice of organ retention, in favour of the NHS. My emotional state at the time of reading it also played a part in my outlook.

I have to say though that the report itself reflected Matt Redmond's optimistic view that it would be a well-balanced and non-biased report on the whole issue, and it was. I briefly spoke with John Alder, the chairman of the commission, at one of the meetings for the parents and found him to be an intelligent, down-to-earth man and I felt at the time that he would seek a just outcome to the final content of the report.

I contacted the local paper for our area and told the reporter to whom I spoke that we had received the long-awaited results of the retained organs commission's labours, but that due to the embargo, we couldn't speak publicly until the official release at the meeting in the Aston University in Birmingham. It was here on that morning we found the press and radio and television crews there, ready to record for posterity the findings of the commission. Everyone who had been involved up to yet in this sorry affair was there including the whole membership of the Stolen Hearts Bereaved Parents Group; as well as others such as the 'Rest In Pieces' group and notably a lady to whom I spoke from the 'PITY 2' group called Jan Robinson. The group name stood for 'Parents who Interred Their Young Twice'. The atmosphere was one of expectancy and all were in readiness for the meeting to begin and the announcements of the findings of the commission to be aired. The panel before us consisted of the membership of the Retained Organs Commission plus NHS personnel; among these were professionals there to answer questions put to them from the parent groups. It was just off to my right-hand side from where I was sitting that I noticed a familiar couple sitting side by side, the husband with his arm around his wife's shoulder in an unending sign of support. I felt my heart go out to them as they sat quietly, patiently and politely, waiting for the start of the meeting. The older couple I had met briefly at one of the other meetings were for me a symbol of unfairness in the way that this tragic scene had affected them. I was lucky in that I had three children at home, I could at least comfort myself with their love. They though, had no-one but each other and the child they had lost twenty-five years earlier still motivated them to sit attentively; patiently awaiting the outcome of these proceedings. I instinctively felt protective of them even-though I hardly knew them and hadn't even got their names the last time we had spoken.

The meeting began and with the formalities of introduction over, the rules of the meeting were discussed and the time for questions to be taken designated. We all listened as the chairman John Alder read through the main topics and revealed the findings from the deeply complex and painful issues thoroughly examined in the year or so that the commission had been functioning. Regret was expressed at the handling of the whole enquiry. Looking back now, I have to say that the group did an excellent job tackling an extremely distressing subject and putting it all into total perspective for the very upset and confused parents and relatives of all those affected.

When all that had been said it was time for the questions that parents had for the commission and those present before us. The usual ones that had always been asked were asked again; evidence that it could never be accepted by some as to why their child's organs were taken in the first place. It was then that I noticed the lady of the couple I referred to had her hand raised timidly in anticipation of being asked to air her question for the panel.

"Yes, the lady in the dark cardigan," asked the owner of the shiny suit and the slicked back hair; he seemed to be the answer man for the whole panel so far and was enjoying his role by the looks of things.

"Our child died along time ago and we have only recently found out about all these things," she said in the quiet unassuming way that every fibre of this woman represented;

"Would it be possible that the NHS might build a memorial to all those children affected by this?"

"I'm sorry but we're here to discuss the Retained Organs Commission's findings on the practice of organ retention; the building of memorials is not on the agenda."

Mr. Personality smiled sweetly back at the woman whose only request for compensation in return for the retention of her only child's organs was that the NHS might find it in their hearts to build a lasting reminder of their guilt. Well that's how I imagined Mr. Personality saw it I thought, and the ease with which he dismissed the woman's timid question had answered my own so-far unuttered enquiry as to why this hitherto unknown face was now the centre of attention.

Enraged, my arm flew up and without being asked for my question my previously unheard voice was now louder than all the others.

"I got a question for you, mate," I said, being deliberately disrespectful.

"Err, yes, the 'em gentleman to the left," he said. The room fell silent as the force of the word 'mate' registered the fact that that was the last thing I wanted of that man.

"How did you manage to come up with the twelve quid?" I asked forcefully. I had found out that the average cost of the organs sent to Aventis Pasteur ranged from ten to twelve pounds. There was no way I was going to be parried with the apparent ease at which my fellow parent's question was.

"I'm sorry, I don't understand the question."

"Well you're right, you should be sorry, but that's another matter. I want to know how the NHS came up with twelve pounds per organ in the cash exchange to the pharmaceutical companies?" If a pin had dropped it would have resounded around the room.

"I'm afraid I still don't quite understand your question," he answered, still smiling but shifting uneasily in his seat which I imagined was getting warmer by the second.

"It's a simple question, how was the sum of twelve pounds per item arrived at? Was it by weight? By bulk? Come on, I used to be a butcher, we always sold by weight, I can understand these things. I'm interested to know how the sum of twelve pounds came about. Why not a tenner or fifteen quid? It strikes me as an unusual sum, and I'd really like to know how you got it to twelve quid." He was looking at me in such a way as though he was trying to figure out if I was indeed serious; my face left that fact in no doubt whatsoever. I also knew that this man was prepared with every possible answer available legally and scientifically, but to answer my question seemed beyond him. Of course I knew the answer, I just wanted to see if they were prepared to answer the question.

"Well p-p-perhaps one, eh one of my colleagues might have the answer to the gentleman's question." He lost his poised manner as the simplicity of my seemingly innocuous question appeared to have affected his ability to speak. They all looked at each other, I could almost see the imaginary hot potato being thrown from one to the other and back again. The other parents present smiled in delight at the sight of this unflappable representation of the NHS unable to answer the most simplest of questions, yet one totally pertinent to the entire proceedings. The task fell to one man who looked me directly in the eye and said,

"The twelve pounds was simply an administration fee to the pharmaceutical companies involved."

"Post and packing?" I asked.

"Yes, that's correct sir."

"Thank you for your honesty sir." I said in return to him. I respected a straight answer and gave the man his due respect for that.

Eventually the stormy exchange drew to a close and the meeting ended. Later John Alder later shook me by the hand and smiled that knowing smile at me as if to say, 'you had 'em there with that one'. The commission had done it's job, with a final addendum to the report to follow on at a later date. The press moved in and I found myself, with others, the focus of the attention of BRMB radio and HEART FM, for an interview for their news slots. I'd sat in the mornings in the years gone by listening to Les Ross in the morning breakfast show, eating my cornflakes before heading off to work; and here I was being interviewed by the very radio station that in years gone by, I would laugh at heartily as the breakfast DJ Les Ross was one amusing guy in his day. Funny how life changes I thought, as the most serious of subjects was now discussed and questions were put to me by the interview news teams of both stations. Central Television was present also but I wasn't interviewed by them then, that was to come later. On my way home later in the car I had the unsettling experience of listening to myself on the radio on the five o' clock news. Strange I thought, that doesn't sound like a building site worker. Who was I? The whole experience had changed me completely. I wanted my old life back, the one where there were no meetings and parents bereavement groups or newspaper reports. The last thing I wanted was to hear myself on the radio talking about Kaine who had been laid to rest but not in peace, thirteen years ago.

The next ordeal we had to face was the coming court case now that the reports had been completed, and these things, as they are prone to, do take their time in coming round.

The press hadn't finished with me however as news of my pointed question to the panel which had flapped the unflappable spread and the next day I had a phone call from the 'Express and Star' newspaper asking me if we would do an interview regarding our daughter. Within an hour a photographer and a reporter were at our home, we duly gave our interview and that evening, much to my surprise, we found out we had made the front page main headline story, with a full colour photograph accompanying the transcript. The massive headline in the 'Express and Star' dated Saturday November

30th 2002. read.-

NEW AGONY OVER BABY!

The piece written by Steve Castle read.- Organs from an 18 month old Willenhall girl who died from meningitis may have been sold on without permission.

Her anguished parents have been told her organs may have been sold to pharmaceutical companies for just £12 each. Now they want to know exactly what has happened.

Joseph and Karen Lawlor are demanding further answers from the hospital at the centre of the retained organs scandal despite the publication yesterday of a report which criticises the handling of the affair. The couple, from Villiers Street, Willenhall, have now joined other grief stricken families across the West Midlands in calling for a public enquiry into practices at the Diana Princess of Wales Children's Hospital in Birmingham. The Lawlor's claim the report by the retained organs commission is a whitewash. It was when they the couple read the transcript they learned that some organs had been sold to companies. Their daughter Kaine died in November 1989 from meningitis after the decision was taken to switch off her life-support machine. Mr. Lawlor said that hours before she died he was asked by the hospital if live organs could be taken from his little girl's body for transplant. He refused permission, but twelve years later it emerged that organs had been taken from her after death.

"This was bad enough but yesterday we learned that some organs had been taken and sold on to pharmaceutical companies for £12 each," he said

"We don't know specifically that Kaine's were used and this is where the independent report has failed us and we want answers."

"It is bad enough that her brain, heart, kidneys, and ovaries were taken in the first place, but now we have learned that some organs of dead children have been sold."

And so here we were, front page of the paper, now firmly in the public eye, somewhere I didn't want to be, but found I had to be if I wanted to make our case known. We never did get to the bottom of our enquiry at that time regarding whether Kaine's organs were actually used by Aventis Pasteur or not, but it was clear that the practice was quite widespread and along with the earlier Harwell Atomic Research report of children's thigh bones being used for experimentation, made for some very uncomfortable reading about the NHS. Stories of parents having to go to the hospitals involved to pick up their children's body parts and being handed these in cardboard boxes were bad enough but in the early part of the scandal breaking it was reported that some parents had had their child's grave opened and had interred the organs retained, had laid them finally to rest only to be notified that the hospital had found some more organs that had been missed in the first searches. And so multiple burials of the same child had occurred. In other cases also it was reported that in some graveyards the grave could not be opened and that another location had had to be found in another part of the same graveyard. I even heard of one case where the same child was interred in different cemeteries a few miles apart! How the parents involved in these cases coped I'll never know. I was struggling with what had happened to us and hearing the horror stories attached to the other cases, such as caves with organ banks on the south coast of England; these filled me with revulsion.

I felt trapped. However there was no way back only forward, but for now I felt as though I was in limbo. The report of the Retained Organ Commission had established that the practice of organ retention and the sale of organs had occurred. The only good thing for us was that by the time the Children's Hospital's involvement had been established lessons had been learned in the handling of the whole issue; mainly from the Alder Hey debacle and we weren't the subject of the same shambolic episodes that I alluded to above.

We were entering the year 2003, the legal eagles were lining up opposite each other now for the coming court case. This for me was the most frustrating time, we were part of a huge litigation process formed to take the NHS to court. 2000 families were involved. I felt that the huge size of the collective action against the NHS was a hindrance; as the action grew details would be lost as to the individual suffering of each and every parent. Three battles were about to be fought; one was for compensation to the families affected by the past practice of organ retention, a second was to stop it if it was still continuing, and a third also to change the law to prevent the scale of woe from occurring ever again. In this respect doctors and pathologists now started to raise their voices in protest over the drying-up of sources of organ donation; they were in a sense victims of their own culpability in the whole affair. I can only speak for myself personally here, and I did go on record as to how I thought in a further television interview I gave sometime later; my opinion being that what had been done by the NHS pathology department had hamstrung the whole system for scientific research and the discovery of cures to the various afflictions that continue to cause mortality amongst us as humans. The fact that organ retention had gone on for decades in secrecy and was now exposed had altered the general public's view of what should have been, if handled properly, a decent and dignified matter of research to cure and prevent the loss of further human life. People tended to react with knee-jerk emotion to the suddenly exposed grotesque and often repulsive practices that were now coming to light. All medical personnel were viewed with suspicion. Necessary post-mortems were now objected to with great ferocity as parents who lost children in the middle of the exposure of this scandal were now painfully aware of what went on in the mortuary rooms due to the revealing articles in the news and press. Organ donation declined as a failure to educate was replaced by the horror stories surfacing every few weeks in the newspapers; the whole matter of organ retention without consent was threatening lives. I could see this myself but, at the time I had little sympathy for the pathologists who had now started to bleat on about the lack of material available to carry out vital research and, worse yet, live transplants were being affected. The prevalent view I had at the time was 'it's your own fault, you should have been more honest with people in the first place and maybe you wouldn't have all this problem of getting folks to agree to transplant operations.' That was how I felt at the time. I remember thinking though that if I had been in the position of a parent whose child was waiting for a life-saving transplant or facing death, how would I have felt being caught in the middle of all this? My own child's organs had been removed without our consent and retained for a purpose unknown to me at the time. Our efforts so far to find out exactly all that had been taken and what remained at the hospital had been fruitless as the searches were extensive and painstakingly slow. I had of course read the entire contents of the medical records regarding Kaine and had seen the coroners report in detail, I knew what had been removed but not specifically what had been retained. To make our case in the coming litigation process against the NHS it was necessary to find this information, and to that end a letter dated the 20th February 2002 was sent to the Children's Hospital. It read.- Dear Sirs,

RE Kaine Helena Lawlor (deceased) We act on behalf of Joseph and Karen Lawlor in connection with the retention of organs from their daughter Kaine Helena Lawlor. Our clients instruct us that they do not yet have answer to all the questions they have raised with yourselves. We should therefore be grateful if you could respond to the following:- Please confirm which whole organs were retained from Kaine's body at post mortem.

2. Please confirm and identify further tissue samples taken from other organs or parts of the body. 3. Please

confirm whether any body parts were retained. In relation to 1, 2 and 3 above please confirm which items are still in your possession. In relation to 1, 2 or 3 above please confirm which items were disposed of. If any items in 1, 2 or 3 above were disposed of provide details of the method of disposal and the dates.

We look forward to hearing from you.

Yours faithfully, Catherine Godfrey, Irwin Mitchell.

It was nearly twelve months later that a response to our enquiry was forthcoming; the letter dated the 23rd of January 2003 was from Doctor J Sandy Bradbrook chief executive of the Birmingham Children's Hospital. In the letter he apologised for the delay in the response to our enquiry. It was harrowing reading for me. Multiple organs and pieces had been taken and retained at Kaine's post-mortem. In answer to question 6 he said that all the retained items were disposed of by incineration; no dates for this were kept. The answer to question 4 was that 17 wax blocks and 19 slides were still in the hospital's possession. But no use of her organs or glands had been made or sent to Aventis Pasteur, the pharmaceutical company.

So thirteen years after Kaine died I had finally found out what had become of her. Was I angry? Yes I was. Not only did I feel misinformed and cheated, I also felt that the disrespectful way my daughter's remains had been treated by the hospital and casually spoken about as being 'disposed of by incineration' like so much rubbish, was an insult to human dignity. As to the wax blocks and slides referred to in the letter and still in the hospital's possession they sent a handy booklet to us explaining exactly what these were. That was nice of them. Rather like someone beating you around the head with a baseball bat then taking the time to phone an ambulance, and holding your hand until it arrived. On the night they had asked me about transplanting Kaine's organs knowing what was going to happen as soon as she arrived on the mortuary slab with the resulting retention of her organs and, in my eyes, wasting them by incineration; the question arose in me as to why hadn't they just transplanted them into another little person? The fact that we'd refused permission (in our grief) to take her organs was ignored anyway so what's the difference? If a letter from the hospital had arrived thirteen years later stating that against your wishes we took your little girl's organs and because of this little 'Jenny Smith' or 'Johnny Arkwright' are fine healthy young people today because we put the organs to good use; do you still want to take us to court? The answer would have been a resounding 'No.'

No doubt a plethora of medics would give me the response 'unethical' and 'impractical' to why this wasn't done; but they probably would have done that if the chances of discovery had been as slight at the time as for those whose deeds had gone on in the mortuary room. However the point I'm making is that if a wrong was to have been perpetrated anyway, I would have preferred it to have been that one.

The fact was that I could see no benefit in what they had done. I was now on anti-depressant tablets for the first time in my life. Every time I went to Kaine's grave the knowledge that not all of her was laid there now, tore at me. If another child had lived because Kaine had died that at least would have been something to feel even a degree of happiness for, but not this. Had I known what was to become of Kaine's organs after she had reached the mortuary room, all that they took without our consent I would willingly have donated for live transplant for the benefit of other children.

I wonder how many other parents would have felt the same as me? I can't help but feel that had the NHS come clean in the first place as to what happens in post-mortem procedures, that many more children, perhaps into the thousands, would have benefited from consented organ transplants by parents who would have preferred to go down that route rather than years later to have found out that their children's organs were sitting in a jar on a shelf, a part of some forgotten organ bank hidden from view. Or indeed had ended up on display at a medical museum for all to see.

Of course I'm aware that this is a simplistic outlook on things of that nature, the sensitivity required in dealing with parents about to lose a child must make the broaching of the subject (asking for the donation of the child's organs) one of the hardest tasks imaginable. But the old lady who was my grandmother always impressed upon me that education was the best form of enlightenment; it would be a mistake to assume that people of ordinary backgrounds, when faced with terrible circumstances and having to make decisions based on those, are incapable of making informed choices; but they must know the facts. I was totally unaware that the post-mortem to be performed on Kaine involved the removing of her organs. It was the thought of any more intrusive surgery that was the catalyst for the refusal of donation of her organs on the night she was declared brain stem dead; that prevented us from saying 'yes'. Hard though that might have been, the fact remains that Kaine's body was as precious to us in death as it had been in life. If by order of the coroner her body was to have been dissected then it would have been my unequivocal choice for her precious parts to have been used for the purpose of life rather than incineration. And I don't feel that I would have been alone in that way of thinking.

Clearly a new way of thinking had to be implemented; the almost Masonic secrecy of the Health Service vaults were now being forced wide open to let the stink out. Change was now coming from the top due to the outrage of not only the parents involved but also the horrified populace of the country. The then Health Secretary Alan Milburn set the tone in a speech he made when he said, 'The days have gone when the NHS could act as a secret society; it cannot operate behind closed doors. It cannot keep people in the dark. It has to actively earn the trust of patients.' He went on to say, 'And if things go wrong it needs to explain why, it needs to be quicker to say 'sorry.' In short the NHS has to be open and honest in dealing with the people it serves. It is the right of the individual, not the right of the institution, that counts.' He said this in expectation of the new laws that pressure groups such as the 'Stolen Hearts' group (of which we were members) and the 'Pity 2' group, among others, were calling for in relation to the past practices of the NHS. The new laws were expected to govern consent to post-mortems including forcing doctors to explain exactly what the procedure involved and to ask what patients wanted to happen to the organs when they had finished. The government had taken notice of the way it's citizens had been treated by what is, by and large, a servant of the public; it had all smacked a bit like a case of the tail wagging the dog. A Whitehall source was quoted in the Observer newspaper bringing to notice to the wider public what the parents involved in the Alder Hey and Bristol Royal Infirmary scandals were already painfully aware of, when he said,

'It was shambolic. The way the parents were treated was with a total lack of respect and fairness, it was as though somehow they were part of what had gone wrong at the hospital, not the victims. What we think they want is acknowledgement that they have suffered, a recognition that what has happened was profoundly wrong, and some reassurance that we will put in place the necessary changes to ensure it does not ever happen again.'

Fine words well spoken, the subject was like a rabbit out of the hat and running around with everyone diving to grab the elusive creature. As in every controversy sides were taken, and members of the press lined up to give their thoughts and views an airing in the turbulent wake of this seemingly never-ending story. For some the story gave the opportunity to print the copy needed to do a little political bashing over the head. Mary Riddell, writing for the Society Guardian gave Mr. Millburn a subtle telling off in her piece 'Demonising doctors' in which she acknowledged the Gothic practices of Professor van Velzen, brought in comparisons of Burke and Hare, with Mengele and Hannibal Lector thrown in for good measure. Leaving aside the political cut and thrust it has to be said that the practice of organ retention stretched back over many decades, under the noses of both Labour and Tory administrations, I don't wish to join a political debate but the fact is that Alan Millburn's condemnation of the practices that have had the effect of outright harm on the people whose trust was in the institution of the NHS was quite correct, and the resulting change to the law required by us as citizens of the country for the protection of our collective interests was the correct course to take. It seems sad that any politician could or would use this kind of platform to score points with the electorate, but I have to say that that was not the impression I got. Demonising doctors with the resulting witch hunts generated by the exposure of the collection of organs held by the NHS trusts could be of no possible good to anyone. Mary Riddell was quite

correct though where she states, 'The parents will sue for £10 million compensation. Two rival firms of solicitors vie for rights to this lucrative business. Hospital switchboards are jammed by those who fear their children's organs lie in a glass jar. A commission is assembled to hand back sad relics whose discovery serves little purpose, beyond eclipsing joyful memories of a living child. (And this is the point) Pathologists warn that life-saving operations are already ceasing for lack of donor organs and that medical research will be gravely affected. There are no winners here!'

Precisely so, doctors and medical staff are an essential part of society. As far as I can see there are two sections of the medical profession involved in this issue whose roles need clarifying. There are those who are involved with the treatment of patients and those involved with what happens when a patient dies. It would seem that the problem stemmed from those dealing with the remains of those who have been pronounced 'life extinct', and that is where the treatment of the now dead individual ceases to be one of care and more one of objectivity and practical curiosity for those involved in trying to establish both cause of death and the prevention of such a state. I thought long and hard about the paradox involved in the nature of the medical professional. On the one hand I saw with my own two eyes the outright care and professionalism involved when Kaine was in the hospital on the occasions when she became ill and in the latter stages of her life in the intensive care ward and the attitudes of the nursing staff and doctors involved when we had to switch her life support off. On the other I have come to know what happens to a body that has no life in it and arrives on the slab. What happens then? Does the individual presiding over the scene suddenly turn into an uncaring monster? Uncaring and unfeeling to the fact that the subject to be dissected and studied was once, only a very short time ago, a child loved and cared for by its devastated parents? In all honesty I don't think so; from what I read in Kaine's post-mortem report all was conducted with professionalism; the only shock to me was of not knowing what had to be done at such times. To juxtapose the two sides of this coin, the argument could be put forward that they, although working in different spheres, one with the living the other with the dead, are yet both working toward a common cause; that being, for the benefit of future patients through the expertise gained by medical research. In the case of the Alder Hey Inquiry however, the actions by Professor van Velzen threw the medical profession into complete disarray.

Mary Riddell had also made the comparison of van Velzen to the notorious and infamous Doctor Mengele. [From the book 'The SS a warning from History,' written by Guido Knopp,] a curious comparison can be drawn. Miss Riddell said that for all his flaws van Velzen never killed anyone in order to conduct his research. This is true, but a brief look at the way Doctor Mengele viewed his patients begs the question as to what a close comparison drawn between these two men might actually reveal.

Doctor Ella Lingens was a prisoner at Auschwitz forced to assist Doctor Mengele in his work, she witnessed first hand the appalling cruelty dished out by the 'Doctor of Death.' After the war she gave a unique insight into the mindset of the man. 'It is in the nature of a sadist to enjoy inflicting pain on his victim. With Mengele one had the feeling that he *simply didn't notice the pain.* It never occurred to him; to him the prisoners were *guinea-pigs, laboratory rats,* whose inner life and suffering was of absolutely no concern to him.' She further went on to say of him, and this is where I think the drive behind his thinking lay, '*He wanted to be immortalised in the medical textbooks for his theory on twins. In the name of 'research' he injected chemicals into the children's eyes, to see whether brown eyes could be turned permanently blue. He killed others with injections of Evipan or phenol and removed their organs.*' (Italics in both paragraphs mine)

I am not suggesting for a moment that professor van Velzen would be capable of the same crimes of murder that Mengele was, but the same non- caring, all consuming preoccupation with 'research' for medical glory and the removal of organs bear an uncomfortably close resemblance. Did van Velzen see his appointment at Alder Hey as an opportunity to use the thousands of children's organs that came his way without thought for the parents of those children, in the same way as Mengele viewed his appointment to Auschwitz as a heaven-sent opportunity to conduct experimentation without fear of retribution? Just how thin really is the line between genius and madness? Professor van Velzen was consumed with his research into cot death, but what was the motivation? Was it to help those unfortunate ones who had discovered their child had died for seemingly no apparent reason? Or was it to immortalise himself as the genius who discovered the cause and cure for this affliction?

CHAPTER 37.

van Velzen's sins seek him out.

Professor van Velzen's less than illustrious career had some mileage to run yet though. As early as 1994 van Velzen's bosses at Alder Hey decided to restrict his activities, he was confined to foetal and pre-natal work only. This news didn't sit well with the professor and on hearing this he decided to take unauthorised leave from Alder Hey.

Within the walls of Alder Hey his activities must have been giving some cause for alarm because the following year in February, he was ordered to stop any and all research undertaken without ethical approval. Clearly the professor's research being brought to a standstill would not do and in December of the same year he decided to leave Alder Hey and not only to change hospitals but also to change countries. He emigrated to Canada where he began 'work' at the IKW Grace Hospital in Nova Scotia. As yet he had no idea that his order to strip organs from children's bodies back in the UK was like a ticking time bomb. Habits can be hard to break however and the professor resumed his work in the same vein in Canada.

The Canadian hospital authorities took a more controlled approach to his work and discovered that his research didn't add up to much and in 1998 he was fired from Halifax IKW hospital for incompetence. But it still took two years to arrive at this conclusion; what had he been up to? van Velzen decided to return to his native Holland.

It was close to this time that the whole affair at Alder Hey was about to be exposed through the Inquiries being conducted due to the questions being asked at Bristol Royal Infirmary, the Professor's world was to come crashing about his ears with the scale of his 'work' creating horror on both sides of the Atlantic ocean. Whilst in Canada, he had rented some storage lock-up facilities and in his absence a worker there discovered the organs of a young girl in heat sealed bags. The game was up for him in Canada. The past was about to catch up with the man who had brought heartache to thousands of people and like dominoes falling, one authority after the other was coming down upon him. In 2001 the General Medical Council in the United Kingdom ruled that van Velzen should be temporarily banned from practicing medicine in the UK. On January 30th of the same year the Redfern report was released highlighting his unethical and illegal stripping of organs from children's bodies.

On the 4th of February the same year, prosecutors in Halifax Nova Scotia sought the extradition of van Velzen from his native Holland, on charges relating to the discovery of children's organs in the sealed bags in the storage facility rented by him during his stay in Canada. The authorities in Canada acted swiftly and in July 2001 he was convicted of improperly storing body parts removed from the child in the Halifax case. He received twelve months probation and was ordered to pay two thousand Canadian dollars to charity. No mention was made of him being banned from practicing in the country but it would be safe to say that he was not welcome there after that. His troubles were not yet over however as the sins of van Velzen had sought him out.

His activities on both sides of the Atlantic had ensured that his face had been splashed all over every newspaper eager to cover the story that horrified the nation. The parents of the children affected at Alder Hey were screaming for the head of van Velzen; if not in a jar then at least on a platter. The British authorities had to act, as the public outcry was such that public disorder was envisaged over the scale of the scandal. The police became involved investigating possible criminal charges against him. In this respect however he was lucky. His incompetence may have saved his skin through his not having properly catalogued the organs retained at Alder Hey, and in December of 2004 the Crown Prosecution Service reluctantly decided that there could be no prosecution of van Velzen for criminal offences. The reason given was that there were no guarantees that the remaining organs in containers at Alder Hey were obtained illegally. The police to their credit sought to find a solution to this problem but alas were unable to do so. The families affected were naturally dismayed and appalled that he would not face criminal charges, but had to take solace instead with the General Medical Council's ruling on Monday the 20th of June 2005 that the Dutch pathologist would never be able to practice medicine within these shores again. Throughout all this van Velzen protested that he never knowingly removed organs without consent. This was dismissed outright by the hospital, and in the end he finally admitted that what he had done was wrong. Did he finally see the light?

No matter what the answer to that question might be, van Velzen it seems 'didn't notice the pain' in the midst of all he was doing. It was clear that the Law had to be changed to prevent arbitrary harvesting of children's body parts by 'rogue' pathologists. The Law however turned up some surprising information that the average man in the street may not have been aware of, and despite the vilification of, and absconding of van Velzen, the legal department of the NHS decided to launch a defence of the practice of organ retention by invoking an old law that went back to the time of Burke and Hare the grave robbers (also known as the 'Ressurectionists' or the 'Resurrection Men.') That law was, 'that there is no property in the human body.' Put another way, when a person dies regardless of age or sex, no one can lay claim to the remains as 'theirs'.

This law had been exploited by unscrupulous individuals in an effort to make money. I was at home one evening watching the television when a programme advertised on the 'History Channel' called the 'Body Snatchers' caught my interest. The programme itself was about the notorious grave robbers from Edinburgh in Scotland the afore-mentioned Burke and Hare. It highlighted for me the lengths to which medical students were prepared to go to procure human remains for dissection and anatomical study. A brief history of body-snatching in the United Kingdom would leave one in no doubt as to how highly sought after the remains of human beings were for early medical schools. And equally, how strongly opposed the common folk of the day were to the practice.

Before the Anatomy Act of 1832, the only legal supply of corpses for anatomical study in the land came from those unfortunate enough to be condemned to death and dissection by the courts of the day. Those who were sentenced to this horrific fate were often guilty of comparatively harsher crimes. Due to the nature of the sentencing the deterrent was such that these sentences did not provide nearly enough bodies for the emerging medical schools and the private anatomical schools which did not require a licence to operate before the year 1832.

In the previous century hundreds had been executed for relatively minor crimes. But by the nineteenth century there were only about fifty-five people being hanged per annum; this created a problem for the growing medical institutions because they needed upwards of five hundred corpses to accommodate their needs.

The problem was exacerbated by the rapid decay of the bodies due to the lack of electric refrigeration in those days. Very soon after procurement the cadavers became unusable for study. This spawned the body-snatching phenomena as a means to counter the deficiency of bodies fresh enough to be studied. Surprisingly the stealing of a body was only a misdemeanour at Common Law, and not a felony; this therefore meant only a punishment of a fine and incarceration as opposed to the more serious punishment of transportation or even death. The profession of body-snatching was a good enough earner to run the risks of being caught doing it; aided by the fact that the authorities tended to turn a blind eye to what was considered at the time necessary, even though repulsive.

Body snatching became so commonplace that it was not at all an unusual sight to see the next-of-kin of the deceased watching over the corpse until its interment, and then to keep watch over the burial site for days after to stop it being raided. Coffins made of iron were used as a defence against these body-snatchers, or the grave itself was protected by an iron bar framework called mort-safes; this protection can still be seen in Greyfriars churchyard Edinburgh, no doubt to deter the likes of Burke and Hare who were active at the time.

In Holland the Poorhouses were accustomed to receiving a small fee from undertakers who paid a fine for ignoring burial laws and resold the bodies to doctors. Sound familiar?

The programme ended with the unsurprising leap by the main characters of Burke and Hare to simply murdering people to procure their ill gotten gains; this instead of going to the trouble of digging up freshly buried corpses with all the hard work that entailed. And also the fact they were paid more for very fresh corpses no doubt hastened the enterprising move. Their activities and those of the London Burkers who copied them resulted in the passage of the Anatomy Act of 1832. This Act allowed unclaimed bodies and those donated by relatives to be used for the study of Anatomy; and this in turn required the licensing of anatomy teachers, effectively ending the body- snatching trade. The use of bodies for scientific research in the United Kingdom is now governed by the Human Tissue Authority.

The lengths to which the deceased persons' relatives went in order to try and prevent the theft of their loved one's remains, gives an indication that the human feelings displayed in the previous two centuries are no different than those of today, but it would seem that the procurement of anatomy for study still went on with the same zeal, the only difference being that the likes of the 'Resurrection Men' were the only persons that were now 'superfluous to requirements'. The 'grave robbing' still continued, the only difference being that shady characters no longer visited the graveyard in the dead of night to disinter the deceased, the items required were now procured well before then. There can be no doubt in my mind that the practice of keeping organs from deceased humans was not viewed as anything other than being wrong by those involved, as otherwise it would have been common knowledge to the public. The fact that it wasn't, probably due to the highly sensitive feelings of the surviving relatives, gives clear indication that it was only when the harvesting of organs on the scale being implemented throughout the NHS became so commonplace that clearly it was, it became only a matter of time before someone desensitised to the whole process let it slip.

And the heart specialist giving evidence at the Kennedy inquiry did just that. I imagined that the resulting explosion of public and parental fury gave rise to a lot of head scratching within the NHS pathology departments as the bemused protagonists of this practice asked themselves 'What's all the fuss about? We've being doing this sort of thing for years.'

Well just because it's gone on for a long time didn't make it right. Margot Brazier, chair of the Retained Organs Commission, wrote a paper on the outlining of the Human Tissue Bill. I want to quote directly from that paper a section that for me clarifies the feelings displayed by humans throughout the ages towards our deceased loved ones. The section of the paper I want to highlight is on page 3 under the heading, 'ARE THE SCOTS RIGHT?'

This section leads off with the question that was being asked at the time as fears were growing that due to the scandal and the public awareness as to what could happen to their bodies after death that organ donation would slow to the point where lives were put at risk. The British Medical Association were calling for a 'presumed consent'; put simply this means that if you haven't specifically not consented to your organs being used for transplant then it was assumed that you didn't mind if they were. It was a little bit like a burglar turning your house over and then using the defence that, 'you never actually said that you didn't want to be robbed.'

This though was too fraught with difficulties to be made law. In Margot Brazier's paper she attempts to highlight the difference between organ donation for transplant and organ retention for teaching. 'A number of families affected by organ retention have argued that organ retention ought to be dealt with quite separately from organ transplantation. The independent review group on retention of organs at post-mortem in Scotland agrees. ***"...... the review group does not believe it to be appropriate that new legislation should contain provisions dealing both with transplantation and retention of organ."*** (Italics hers) Separate legislation is thus likely to be introduced in Scotland. Are the Scots right? This is a difficult question. Attempts to introduce 'presumed consent' in relation to transplants, placing the Bill at some risk, may offer support for the Scottish approach. There is no doubt that many people do see the questions of donating an organ to save someone else's life, and giving organs to be used in teaching and research as different. Two compelling reasons convince me that the Human Tissue Bill is right to provide a comprehensive coverage of all uses of body parts. It is the right principle. English (and Irish) Law has long proclaimed that there is no property in the human body. Alas the 'no property' rule has been used from the time of Burke and Hare (the grave robbers) to the tragic history of organ retention in the 20th century, to take and use body parts without any 'by your leave'. Paradoxically the rule derived not from a lack of regard for the human body but from a judicial view that the body and its parts *have such incalculable value that they could not be regarded as mere property. Our bodies and their parts are integral to our existence. The bodies of those we lose do not suddenly become mere things- of less interest than our dead child's toys or deceased husband's possessions.* (Italics mine).…. The gift of something that is the essence of your family is an incalculable gift. The rules governing that gift should be one and the same.

(2) To introduce new rules for organ retention, the Human Tissue act 1961 had to be repealed either wholly or in part. That means that the unsatisfactory 1961 Act would continue to apply to transplants, or a second Bill on transplants would have to be prepared and introduced into Parliament. Two controversial and complicated pieces of legislation were just not practical. The whole point for me was in the section of text that I have italicised; the bodies of those we lose do not suddenly become mere things. Clearly there was an attitude problem within the NHS; the thought processes that govern the minds of

the recently bereaved and those whose every day role was dealing with the bodies of those who had died were clearly in different corners. We as bereaved parents assumed that the precious body of our child Kaine would be treated with the same degree of profound loss and grief that we were feeling by all concerned; she wasn't. To the staff on the day of her post-mortem she was just another sad fact of life that now had to be processed. I was left in no doubt of that when I read the opening line of her post-mortem report years later. It began with her name, a serial number, her date of birth, and the date she expired.

'External appearance.'

'The body is that of an 18 month old female infant'......
No it wasn't, she was my daughter Kaine......

It was not hard to see where the human feelings ended and the job began for the pathologist, and the desensitising of the individuals within that sphere of work would have to be governed by a law that protected the rights of the public. If one was in any doubt as to why we needed a law, I have picked two news reports from the 'Guardian' of Thursday 1st of February 2001. The piece is a special report on Alder Hey written by two people one described as an NHS insider Meg Henderson; the second piece was written by Charles Burgess.

I have decided to reproduce the entire two pieces and comment on each after. For me both pieces highlight the dangers of complacency in a job and the accompanying non existent empathy. The report has as its title, **'Most women would not like their baby in a jar' by Meg Henderson. 'As an NHS insider Meg Henderson saw some shocking things involving organ removal. They were, she said, an affront to human dignity. But former**

mortuary attendant Charles Burgess finds the outcry over Alder Hey mawkish (sentimental).

'There is public horror at the stories of children's heads in jars, shelves of babies' body parts. And all over the country, doctors stare at their newspapers and TV screens, bemused and unable to comprehend what the fuss is all about. The hospitals talk about "outdated bad practice in one or two pockets", which is intended to convey the impression that it used to happen and perhaps still does in some isolated areas, but of course it isn't the norm.' 'the truth is that snipping out bits and pieces at post mortems has always been standard practice, one that is so entrenched that no one sees anything wrong with it. The reason relatives have never been told is what they don't know won't hurt them.' 'This excuse is part of what the medical profession likes to see as its paternal role-thought for others. Those of us who have seen the profession at close quarters have always known that this is a lie, a cover up for the sheer arrogance and insensitivity. Doctors remain unable to tell the difference between empathy and sympathy yet still try to convince us that they are kindly, golden hearted, caring Dr Camerons.' 'I was once a cardiac technician; all you needed to come within my remit was a pulse or the absence of one. I worked in heart surgery, heart disease, resuscitation, and research in various hospitals here and abroad, rising to chief tech before I changed careers. So I know that patients belong to the medical profession from the moment doctors lay stethoscopes on them. We're not talking about the removal and retention of organs from a few babies and children, or a few hundred even; we are talking about patients of all ages and sizes. That is what that desperate smokescreen is intended to cover, that the situation is across the board, adults as well as children.' 'Organs are retained for a variety of reasons. For instance, there is great rivalry between medics and surgeons, and if something goes wrong in a case they share, one lot will try to blame the other. I often collected someone's heart from pathology and took it to my medic colleagues for examination, in the hope that a badly sutured plastic valve could be identified, or maybe a leaking vein or artery, so that the pointed finger could be pointed back to the surgeons. No one ever thought to ask the relatives; medicine just doesn't work like that, and anyway, what they don't know won't hurt them.' 'And medical research needs supplies of organs, and there are papers to be written to enhance and further medical careers. There is always someone looking for some little piece and another perfectly willing to supply it. And who will ever know?' 'Sometimes pathology technicians have been known to make extra money selling items to drug companies who do their own research, and however hotly denied this may be, it is true all the same. After all the patient no longer needs it, so where's the harm? I have yet to meet to meet anyone who was asked to donate a piece of a loved one, let alone their unborn or stillborn child. Most women would not react well to a request that their lost baby should be kept in a glass jar for the foreseeable future, or dissected with bits sent to various interested parties so that they can submit a paper to one of the journals or get more letters after their names. So no one asks.' 'I lost five babies and, knowing what I knew, the first thing on my mind each time was what would be done with them; however incomplete they were, they were still human, still my children. It's a sad indictment of the medical profession that what became of my child was uppermost in my mind each time, when I should have been coming to terms with my loss. Other women in similar situations were spared that knowledge. Until now, of course; all over the country women today must be wondering if their lost baby is part of that collection at Alder Hey, and how can they ever be sure?' 'Most of these cases are outside the retention of organs for teaching purposes, to be kept in medical museums, where there might be some justification; though even when I was in medicine I used to look at these preserved oddities and grotesques, but human beings for all that, and feel guilty for staring at them, the babies with two heads, and the other little bodies at different stages of normal development floating in jars forever. I often wondered if their mothers were aware that their children were here on our dusty shelves and I had an almost irresistible urge to cover them up to stop idle eyes gazing at them. Indeed I once shared an office with a brain in a jar that had been used as a paper weight for so long it wasn't even questioned. I used to look at it occasionally and wonder if this was what the owner had envisaged for it, even if he or she had given written consent, which I doubted.' 'When my mother died some years ago an over-zealous official decided that she should have a post-mortem and I vainly tried to stop it happening. Before it went ahead, I vowed dreadful vengeance if any part of her should be removed. Of course, as those conducting the post-mortem knew perfectly well, unless I'd been standing beside them throughout I could and would never be certain. Somewhere in the dark recesses of my mind it still bothers me occasionally, though that won't change whatever did happen. But she was my mother, she deserved respect in death, just like all those mothers I know didn't get it, and the same applies to the babies I lost.' 'You try not to think that they too might be on shelves somewhere or used for some experiment, but the thought is there, because I saw it happening to other babies, and now even those emotional creatures outside know too it has all turned into a nightmare for the medical profession, though some of us see it as the chickens rightly coming home to roost.'

_____ **'All that's there is the shell – nothing more.' By Charles Burgess.** 'When I worked in a mortuary as a transporter and cleaner nearly thirty years ago bodies used to be stuffed with roll up copies of the local newspaper when the autopsies were finished and the next stop was the undertaker.' 'And I did not – and still do not – see anything wrong with that.' 'It was the end of a precise process which may seem appalling to those who have never thought about it before but which I came to realise was absolutely necessary. All the internal organs were taken out and looked at; some were kept and some were thrown away into black plastic bags which one of us then took to the incinerator. I remember once an amputated foot looking rather odd, sticking up as if someone was stuffed whole in the bag. And I remember too what looked like a fully formed baby making that functional final journey.' 'The noise of an electric saw (or the smell of formaldehyde, for that matter) still takes me back to that autopsy room where the saw was used to cut the skull so that the brain could be taken out. And then paper would go into the head and the skin would be flipped back and sometimes you had to hit the forehead to get the skull into line so that the body would not look like

Frankenstein's monster. And sometimes when an intestine had been rolled into a concentric circle on a plate we would put one end into the bin and watch it unwind until the final plop.' 'Then we would comb the hair, put a white shroud over the body and wheel it into a room off the chapel. And the relatives would come and you could hear them crying for their dead loved ones. And we knew that all that was there was a shell – nothing more.' 'It taught me, as an eighteen year old, that once you are dead that's it with the body you have been carrying around all your life. If there is a spirit then it took a hike straight away.' 'That is why I find the reaction to this week's Alder Hey story mawkish, I appreciate that people are upset that they never knew what was happening to their children's bodies. If they had read the above they probably would not want to know anyway. At Alder Hey the organs are kept in tubs in a room, which some seem to think is an outrage. But how else should they be kept? It seems we care more about the dead than the living – or certainly the elderly. How can we talk about "dignity in death" when we allow our elderly to die in conditions stripped of dignity?' 'And is it better to bury the remains of a human being, to let it rot in the earth, than to have it used to try and help someone else's life?' 'Pathologists are not murderers, although it seems some have not been playing by the rules. Society can't have it both ways and say we want to find a cure for a plethora of diseases but then get squeamish when we know what is involved. Pathologists use dead people's organs for research. The process involves some butchery. But it is worth it.' 'And don't forget to carry a donor card.'

_____

When I had first read those two pieces a mixture of emotions had swept through me. I have to say my predominant reaction to Charles Burgess's piece had been initially one of anger, but in all honesty I was grateful to both writers for their candour in writing on such a sensitive issue. I wouldn't have recommended either person for the Diplomatic Corps, especially 'Chuck'; but I appreciated their honesty, the only important criticism I had really of Meg Henderson and Charles Burgess was that prior to the whole Alder Hey affair exploding into a nationwide story of keen public interest, neither had felt compelled to enlighten us with their memories. In Mr. Burgess's case, he stated that he still saw nothing wrong with the practice of organ retention. In Meg Henderson's case she clearly had, but it was only when the practice involved her own mother had she felt stirred enough to try and do something about it. But it has to be said that Meg Henderson did confirm what I had long suspected existed in human nature. We now know that arrogance and insensitivity were the rule rather than the exception. The 'God' complex was clearly alive amongst those who had the capability to keep us mere 'emotional creatures' and our offspring alive, and if the worst did happen, a few bob could be made on the side from the bits that were no longer needed by the former owner. 'Who'd know?' Well eventually the whole country knew, and shock horror, they hadn't liked it.

Mr. Burgess on the other hand took a more practical standpoint. He had answered two particular questions for me though, ones that had been on my mind for a long time. I mentioned that the day we went to the morgue Kaine had been dressed in what looked to me like a sleeveless cotton night dress; I now knew that that was a shroud. The other question answered was that when Karen and myself had sat there destroyed by what had happened to our child, it's entirely possible that some-spotty faced eighteen year old had been listening to our grief having all the sensitivity of a toilet brush.

It infuriated me to have had to read some of the journalistic comments along the lines of 'you want a cure for disease but you don't want to know the mechanics of how that's done'. What? Did they really think the whole population of the country was completely stupid? The whole issue concerning the practice of organ retention was the fact that it was done without consent, C-O-N-S-E-N-T! That was the word, nothing to do with being squeamish, Mr. Burgess also mentioned that bodies were stuffed with newspapers, to fill them out I assume, not to use as a handy bin. He also profoundly informed those that might not have known or have guessed, that all that's left was a shell as the spirit had took a hike; I could see why he hadn't considered a career as a man of the cloth. If Mr. Burgess had been fortunate enough never to have taken a walk in my shoes (as I sincerely hoped he hadn't), then he could not have realised how offensive those comments would have been to a parent looking at the shell of a person that had been loved and cherished. His detachment from his work was comparable to the same feelings I had had when I had worked in a butcher's shop many years ago. I hadn't given to much thought either to the mother of the pig or lamb that I had been busy chopping up, the reason being that I hadn't known them, and I had never ever seen one grieving. After all they were just animals for our use to make a profit on, but hang on, hadn't that cat that had gone into that burning building time and again to rescue her babies been an animal as well? I can only say that if the parental instinct and love of a tabby cat for her kittens inspires courage beyond belief in a mere animal, then it speaks volumes for those who have no sentiment whatsoever toward human kind and their children. Oh, and yes, I carry a donor card; for practical, not mawkish reasons.

So no real wonder then that we needed a change in the Law to protect us from attitudes such as those. The 1961 Human Tissue Act was inappropriate and was open to wide abuse which, as we have seen happened on a grand scale. The Bill being read in the House of Commons was pushed ahead in no small way due to the tenacity and bloody-mindedness of that fearless Irish terrier Mr. Matthew Redmond among others.

I will set out briefly under the heading 'What does the Bill do?' what the new Bill entailed by directly quoting again from Professor Margot Brazier's paper on the subject.

The Human Tissue Bill had been long awaited by the families and support groups involved in organ retention. She attempts in the paper to explain some of the principle provisions. The Bill was amended by the Standing Committee of MPs and she has in the paper included those changes. The Bill itself had still a long way to go. It was to be considered by the whole House of Commons and then be debated at a third reading. Once the Bill had completed its passage through the House of Commons, it had to go to the House of Lords. What follows will be a direct quote of her personal account of the Bill up to the 23rd of March 2004. INTRODUCTION.

'The Human Tissue Bill received its second reading on Thursday 15th 2004. The Bill was reviewed by a committee of MPs at Westminster. That review was completed on February 5th. Within, and without parliament, a vocal group of commentators (with the support of the British Medical Association) called for an amendment of the Bill to introduce a system of ***presumed consent*** (italics hers) in relation to organ donation for the purposes of transplantation. It seems very unlikely they will succeed. A growing number of scientists have attacked the Bill as likely to limit medical research especially in relation to its provisions addressing consent to the use of ***surgical tissue*** (italics hers) taken from living patients. Some further amendments may well follow but I hope solely in relation to surgical tissue. It is important to remember that the Bill has been broadly welcomed, notably by the Royal College of Pathologists.' WHAT DOES THE BILL DO? 'The Bill seeks to provide a coherent set of rules to govern all questions concerning the removal and the use of human body parts, except where body parts are removed and retained solely for the purpose of investigating a death under the authority of the coroner. The Bill entirely repeals the wholly unsatisfactory Human Tissue Act of 1961 and the Human Tissue Act (Northern Ireland) 1962. It also repeals the Anatomy Act 1984, incorporating the sensible provisions of that Act into the scheme of regulation for the retention of body parts more generally. The best features of the Anatomy Act will now apply to the retention of body parts overall. As the Human Tissue Bill applies to organs and tissue taken from living patients, as well as from deceased people at post mortem, the Human Organ Transplants Act 1989 is also repealed. One Act of

Parliament should in future set out the rules governing uses of our bodies and their component parts.'

'It follows that the Human Tissue Bill (which if passed will apply in England Wales and Northern Ireland) extends beyond reforming the law relating to organ retention. The Bill is more than a response to the controversy which exploded in the wake of the Bristol inquiry Interim Report and the Redfern Report.' That section ends with a comment by Professor Brazier where she says, 'A number of families affected by organ retention have argued that 'organ retention' ought to be dealt with quite separately from 'organ transplantation'. I am personally of the opinion that that is quite right. For me there are two clear distinctions between both practices, one for live transplants, the other for organ donation for research, and the thoughts generated by each although linked, convey two different levels of emotion within the affected party. Number one being, to donate organs for research with the full knowledge of such a decision would only bring satisfaction if the results were that a disease of some kind may be eradicated because of that gift, and number two, on the other hand, to be aware that a gift of an organ or their multiples has saved the lives of another or others in some way assuages the grief felt at the loss of a child or adult, and the ongoing years are made easier by believing that a part of that person lives on. When my mother was the recipient of a kidney donated by a young man who had died in a car accident, his parents found immeasurable comfort in the fact that his death hadn't been for nothing and they corresponded regularly with my mother up until she passed away in 2001. It is my one sincere regret that we did not take that step with

449

our daughter's organs in 1989, but as I have said we were unaware of the procedures of post-mortem. If we had been told what was to happen, (and this is where my criticism of Meg Henderson and the practical Charles Burgess kicks in; they knew but had said nothing.) then instead of the outcome of retention going to waste, the comfort derived from the fact that someone else might have lived would have done me fine. That was where the amendments to the Bill pushing for 'informed' consent were important; more so than 'presumed' consent which in my opinion would still have been open to abuse. The fears of the scientific community that organs would not be donated by those who knew what was to happen to them were still rooted in the mindset that looked upon us as the ill-educated who couldn't be trusted to make the right decision. Time has proved that theory wrong as the levels of donation to both areas of live transplant and research have remained unchanged despite the coming to light of the practices of the past.

On the 4th of December 2004 the office of the then Health Secretary John Reid released a briefing on the Human Tissue Bill. In summarisation I will use five key points that the Bill was created to achieve. To ensure that no human bodies, body parts, organs or tissue will be taken without the consent of relatives or parents. Once Coroner's enquiries have concluded then organs and tissue taken will come under the authority of the Bill. Prevent a recurrence of the distress caused by retention of tissue and organs without proper consent by providing safeguards and penalties; (including jail terms and fines for breaches of the law) Help improve public confidence so that people will be more willing to agree to valuable uses of tissue and organs like research and transplantation; Improve professional confidence so that properly authorised supplies of tissue for research, education and transplantation can be maintained and improved; Allow national museums to repatriate human remains in response to claims from the descendants of indigenous people whose remains are held in museums. So victory was to be achieved through the banning of the practice of taking without consent; future generations were to benefit from what had been fought for in the House of Commons. The representatives of the people had listened and had acted to ensure that no others would have to go through what we as a collective parenthood had had to experience. The voices raised against the NHS had recognised the need for teaching and research and even more-so live transplants as a means to save lives, this had been achieved; but at what cost?

The secondary issue to be put forward to the courts of the land was what damage had been done to those whose lives had been destroyed by a child's death followed by the discovery that they would have to re-live the painful memories and re-open wounds. Then there was the shocking way they had been treated by an institution, whose staff had found that they had to return that which had illegally been taken, with no clear framework put in place by their employer for those involved, for the correct procedure to go about returning the organs. And more so, what had been the effect on the minds of those who were handed their child's organs back to them in a box? And had to relive the burials all over again? The courts were to decide how the parents coped with what had happened…..

CHAPTER 38.
Our day in court.

As for myself, being embroiled in the middle of all that was going on made me feel helpless and powerless. It was much the same feeling as I had experienced all those years ago when Kaine had been seriously ill and I had felt unable to do anything. My work and business lay in ruins due to the effects the whole process was having on my mind; at the family meetings I was just another face in a sea of faces and another voice amongst the babble of other voices of angry fellow-parents. We were dealing with academics. As ordinary people we didn't stand much of a chance of our opinions being recognised individually. Collectively our voices were louder it was true, and that in itself made the Establishment take notice; but a broad sword penetrates firstly with a fine tip. And as I sat at those meetings I felt the inadequacy of my education to counter the growing importance of the whole issue surrounding me.

It was in 2002 that I decided to start studying again; I decided to study Humanities and then Law. The on-going procedures of the case in the battle against the

NHS inspired me to do so, I wanted to be able to do something for Kaine. I hadn't been able to save her life that night in 1989, and I had been powerless to prevent her organs being taken. When I had found out I had felt a fool to have been deceived for all those years. So I decided to arm myself with knowledge. I could also feel Karen and myself growing ever more apart at this time and felt powerless to do anything about that also. I wanted to be able to do something but what exactly was eluding me, my demons plagued my sleep still; and drink was my solace. Frustration at my inadequacy tortured me as I had to sit and wait for the judgment of others to tell me how I should have felt.

I completed my studies in Humanities and progressed into studying 'the understanding of law'. I thoroughly enjoyed this and was able to use this knowledge to decipher the complex issues that were now being thrown up as the case against the NHS moved along. Notice of the impending litigation process was being sent to all families involved in the fight for compensation from the institution. I was in all honesty feeling pretty jaded as the family meetings and letters from the solicitors were constant reminders of our lost child. I should have been concentrating more on my living children but found the whole organ retention scandal had driven a huge wedge right through the middle of my life.

No earthly compensation could bring Kaine back to us, no human was responsible for her death, and yet we were made to re-live the terrible experience all over again, as if the first time hadn't been bad enough. The plain truth is that losing a child is life-altering beyond comprehension, and to those lucky enough not to have experienced it, I can tell them that the wound can never ever heal. But here we were chasing compensation; for what? Would it do any good? Would I feel any better? No. 'But you can't let 'em get away with it.' In this I wish I had. No single person could be brought to book for the failings of an entire institution made up of thousands of individuals following orders from the top. Professor van Velzen was guilty of excess in the extreme but he had not been alone in his actions. Who was to blame?

The legal teams representing the parents, including ourselves, were putting together the cases thought to have the strongest chance of success in court, and the opposition, the NSHLA (National Health Service Litigation Authority) were preparing their defence against the concerted efforts of solicitors around the country representing parents' groups. All this was going on as the new Human Tissue Bill was being pushed through Parliament.

Many people involved would have settled for a written apology, an admission of guilt and some kind of memorial built in remembrance of the children and families affected. Others sought rightful monetary recompense. The NHSLA didn't want to admit guilt or pay out any money despite of the findings of the Kennedy, Redfern, and ultimately the Retained Organs Commission external review reports. And so confrontation was inevitable.

In the case of the Alder Hey litigation the NHS settled with the families involved out of court. In our case the NSHLA were putting up a fight as the scope of culpability was widening against them. They were in fact saying that pathologists performing autopsies on behalf of the coroner and retaining organs were doing so outside of NHS practice and guidelines and therefore the NHS couldn't be held responsible for their actions; and it was being suggested that the individual pathologists might have to answer directly for their actions in these matters rather than the Trusts for which they worked. The NHSLA decided to dig their heels in and not budge, our side were pushing for an out-of-court settlement to avoid lengthy drawn-out court cases and costs. Of course there were also the effects still being felt by the families anxious to draw a line under it all and sink back into normality to consider.

I was one that yearned for the day before I had found out all about this, it had turned my life upside down. A furious argument with my doctor in his surgery one day highlighted to me how much I despised anything I viewed as NHS insensitivity, and this whole thing was having serious consequences in my life. It had to stop, but like a nightmare carousel it just kept on going around and around and I couldn't get off. Nothing could turn the clock back but I was stuck in the middle of this; and as yet, no light was visible at the end of the tunnel.

Mediation was suggested and rejected by the NHSLA, bully-boy tactics were the order of play for them; it sent a message that the litigation department of the National Health Service didn't give a fig for the on-going strain that the whole process was having on the parties involved.

Eventually, and quite out of the blue the opposition changed their outlook on mediation and Mr. Justice Gage, presiding, ordered a halt to all proceedings whilst the two sides began the mediation process scheduled for 25th September 2002. The objectives sought by our legal teams were pretty simple. There were four main points. A personal and unreserved apology to each claimant in relation to the the particular circumstances of individual claims. An undertaking from the NHSLA and the Department of Health that they would actively seek changes in the law (insofar as they had not already been made) to ensure such a practice could never happen again.

(3) An appropriate award for compensation (including compensation for personal injury to parents where appropriate). The continuation of counselling being made available from independent counsellors as appropriate, on a nationwide basis. To me it didn't seem too much to ask for seeing as the NHS had taken our children's organs, dissected, studied, incinerated, and sold them. All this was to no avail though, the mediation talks ground to a complete standstill; the Alder Hey settlement was a separate issue to the nationwide group of which we were a small part. And so in January 2003 a letter from our solicitors informed us that as the mediation route was no longer an option, we as a group would now have to fight on through the courts. The letter also informed us of the press releases regarding the Alder Hey settlement with the NHS had been finalised and that a memorial would be built there for them. Our similar request had been rejected out of hand, a much smaller compensation offer had been made and that, in turn, had been rejected out of hand by us as insulting to the memories of our children; derisory had been the word used to describe it. Professor van Velzen had been the catalyst for the settlement as regards the Alder Hey group, but our solicitors argued that although he may have been the extreme example of organ retention, it was in fact a practice of other NHS Trusts up and down the country.

A press release highlighted the immovable stance the NHSLA took against the families involved. ORGAN RETENTION GROUP DISGUST AT BREAKDOWN IN TALKS 'Following the breakdown of a lengthy mediation process, the nationwide organ retention group have today been informed that the action will proceed to trial. Mervyn Fudge of lead solicitors Clarke Willmott and Clarke today said,

"We are bitterly disappointed at the outcome of negotiations and the failure for us to make substantial progress."

"The meeting was at the request of the National Health Service Litigation Authority, who are acting on behalf of the numerous Health Authorities involved, yet were not willing to shift their position."

"We believe that it is totally unnecessary to proceed to timely and costly litigation on this case but if we have to on behalf of our clients we will litigate to the fullest extent and the matter will be resolved by a judge. The NHSLA position is adversarial and obstructive in the extreme forcing the claimants into litigation despite having received numerous constructive and objective proposals to bring this to a suitable conclusion. It is going to cost a considerable amount of money if this case runs to trial, something we feel is completely unwarranted." One area which had caused great surprise and consternation for the claimants was that the Department of Health, via the NHSLA, reached an overall settlement of £5million with the Royal Liverpool Group following the Alder Hey Inquiry. Yet they were offering to the nationwide group, which was double the size of the Royal Liverpool Group, a derisory sum of less than half of that amount. Mervyn

Fudge said, "We have been extremely generous in our dealings with the defendants but now find ourselves in an impossible position where litigation is the only option. Our Focus Group feels extremely disillusioned and disgusted." The court hearing for directions to bring the case to trial is to take place on the 31st of January 2003 at the High Court in Nottingham before Mr. Justice Gage.' So there we had it, we knew what the NHS and the lawyers really thought about us and what they had done to our children. The scant respect shown to us as parents was evident in the attitudes they had displayed towards a situation in which their position had been in my mind untenable; to try and defend the indefensible was for me a puzzlement. It meant that public and private money was now to be used to fight our corners and for us the whole affair went on.

A further letter from Irwin Mitchell now informed us that a trial date had been set for the 26th of January 2004 to take place at the Royal Courts of Justice in London. The trial itself was expected to last between four to six weeks. This was later amended to six to eight weeks.

So we had a wait of over twelve months to see where we stood, would we find out if our Human Rights as parents to our child would be thrown out? Much like our daughter's remains were by an unfeeling, uncaring, unknown person acting under orders from the NHS who now in turn ordered their lawyers to contest our protest. There were too many cases to be put before the court and so a selection of eight were sought to represent the broad attributes of the entire group. Our opponents had the choice of choosing four of these cases and defending their clients actions toward them. If the judge found in favour of the families then compensation would be made on the basis of the effect psychologically that the experience of all this had had on the families, provided that proof of damage was available. The case would be intended to centre on four categories of retention. A hospital post-mortem on a child. A hospital post-mortem on a foetus. A coroner's post-mortem on a child. A coroner's post-mortem on an adult.

All claims had to be registered by the 31st of July 2003, which meant that all information needed by the lawyers acting for the families had to be in place by then for the test cases to be chosen from those categories. All we could do was wait, there was a lot of work to be done by the legal teams in readiness for the court date in London. We weren't alone, over two thousand families affected by the practice waited with us for that day to arrive and for the trial to begin. Just prior to the commencement of the court case we had further notification that one of the lead cases selected had been deemed unsuitable to proceed with; this was the coroner's post-mortem on an adult. A further offer to settle out of court was rejected by the NHSLA in favour of a trial by judgment. Our case hadn't been selected as one of the lead cases but we were invited to attend court to listen to the proceedings. At the time this was impossible for us to due to the financial burden this would have imposed (staying in London for weeks until the trial ended) and so I listened intently to the news as it was announced on the morning of the 26th of March 2004, ironically my mothers anniversary, as judgment was given on the case against the NHS. The trial had actually finished on the 18th of February 2004 and the delay in passing judgment had been for all the legal arguments to be weighed on both sides.

In such a complex issue a straightforward judgment was never to be expected. I had personally been afraid that we would lose outright as I couldn't quite understand why the NHSLA had gone all the way into court with the argument, had they had something up their sleeves? Well yes they did have, for them it had been a case of damage limitation, the law on coroner's post-mortems doesn't apply in the same way as hospital post-mortems.

The outright ruling of the case was this; yes, the NHS were found guilty of negligence, the judge's ruling had been

that the NHS had participated in a 'morally and ethically objectionable practice.' However one out of the three claims was dismissed as this was a coroner's post-mortem. Mervyn Fudge said after the case, 'in the hospital post-mortem cases the judge has found that the claimant was owed a duty of care, and that was breached.'

'The doctors were guilty of negligence and provided we can show psychiatric damage then they are entitled to damages.' And so we had a split decision, based on a point of law. The coroner's post- mortem was outside of the rule of 'interference' with a child's body even though the same practice was followed and the organs retained in the same way.

We had won but we hadn't, Kaine's post-mortem had fallen under the authority of the coroner, and so we couldn't claim damages against the NHS. There would be no apology for what had happened to her......

It was for me, a bitter sweet result.

POSTSCRIPT.
To all the world a baby.

My compensation for what happened to my daughter lies within the pages of this very personal book. Victory can be attained in more ways than by just winning one battle. I feel now, at last, I have attained such a victory. Nothing in the way of compensation could put right what the courts of the land had said was wrong. Just because the coroner had ordered Kaine's post-mortem as opposed to the hospital didn't make what they did to her right; it was just a category, the outcome was the same. It was over; all I wanted now was peace at last for my little girl. It was finally at an end. But the damage had been well and truly done. There was no cure for what had happened and the strain of the last few years during which we had waited and waited for the end of it all took its toll on Karen and myself, to the point where in 2005, after 18 years together, we decided to call it a day. The new victims were our kids in my eyes; they were the ones whose hearts the NHS really took. I can't blame everything on what happened in the hospital but I would say it was a major contributor.

I can look back now with memories of the past when I was younger and still be grateful that I had Kaine in my life. If I were to change anything it would be that if I could have done anything to have kept her with us, I would have done so without question. But that is the past, and the past is like a country to which one has been and can never return. I have endeavoured to make my peace with God and the answers to the questions that at one time perplexed me, I feel now that I have attained those also. Alcohol played its part in my downward spiral for a few years but thankfully that is now past as well. The last six months writing this book has been a journey for me, one of heartache mixed with happiness and now finally peace. The tears I've shed for my lost daughter and wiped away in the early mornings and late evenings whilst writing this book are testimony that love never dies. I love her now as I loved her then. My sincere hope is, that if this book is published it will allow others in the same position a degree of comfort to know that they were not alone, and our feelings in the loss of our children and what was done to them will be a unique experience that, hopefully now no others will have to pass through. This is due in no small part to the fearless efforts of Matthew Redmond, a true Irishman if ever I met one, and also those people who gathered to themselves other parents in other groups to fight an injustice that may have otherwise continued for god knows how long.

For the parents of the children who shared in Kaine's fate I can only offer this as my personal opinion; I know that in Almighty God's due time, all the wrongs that are committed on this earth will be put right and that the children we lost will see the sun once more. For Kaine my beautiful girl, she would have been twenty-one years of age this year; this book is my gift to her. I want you to know Kaine that the words we put on your headstone have true meaning always, and even though the world still turns with supreme indifference, I know that 'to all the world you were just a baby, but to me, you were my world.'

If I ever.

By
N. Lowe.
J. Lawlor.

If I ever met the sun, in his home up in the sky,
I would ask him why the sky gets scratched
When an aeroplane flies by.
If I ever met the sun,
I'd whisper in his ear and say
Thanks for giving us your shining light
On the summer days I play.
And if I ever met the sun in winter,
When his days are not so long,
I'd thank him for making a snowflake glisten,
As I catch it on my tongue.

The end. X

Lightning Source UK Ltd.
Milton Keynes UK
171251UK00001B/1/P